let's read

A LINGUISTIC APPROACH

Second Edition, Revised and Updated

Cynthia A. Barnhart and Robert K. Barnhart

Based on the original work of Leonard Bloomfield and Clarence L. Barnhart

Wayne State University Press · Detroit

19   18   17   16   15   7   6   5   4   3

LIBRARY OF CONGRESS CATALOGING-IN-PUBLICATION DATA
Barnhart, Cynthia A.
Let's read : a linguistic approach / Cynthia A. Barnhart and Robert K. Barnhart.
— 2nd ed., Rev. and updated.
p. cm.
Includes index.
"Based on the original work of Leonard Bloomfield and Clarence L. Barnhart."
ISBN 978-0-8143-3455-3 (pbk. : alk. paper)
1. Reading—Phonetic method. 2. Readers (Primary) I. Barnhart, Robert K. II. Title.
PE1119.B388 2010
372.46'5—dc22
2009026959

Cover and interior illustrations for this edition
by John R. Barnhart

Designed and typeset by Charlie Sharp,
Sharp Des!gns, Lansing, Michigan
Composed in ITC Century

*This revised edition is dedicated to the memory of
Robert K. Barnhart, for whom all things were possible.*
C. A. B.

*To my mother, Frances Barnhart, who read to me and taught me
to read, and to the memory of Leonard Bloomfield, who evolved
this system by which countless children can learn to read.*
C. L. B.

Contents

Foreword

By publishing *Let's Read: A Linguistic Approach* in 1961, Wayne State University Press forever changed the national educational dialogue about basic reading. No longer was a reading program based on linguistic principles a figment or an unfulfilled desire; it was a reality. And because this approach to teaching basic reading was developed by Leonard Bloomfield, one of the most eminent linguists of the twentieth century, it could not be ignored. After publication of *Let's Read*, even the publishers of reading series widely used in schools felt compelled to include something "linguistic" in their materials. At that more hopeful time, a contagious intellectual enthusiasm resulted in administrators and teachers initiating reading experiments, and, often with funds supplied by the federal government, educators tried out new materials, including *Let's Read*, in thousands of classrooms to see if any of them would yield greater instructional success.

The history of *Let's Read* mirrors our national educational life story of hope, advance, retreat, success, failure, and endurance. While experiments involving the Bloomfield-Barnhart materials were successful, especially for a new and different reading program, *Let's Read* did not cause a revolution in the methodologies of reading instruction. The reading establishment in fact appeared to react somewhat nervously to it. *Let's Read* did, however, become the program teachers turned to as a last resort for pupils who were highly resistant to more traditional methods of reading instruction, possibly for the same reasons that impelled Leonard Bloomfield to set down his ideas about the discipline in the first place.

While it has remained among the alternative players of the major league reading programs, *Let's Read* nonetheless has kept its place as a failsafe approach to basic reading.

The program has endured largely because it is a logical and simple way to teach someone to read. It has also endured because it was written for parents to use with their children, and it continues today to appeal to the many parents who want not only to ensure that their children learn to read but also want to share the achievement of that intellectual benchmark with them. Most of us recognize reading as the first step to literacy, the key to getting on with the business of life, and most especially the key that opens the door to all other learning: the youngster who can read has the tools needed to explore all other subject areas and is limited only by affinity and interest.

The other part of the *Let's Read* story is the people of Wayne State University Press, who have been its steadfast supporters. I recall Harold Basilius, the director who undertook its publication, and Mike Ware, who oversaw its fortunes for many years, with great affection. I am most grateful for the encouragement and support of the present director, Jane Hoehner, who suggested this revision.

Over the years, Robert Barnhart and I thought about a revision of *Let's Read* and set down various ideas. This revision is based on those preliminary plans, as well as the rich lode of experience shared with the Barnharts by parents and teachers. I also need to thank Katherine Barnhart for her insights on teaching the nonnative speaker and John Barnhart for his drawings.

I very much hope *Let's Read* revised will meet the needs of learners and teachers as well and for as long as the first edition.

Cynthia A. Barnhart
Los Angeles, California
2010

The *Let's Read* Linguistic Approach

Introduction

Cynthia A. Barnhart and Robert K. Barnhart

A Short History

When Wayne State University Press first published *Let's Read* in 1961, the Bloomfield System, as the method was often referred to, already had accumulated a history. Developed by the eminent American linguist Leonard Bloomfield (1887–1949) in the 1920s, in its first form Bloomfield's program was essentially a series of lists from which the learner was taught to read by learning the basic spelling patterns of English. Bloomfield had concluded that, from the linguist's point of view, the majority of school reading programs were illogical and unnecessarily difficult. His conclusion was based on an analysis of the underlying principles and organization of these programs. At that time, reading texts could be roughly described—and might still be described—as based on either the concept of sight-to-sense (visual recognition) or sound-to-sense (phonics), *sense* here meaning comprehension.

Sight-based, or look-say, programs rely upon the pupil's memorization of a limited collection of vocabulary words that serve as an introduction to reading. Early sight-based texts were frequently composed of familiar biblical passages that a pupil memorized. After having "learned" them, the pupil was able to read, largely by analogy.[1] In later and more sophisticated look-say reading texts, the vocabulary was chosen because students were familiar with it through usage, but the words themselves were unrelated

---

1. This method is also used by children who teach themselves to read. Essentially, they memorize words from favorite stories that have been read to them often and then transfer their recognition of these words to the same combination of letters in other contexts. By analogy they break the code.

to each other in orthographic structure, or how their sounds are represented by letters. All such reading programs assume that by reading and rereading, writing and rewriting a particular and limited vocabulary, the pupil gradually will come to infer the phonetic system of written English. In other words, over time the pupil will utilize the vocabulary already learned (or memorized) to form an idea of how written English translates into the language we speak.

Sound-based, or phonics, programs have long been available as well. Early phonics texts were simply lists of rhyming words, some including pronunciation keys. Sound-based approaches recognize that written English has an alphabetic structure, and they attempt to apply that understanding of its phonetic structure to reading instruction. The difficulty of teaching reading by means of phonics only is that it assigns to individual letters a particular sound, or often many individual sounds, with rules explaining why pronunciations of certain combinations of letters are not consistent in actual spoken language. Phonics, in a sense, sets up a conflict between individual pronunciation systems and a synthetic (idealized) representation of actual language, which quite naturally can complicate learning to read.

Bloomfield recognized that while these approaches differed in how they introduced reading to the pupil (either by looking or by sound), they both drew on vocabulary that was not representative of the alphabetic structure of English spelling. They also shared a patchy record of success in teaching large numbers of children and adults to read. Nevertheless, contemporary reading texts continue to embrace these methodologies.

Although today's phonics- and sight-based texts pay more attention to word structure and spelling patterns, they remain largely interest-based; that is, they try to capture the pupil's attention through attractive designs and a selection of familiar vocabulary embedded in simple reading that deals with familiar situations.

Bloomfield looked at the task of learning to read differently. He viewed written language as a code and therefore decipherable. Contrary to the belief held at the time (and still prevalent today), that the English spelling system is chaotic, Bloomfield's analysis showed that English spelling is at least 80 percent predictable or alphabetic. This regularity allowed him to design a method that capitalizes on the alphabetic nature of written English. He believed that if there were greater emphasis upon teaching the phonemic sound-letter correlations of English—how the alphabet is used to represent various sound patterns in the language—the pupil would have a much easier road toward mastery of the code.

He also divided the task of reading into two parts, which other approaches to reading did not and still do not do: he separated comprehension—which has many aspects and is in essence an ongoing, lifelong process—from the task of decoding. It is a sad fact that a shaky reader is an unsure decoder and a decidedly imperfect comprehender: unless and until a pupil is able to decode words easily, comprehension of the message the words convey will be a slow, inexact, and fitful process.

In the early twentieth century, many American linguists shared Bloomfield's opinion that the emerging science of linguistics had much to contribute to the process of teaching reading, and this belief encouraged Bloomfield and others to develop ideas for linguistics-based programs. While Bloomfield's approach sprang from a linguistic analysis very different from the various programs that had already been used in schools and homes, its presentation of material was and is not particularly revolutionary. Historically, reading texts drew upon a limited, controlled vocabulary either from familiar spoken vocabulary or dictated by rhyme, phonics rules, and, to some extent, pattern to introduce reading to pupils. Nor was resorting to lists of words an unknown practice in reading texts. What remains revolutionary about Bloomfield's approach is its resolute adherence to spelling pattern; its design as a skill-centered rather than an interest-centered approach; and its emphasis on mastery of the basic alphabetic code of English.

In fact, if we think about the process of reading, it becomes clear that all of us, regardless of how we are taught to read, naturally and necessarily engage in the very process that Bloomfield incorporated into a coherent pedagogical scheme. All practiced readers visually gulp down syllables. But in the fluent reader, the skill is so practiced and the alphabetic habit so ingrained that the reader is unaware of how or when or if phonic values are assigned to the individual letters and syllables so rapidly processed. A practiced reader is unaware of the underlying process, that is, until confronted by an unfamiliar word or a foreignism or a technical term, which usually requires the reader to slow down (as the learner must) and travel along the letters syllable by syllable, often drawing upon knowledge of more rarefied vocabulary, other languages, or other disciplines to decode the word. Imagine for a moment the effort required for the pupil who does not and appears unable to acquire that facility to unlock the sequence of letters and syllables. Imagine the additional effort of gleaning the meaning from imperfectly decoded words. It is stupefyingly difficult. And yet, as an accomplished speaker, that groping reader has performed the acrobatic intellectual feat of mastering and internalizing the vocabulary, pronunciation, grammatical structure, rules, and stress patterns of spoken language. Mastering the relatively simple code of the written language should therefore be an attainable, reasonable goal for most beginners. Once the code has been mastered, the reader should be able to comprehend any written material at a level appropriate to his or her age and experience. *Let's Read* offers to the pupil and the teacher the means to do that.

THE BLOOMFIELD-BARNHART COLLABORATION

Once Bloomfield had set down his lists in an order determined by the frequency of their appearance in written English, he used them to teach his son. All we know about that family experiment is that the boy did learn to read, as Bloomfield reveals in his rather laconic observation to Clarence Barnhart that his son, having learned Bloomfield's first lists, moved on to reading ordinary texts offered in school.

From the late 1920s until 1940, Bloomfield was a professor and the chairman of the Department of Linguistics at the University of Chicago; he later was Sterling Professor of Linguistics at Yale University. One of his students at Chicago was Clarence Barnhart (1900–1993), who later achieved renown as an innovative dictionary maker, most particularly for his role as editor of the Thorndike-Century school dictionaries (later, the Thorndike-Barnhart school dictionaries).

While an undergraduate and graduate student at the University, Barnhart developed a professional and personal friendship with Bloomfield. It was a complex collaboration. Barnhart's editorial designs for his school dictionaries drew upon the disciplines of linguistics and psychology (he was the psychologist E. L. Thorndike's editor), and certainly basic reading was a logical extension of his work. Also, as Barnhart was then working at Scott Foresman and had many acquaintances in the publishing world, he could act on Bloomfield's behalf to find a publisher for the reading program. Little did either man know that it would take more than twenty years to succeed.

Barnhart's experience in commercial publishing made him sensitive to the commercial possibilities of Bloomfield's approach to reading instruction, which was initially simply an exploration of his ideas. As Bloomfield wrote in a 1937 letter to Barnhart,

> Without hope of publication, I wrote out what I thought and what I had done with my boy. If there is any chance of publication, the present essay [see pages 21–45] could form the basis of the teacher's handbook, and a child's reader, containing material very much like the illustrative sentences now given, would have to be added.
>
> My son went from the one-syllable reading that is in the essay, directly to ordinary readers; probably no change in later readers would be needed, once the pupils had learned what is in the essay. On the other hand, it might turn out that a systematized vocabulary in later reading would speed things up. If you think the thing has commercial possibilities, perhaps the thing should be tried out in a school.[2]

In their unpublished form, the Bloomfield materials eventually included seventy-two lists of words, each illustrating a spelling pattern of English. At Barnhart's urging, Bloomfield wrote out sentences to give the pupil reading practice and later added some stories, most of which are still a part of the lessons in this book, although they have been revised and many of them expanded.

---

2. As quoted by C. L. Barnhart in "The Story of the Bloomfield System," *Let's Read: A Linguistic Approach*, 1st ed. (Detroit: Wayne State University Press, 1961), 9; originally drawn from the Barnhart files.

This sporadic process of development coincided with Barnhart's rising expectation that he would find a publisher willing to back an interesting and potentially profitable undertaking. It remained a puzzle to Barnhart that there was little enthusiasm in educational circles for Bloomfield's program, and not one of the American textbook publishers he approached would accept it. As he wrote in his introduction to the first edition of *Let's Read*, "It is a remarkable fact that a [reading] system worked out by one of the great linguists of the twentieth century could get no hearing in educational circles, and that there was only one attempt to try out his ideas of how to teach reading in schools."[3] Bloomfield seemed more philosophical—or resigned—writing to Barnhart after arrival of yet another publisher's rejection in 1948, "I hope you won't feel bad about the reading system. The Press's adverse letter is merely one of the occasional penalties you, as an optimist, have to pay in amends for being in a more favorable world than the pessimist's."[4]

Two fortuitous events coincided to bring *Let's Read* to publication. One was a grant provided to Barnhart to develop the Bloomfield manuscript into a fully worked-out and complete program. The second was the interest of Dr. Harold Basilius, director of Wayne State University Press, in publishing it. Basilius had been an associate of Bloomfield's at Ohio State University before Bloomfield left for the University of Chicago, and he knew of Bloomfield's manuscript and the essay explaining his ideas.

Thus ended the twenty-year quest to find a publisher. By this time, sadly, Bloomfield had died. It was left to Barnhart, as the survivor of the partnership, to add "a systematized vocabulary in later reading" (as Bloomfield described the fuller development of his idea), effectively raising Bloomfield's preliminary manuscript to the level of a complete program.

BLOOMFIELD-BARNHART *LET'S READ*

Let's Read, both in this new revision and in its first edition, is not structurally different from those original seventy-two lists. Barnhart and other linguists who consulted on the first edition believed it should be emphatically experimental. They shared the opinion that it would not be offered as *the* solution to the increasingly obvious lack of success in teaching basic reading in America's schools. *Let's Read* was not thought of by anyone involved in its publication as linguistics' call to arms nor an attack upon the reading establishment; the genuine desire of both Barnhart and the contributors to the book was to offer educators and parents a fully developed scheme based on the science of linguistics that could be used—most especially in the public classroom (where it could be evaluated) but also by parents—as a reliable tool to teach children to read. Therefore, in the front matter of the

---

3. Ibid., p. 12.
4. Ibid., p. 16.

original edition, thoughtful attention was paid to the important, unanswered questions raised by the Bloomfield scheme:

- What about comprehension?
- What about the many words of vocabulary (*Let's Read* includes the 5,000 most common words of English) unfamiliar to most children of school age?
- What about the interest factor?
- What about variant, dialect pronunciations that abound in the United States?[5]

By the time of publication, however, much was, in fact, known about the potential of the Bloomfield scheme as an instructional tool that addressed comprehension, vocabulary, interest, and variant pronunciations. For a number of years, there had been an ongoing experiment in the Archdiocese of Chicago undertaken by Father Stanley Stoga, superintendent of the schools in that archdiocese. In some of those parochial schools, there were many pupils for whom English was a second language, their first being Polish. Understandably, many of these pupils seemed to be chronic underachievers in reading and comprehending English. Father Stoga was anxious to see if Bloomfield's approach might ease their path to reading English. Sister Mary Fidelia, who oversaw the Bloomfield experiment, wrote of her first reaction and subsequent experience:[6]

> Several problems stood out. First, there were no materials prepared for group teaching in the comparatively large classes of forty or more children; second, Dr. Bloomfield furnished no models of lessons in his manuscript which would suggest to the teacher how she was to go about presenting this linguistic approach to word-attack[7] in reading; and third, it would take a good deal of courage to leave the beaten path of conventional practices to venture unequipped and unguided on the strange seas of linguistic waters. But nothing ventured, nothing gained.

---

5. The contributors who provided thoughtful essays for the original edition of *Let's Read* about these unknowns were Robert C. Pooley and George P. Faust. Dr. Pooley, a longtime associate of C. L. Barnhart, was a professor at the University of Wisconsin and had written widely on English usage and grammar. His contribution to *Let's Read* was the encouraging "Introduction for Teachers." Dr. Faust, who also worked with C. L. Barnhart over a long period of time, was a professor of linguistics at the University of Kentucky and associate editor of the journal *General Linguistics;* he contributed the essay "Speech Variation and the Bloomfield System." These essays raised questions about Bloomfield's approach, questions that have been answered by use over the years and that are addressed in this new introduction.

6. The material included in this passage and all citations are taken from pp. 12–15 of C. L. Barnhart's "Story of the Bloomfield System" (see Note 1).

7. Word-attack is a method designed to help pupils read multisyllable words more easily, principally by specifically teaching them common syllables that make up many words. Such techniques become necessary when a reading scheme fails to teach a pupil the code of the language, especially a program that relies on memorization of specific vocabulary yet provides insufficient information to allow the pupil to infer phonetic "rules." *Let's Read* is emphatically not a stopgap to better decoding, but its underlying principle is similar to word-attack.

Despite being on a voyage of discovery themselves, the resourceful teachers in the archdiocese prepared flash cards, practice exercises, and other materials and sallied forth with results that in retrospect must have surprised everyone. For, as Sister Fidelia continues,

It should be noted at this point that this trial was in the nature of an uncontrolled experiment. According to Dr. Bloomfield, the children were not to be given any books until they mastered by an analogous process the letters of the alphabet to a point of spontaneous association of the correct phoneme [smallest unit of meaningful sound in a language] with the letter [or letters] of the alphabet representing it.

Once the children mastered the short vowel sounds in combination with the regular values of consonants [part I of *Let's Read*], the children read one pre-primer [standard published texts for beginning readers] after another. The teacher did notice an absence of rhythm in their reading, but to her great relief the comprehension was very good—something the experts in reading claim is sacrificed when undue emphasis is placed on word-attack. The disturbing halting reading smoothed out with practice in phrasing, and interest in reading mounted with each day.

The pre-primers to which Sister Fidelia refers were interest-based in their vocabulary, much of which was not included in the Bloomfield lists, suggesting that Bloomfield's method allowed children to successfully read words they had not encountered or been taught before.

At the year's end, the children were tested using standard achievement tests, and among the forty children, scores ranged from 1.5 to 3.5; only five pupils scored below 1.9, the national first-grade norm in 1942. As Sister Fidelia recalled, obviously, the results were satisfying. The fear that the children would gain in word-attack skill at the expense of comprehension—the ultimate goal of reading—was dispelled.[8] The teachers in other diocesan schools not using the plan expressed the desire to try the plan in their classes. And so the following year and for many years after, these inspired teachers provided the materials and led their pupils to mastery of basic reading. As Sister Fidelia observed, "There were a few slow readers, but there were no non-readers." It is especially significant that Sister Fidelia does not mention any difficulties with variant pronunciations, which must have been prolific given the fact that for many of the pupils, English was not their first language.

Subsequent experiments in other locations more or less confirmed the early results in Chicago. One of particular interest was carried out by Wendell Williams, a principal in Paterson, New Jersey, in the 1980s. It involved a school population of teenage pupils who had IQ scores too low to qualify them for special education classes. After a year of reading

---

8. The fear expressed by stalwarts of interest-based pedagogy was that Bloomfield's approach would create "word-callers," not readers. Hence, Sister Fidelia's test results were all the more significant.

instruction based on *Let's Read*, when given district-wide reading tests, these pupils had higher reading scores than students enrolled in the special education classes.

At about the same time, in New Brunswick, Canada, a classroom innovator, Dr. Lal Sharma, persuaded his district to allow him to provide structured instruction in all subjects, especially reading and math, to students whose first language was French and who were challenged by learning to read English. As his pupils progressed through *Let's Read*, they needed more and more supplementary reading material, and by the end of second grade, Dr. Sharma had to go to the fifth-grade classroom to find appropriate resources. Dr. Sharma observed that along with a firm grasp of reading skills, his pupils also showed improved results in all other subject areas.

The use of *Let's Read* for a decade in one school district near Harrisburg, Pennsylvania, allows us to make some generalizations about *Let's Read* as a basic text. During the 1960s, a reading supervisor in the Bethel Park school district designed a district-wide program utilizing *Let's Read* as the only text for beginning reading. By the time a pupil finished *Let's Read*, educators required a third-grade comprehension score on a standardized reading test as the basis for more advanced language-arts instruction. Indeed, pupils participating in the Bethel Park program could not switch to conventional reading texts until they had attained that score, a level most of them achieved by the middle of second grade. A by-product of *Let's Read* was that the children scored so far above the norm in spelling on the test that those scores could not be included in the overall reading scores, as they rendered the average virtually meaningless. Only 3 percent of all pupils in the district required remedial reading instruction, a statistic that did not vary over the years.

Experimentation and use have confirmed that pupils taught according to the principles of *Let's Read* become comprehending, attentive readers rather than "word-callers" who correctly respond to any series of letters in words but do not grasp their meanings. Generally speaking, children instructed from *Let's Read* comprehend what they read at a level consistent with their age and experience. These pupils share two important distinguishing features: they are singularly good spellers, and they are intrepid readers. An explanation for this may be that pupils able to extract the message in their reading without laborious effort experience a growing sense of mastery and a corresponding increase in confidence. It is one reason why *Let's Read* is frequently described as a skill-centered approach.

In addition to addressing initial questions about comprehension, the real-world use of *Let's Read* has, over time, answered the other questions about student interest, unfamiliar vocabulary, and variations in pronunciation in different parts of the United States. Pronunciation difficulties have not materialized, most likely for several reasons. Variant pronunciation systems (as, for example, the Southern tendency to pronounce short *i* and short *e* the same way, as in *Ben* and *bin*) are generally consistent for all words presenting the same consonant-vowel-consonant combinations; the speaker will regularize pronunciation to fit his or her personal pronunciation scheme. A second factor may be that *Let's Read* is primarily a visual approach and does not rely on aural rhyming (pronouncing a particular way to achieve an oral goal) to teach patterns. By the time a pupil reaches rarer patterns in English that can be pronounced in widely varying ways, as with *twelth/twelfth, sikth/sixth, dawg/dahg/dog,* or that old saw *wen/when*—all of which are taught as patterns of similar variants—the pupil is fully accustomed to attend to spelling patterns, the pedagogical basis of *Let's Read:* pronunciation is not the key to unlocking the code but is relegated to its appropriate status of oral response to the code. There is, therefore, no need to force pupils to conform to some hypothetical standard of pronunciation in order to unlock the sequence of spelling patterns presented in *Let's Read*—an unforeseen benefit to nonnative and bilingual English speakers. This focus on patterns rather than pronunciation may explain why Sister Fidelia's pupils, who spoke Polish as their first language, were not hampered by variant pronunciations.

The matter of unfamiliar vocabulary as a stumbling block to reading seems a red herring, too. It has been shown that pupils like to discover new words and meanings, which, once explained, pose no problem for them. In fact, it is most likely an asset of the program that it confronts pupils with multisyllable words made up of monosyllables they have already learned. Adding new words to their vocabularies can be, and often is, a source of pride and pleasure for young readers from both language-advantaged and language-disadvantaged backgrounds.

While Bloomfield's ideas seem to have been validated by more than sixty years of experimentation in the classroom, they have also been substantiated by the legions of special reading teachers who have turned to *Let's Read* as a last resort for pupils who have failed to learn to read from all other approaches and combinations of approaches. The value of Bloomfield's approach has likewise been confirmed by those thousands of parents who have used the program to teach their children to read, and now by their children who have likewise decided to use *Let's Read* to teach the next generation.

Bloomfield-Barnhart Revised

In general, this edition is simply an updated version of the first edition of *Let's Read.* We have not changed the focus or the sequence of the original program, nor have we added illustrations to the stories. Our editorial decisions regarding changes in format and content have been based on experience gained over the years and have been made with the aim of making the program more user- and teacher-friendly.

We have lessened the learning load in the first lessons by presenting patterns in two lessons rather than one and added more connected reading (sentences and stories that use each pattern) throughout the book. We have updated the vocabulary and opted to introduce a selection of sight words earlier in the sequence to provide the pupil with more idiomatic sentences. The revised edition includes stories that are longer and that often continue through several lessons, especially in parts V and VI.

The longer stories in the revised edition are not meant to counter the criticism of a the structured approach, which lies deep within our literary prejudices: How can it be that an approach so unabashedly skill-centered will lead to anything more than simple decoding of the most rudimentary message? Rather, the longer stories are included because their form is integral to the *Let's Read* sequence that builds from the simple to the more complex. The goal of all reading instruction is, insofar as possible, to gradually wean the learner from simple constructions to more complex ones. And in *Let's Read*, just as the simple vocabulary patterns of part I build to the complexity of pattern in all subsequent parts, the reading similarly gradually builds in content. To this end, we have added longer stories later in the program.

The notes that introduce each part of *Let's Read* have been reworked with a view toward making them less tentative and more informative. We have also added a list of multisyllable words at the end of part I that fall within the patterns of the first lessons. Many pupils welcome the challenge of reading long words, and these words provide an effective way to reinforce what has already been learned.

FOR THE TEACHER

The following remarks are suggestions to the teacher, particularly the parent teacher. Over the years since *Let's Read* was first published, it has become abundantly clear there are as many teaching styles, techniques, and philosophies as there are teachers and that the end result is the important thing. *Let's Read* is the first resource for the teacher; how he or she implements the lessons is ultimately an individual matter.

Children who learn to read using *Let's Read* are taught the basic technique of observing *significant difference.* That is, unlike other approaches to learning such a complicated skill, *Let's Read* relies upon inculcating the habit of recognizing one difference between two items, whether it be the difference between the letters *T* and *H* or the words *hit* and *hat.* Careful looking translates into accurate reading at any level and is a skill that will serve pupils well as they progress through all their studies.

If a child can speak fluently and can give full attention to and understand what is being said, he or she is ready to learn to read in the most basic sense, but if that child happens also to like using and listening to language, learning to read is an even more captivating and perhaps more easily acquired skill.

With any pupil, it is probably a good idea on a bad day to make sure a reluctant scholar accomplishes something, even if it is only a very small something. Sometimes young pupils seem to hit a bump in the road and find it difficult to move ahead. Such obstacles require the teacher to ingeniously provide alternative materials, whether a game or flash cards or small, personalized "books" made especially for the pupil.

Some practices should be avoided, however. Most adults are familiar with the practice of "sounding-out," which consists of assigning arbitrary and inaccurate sounds to single letters and then assembling them into the word a pupil is trying to read. We strongly caution that this practice can often mislead the learner. Does *kuh-ah-tuh* actually translate into the word *cat* in the learner's ear, or in anyone's, for that matter? Besides, the phonics detour is unnecessary. What is actually occurring during the learning process in *Let's Read* is that the pupil is inductively translating regular sound-letter correlations into reliable sound patterns in keeping with his or her own speech patterns.

Another practice to avoid, because it invariably works against the learner, is that of assigning a single sound to the first letter of a short-vowel monosyllable and treating the following vowel and consonant as a unit (for example, *kuh-at, cat*). The unintended consequence of relying on this particular device is that, rather than providing a crutch, it can cause a student to develop the habit of reading a monosyllable as a two-syllable word, as if *cat* were *c-at*, which habit the student must then "unlearn."

Once a pupil understands the magical connection between pattern and alphabetic structure, he or she will advance with few crises and little intervention by the teacher, who no doubt is a fluent reader and has formed many sound notions (along with some fanciful ones) about how mastery of reading is actually achieved. The concern that pronunciation can be an impediment to learning to read, especially considering the conflict that often occurs between a child's particular infant speech patterns, or personalisms, and spelling patterns, is not a serious factor. As an example, there was a pupil who regularly pronounced *thunder* as *shunder*. When he encountered the *–er* pattern, including *thunder* (lesson 129), the child was rooted to the spot with wonder at the discrepancy between his pronunciation of *thunder* and its written form. He had already mastered words with *th* (*thin, thump, Smith*, etc.) long before (lesson 61) and did not apply his personal *sh* pronunciation to any of them. This experience caused him to independently recognize his pronunciation error and shortly thereafter to drop *shunder* from his speech. The teacher could have wasted a lot of energy and invention trying to force the child to relearn the pronunciation of *thunder* but wisely chose to allow the child to discover his mistake and correct it on his own.

Before beginning reading instruction, it is necessary that the pupil—in addition to being a fluent speaker and an effective listener—be able to recognize and name all the letters in the alphabet. While this may seem like an obvious requirement, many people mistakenly assume that the pupil can learn to identify the letters as he or she goes along, but in fact, by being asked to combine these two tasks—recognizing the letter itself as well as the letter within the context of a word—the pupil is forced to pay attention to two new and often confusing stimuli rather than one.

LET'S READ AND THE NONNATIVE SPEAKER

For the nonnative speaker, English is generally portrayed as a "difficult" language, a language of "peculiarities" and "irregularities." But what second language for the foreigner is not? Doesn't every language have its oddities and exceptions? Learning to read English is similarly painted as a tough task for the nonnative or bilingual reader, with emphasis often placed on its lack of regular forms and the differences between its spoken and written forms (all those spelling "exceptions" and "silent *e*'s" come to mind).

When considering the process of teaching the nonnative speaker or the bilingual speaker or even the native speaker to read English, we might wonder why we would want to start on such a negative note. Why would the exceptions of written English outweigh in importance its consistencies? Whereas English can be challenging and at times baffling when trying to decode a word using phonics—which attempts to *break down* a word into sounds that simply cannot be realistically "converted" in English—*Let's Read* empowers the reader through its organization. The program leads the reader from the simple to the complex by *putting together* spelling patterns that are regular, constant, and reliable, thus allowing the novice to *build up* his or her reading vocabulary with confidence and assuredness.

Let's Read offers an antidote to the misconception that English is a difficult language to learn to read. The Bloomfield system is a wonderful tool for native, nonnative, and bilingual speakers alike, because it teaches pupils to recognize the patterns that function as building blocks as the reader progressively—and logically—learns to read multisyllable words. *Let's Read* serves not only as a lesson plan based on spelling patterns but also—and simultaneously—as a regularizer of pronunciation, correcting and solidifying the pupil's oral strength (and sense of accomplishment). The benefits of this system for the nonnative and the bilingual speaker are many, for by repeating and revisiting patterns, these pupils strengthen and solidify pronunciation and reading skills alike.

THE ALPHABET

Most Western European languages are written in a form of the Roman alphabet. Within each language system, the letters are understood to represent certain speech sounds. But the *i* in the English word *it* does not stand for the *i* in the French word *livre* (book), rather the latter is closer to our American *i* in *machine*. Think also of the French *r,* which has no English equivalent, or the Castilian Spanish *c,* roughly equivalent to English *th.* Such examples remind us that letters have no intrinsic sounds but usually represent different sounds for each language system. While language systems share the same letters, the written code for each language is unique.

In spite of this evidence to the contrary, the curious idea continues to circulate that words make the language and that letters are undistinguishable building blocks of words—leading some to embrace the notion of "look-say" or "whole-word" pedagogy. Such is the folly of the accomplished reader, who cannot recall not being able to read, because the skill is so automatic that it seems almost to have been imprinted before birth. Anyone just acquiring the skill of reading, however, can distinguish words only by different letters and patterns of letters. The same holds true for the practiced reader, although he or she is not directly conscious of the process. Practiced readers have overlearned the skill of identifying many frequently occurring words by their configurations or sequences of letters (the shape of the word *of* or *does* or *that,* for example). We can all agree that only by changing letters does *put* become *pot* or *personal* become *personnel* or *persecute* become *prosecute* or *exercise* become *exorcise.* While the practiced reader can take in such differences within a nanosecond, the uninitiated must follow the ritual of discrimination with the utmost care. Because distinguishing between letters and patterns of letters is integral to learning to read, it is doubly important for the beginning reader to master letter recognition before embarking upon that journey.

Letter recognition is here defined as knowing the names of letters based on their shapes, as opposed to phonemic recognition, which consists of assigning sounds to letters. Teaching letter recognition allows a great range of technique. Chief among all is approaching the alphabet from its grossest and perhaps easiest advantage: shape, an explanation of how the letters are made according to lines or circles or a combination of both. By this analysis, a reasonable order for teaching the alphabet is described here:

1. I, H, T, L, E, F (straight lines)
2. V, A, N, M, W (angled lines)
3. S, O, C, G, Q (variant circles)
4. D, B, P, R (combinations of lines and rounds)
5. J, U (incomplete round)
6. K, X, Y, Z (crossing angles)

The next task is, naturally, to identify the lowercase letters. The obvious difference between teaching recognition of uppercase and lowercase letters is that some of the lowercase letters have virtually the same shapes as their uppercase counterparts (*c*, *o*, *p*, *s*, *u*, *v*, *w*, *x*, *y*, and *z*). Thus, the pupil's learning load is immediately decreased by the ten shapes already learned, leaving just sixteen whose forms must be learned, along with the variant forms of a/*a* and g/*g*. The sequence for teaching the lowercase letters is based on an analysis similar to that for the uppercase letters: how are they put together? A suggested structural sequence follows:

1. l, t, i (straight lines)
2. v, w, x, z (angled lines)
3. f, k (straight combinations)
4. b, d, h (lines and rounds)
5. o, c, e, a/*a* (circles and variants)
6. m, n, u, r, s (variant rounds)
7. q, p, g/*g*, j, y (descenders)

The lowercase letters can obviously be presented with their equivalent capital letters or as an alphabet of alternate versions of the capital letters.

Sometimes pupils have difficulty distinguishing *b* from *d* and *p*, and even *q* from *p*. Do not assume there is some visual or intellectual impairment in a student if such confusion occurs, as occasionally even adept pupils will stumble long after the alphabet has been firmly learned. Simply show the letters in pairs (as *d/b*; *q/p*) to demonstrate their differences; discernment will come with repetition.

Many children will have learned all their letters—and even words—without such formal intervention. Sometimes children pick out letters on cereal boxes or in much-loved books or recognize them in street signs or newspapers or on the computer or television screen. This development is all to the good and should encourage the teacher to use any means available to make the pupil aware of letters as a conspicuous presence in daily life.

Can the pupil follow the series of drawings but especially recognize and name the letters on pages 54–55? If the answer is yes, it is time to begin reading.

THE READING LESSONS

The following remarks are intended to help the teacher by giving a general idea of how to get started, how the lessons are organized, the sequence in which new patterns are taught, and, most importantly, the basic premises underlying *Let's Read* that influence the way in which the lessons are taught. Additionally, each of the six parts of *Let's Read* begins with a "Guide to Lessons" containing suggestions for the teacher specific to that section.

Once the pupil has mastered letter recognition, it is time to begin reading instruction. *Let's Read* is designed as a visual and oral program: in the beginning, show the student how to spell-and-say by asking the student to name each of the letters in the word in sequence (for example, *c-a-t*) and then identifying the word the student has spelled (Say, simply, "cat."). Later, as the pupil progresses through the lessons, have the student look (carefully)-and-say.

As we advise in teaching the ABCs, the essential pedagogical technique of *Let's Read* is discrimination of significant difference. In the reading lessons, contrast or difference is the means by which the pupil distinguishes between words, that is, the difference between *cat* and *rat*, or *cat* and *cut*, or *cat* and *cot*—all words with discrete meanings. The order in which the spelling patterns are introduced is based on the frequency with which they appear in written English; the appendix to part I lists multisyllable words built upon these foundational patterns and gives an idea of how pervasive they are in the language. Ideally, the basic technique of learning patterns is an indispensable tool for developing those word-attack skills that enable the reader to unlock unfamiliar words.

The reading lessons, in their most basic form, consist of the pupil spelling and saying the words in the list, with the teacher identifying words whenever necessary. All reading in *Let's Read* is done orally. Silent reading will come with mastery but is not a recommended technique to cultivate with beginning pupils, nor is silent reading appropriate for new material throughout the lessons. If it is necessary to emphasize this skill, then the pupil should practice it with connected reading and only after it is clear that he or she can read the same material aloud without hesitation.

Like the original *Let's Read*, this edition is organized into six parts. Each presents particular vocabulary illustrative of related spelling patterns used in written English:

- Part I: The consonant-vowel-consonant "regular," or alphabetic, combinations of both consonants and vowels in English. Alphabetic or regular patterns as defined by Bloomfield's approach are those that are the most consistent in spelling and sound.
- Part II: Alphabetic blends and digraphs
- Part III: The most regular long-vowel spelling patterns
- Part IV: The commonest irregular (nonalphabetic) words, including more of the sight vocabulary (*one, said, were, been, was*); multisyllable words; contractions; suffixes
- Part V: The most common irregular vowel spelling patterns in English
- Part VI: The most common irregular consonant spelling patterns in English

It is not unusual for a teacher to discover that some pupils can read just about any material by the end of part IV of *Let's Read*. However, it is desirable to pursue the *Let's Read* course to its end, because in parts V and VI the pupil will be systematically exposed to important irregular patterns in English. These groups of words (*a* as in *father*, *o* as in *son*) are usually acquired in a helter-skelter fashion, as random words encountered when reading a library book (rather than a reading text) or as happens with an interest-based vocabulary in texts commonly used in classrooms. Continuing instruction through the final two parts of *Let's Read* enhances vocabulary, increases skill, and assures spelling mastery. Such is the benefit to the pupil if the program is followed to its conclusion, and the results are more than worth the modest effort—rather like putting a coat of varnish on a completed oil painting to sharpen its effect and assure its durability.

PRACTICAL SUGGESTIONS FOR TEACHING *LET'S READ*

The most important disadvantage for any teacher beginning a course of reading instruction with a pupil of any age is that the teacher already knows how to read, and it requires a huge leap of imagination to recall that time when one did not have any idea what those marks on a page meant. Learning to read is like solving a mystery. The task of the teacher is to demystify the process.

Remember that *Let's Read* is like a road map to reading. It is more participatory (student-centered) than didactic (teacher-centered). It allows great freedom to both the teacher and the pupil. It does not have workbooks or other ancillary materials that must be used with it. But what does one do about writing, the second requirement of literacy? If a child wants to write, he or she should be encouraged to do so. It is not, however, necessary to write in order to learn to read, and for some young pupils, writing can actually cause frustration and discouragement. The teacher should be sensitive to aspects of the pupil's performance, attitude, and behavior as indicators of his or her comfort with the lessons, spending more or less time on particular lessons as seems appropriate to each pupil.

The following general suggestions may be helpful.

- Conduct reading lessons in a comfortable place.
- Keep the lessons short. Fifteen to twenty minutes is most likely long enough, although with some pupils, it may be too much or too little.
- Allow the pupil to use his or her finger to follow the print on the page, in both the lists and in the connected reading. In the beginning, as the teacher, show the pupil by example how to point to words or use a marker to separate the lines of type. After a time, the pupil will not need either to point or to use a marker to follow the print.
- Have the pupil spell and say each word being introduced. Spelling and saying is how the pupil discovers the relationship between the patterns of letters and the spoken words. In the first lessons, the student will spell the words, the teacher will say them,

and then the student will repeat the word. As pupils progress through the lessons, they will become such masters of the alphabetic patterns of English that they will be able to spell a new pattern and then read it without any cue from the teacher. Spelling and saying also helps develop the left-to-right habit for beginning readers.

- Especially in the beginning, keep paper and pencil on hand, or use a chalkboard as backup if a pupil needs help in recalling a pattern introduced earlier. In general, use the device of pairing (displaying together) words that have only one significant difference (as between *cat* and *can*, the *final –t* and *–n* being the significant difference in the pair) to help a pupil see and recall patterns. In later lessons, the alphabetic habit is so ingrained, usually a pupil requires less and less assistance, and more attention can be paid to the meaning or message.

- Implement creative activities that support the lessons. Teachers usually develop a host of schemes to help a pupil and should not shrink from being inventive. For example, some pupils respond enthusiastically to personalized little books containing perhaps six sentences based on a particular lesson and incorporating the pupil's name. Any proper name should be treated as a sight word, but often even very young children already recognize their names from seeing them at daycare, preschool, and so forth. Letters or cards with words on them can be a very helpful reinforcement, as are word games and spelling games.

- When a pupil wants to read "other books," encourage it; however, guide the pupil to books that will not be too difficult or confusing. The teacher should keep in mind how restricted the *Let's Read* vocabulary is in parts I and II when choosing other books. Of course, some pupils thrive on the challenge of unfamiliar vocabulary, but others can be dismayed by it. The teacher's job is to be sensitive to both possibilities.

- From lesson 1 to lesson 36, vocabulary is restricted to the "regular" spelling patterns (*c* is invariably the *c* in *cat; y* appears only as an initial consonant, as in *yet; g* is always as in *get*, etc.). Gradually and systematically, digraphs and consonant blends (as in *sing*, *spend*) and "irregular" patterns, such as peculiar consonant and vowel combinations (as in *ice, cute, computer*), are taught within patterns. The index at the end of the book shows where particular vocabulary words appear.

Teaching Children to Read*

Leonard Bloomfield

1. WHAT IS READING?

Literacy is the most important factor in keeping up our civilization, and teaching children to read is the most important task of our schools. We perform this task clumsily and with a great waste of labor and time. Even at the end of eight years many of our pupils cannot be said to read; yet eight months ought to suffice.

This is not due to a lack of pedagogic methods. The most excellent teaching technique is bound to give poor results so long as the teacher does not know *what to teach*.

It is generally assumed that a teacher, who knows how to read, understands also the linguistic processes that are involved in the act of reading. No one assumes that a cook who prepares a cup of coffee understands the chemical processes which he has called into use. Everybody knows that there is a science of chemistry—that chemical processes have been systematically observed and analyzed—and everyone who deals with chemistry, in the way of teaching or otherwise, makes use of the knowledge that has been gained by generations of scientific study. In quite the same way, though not everyone knows it, human speech has been systematically observed and analyzed. Generations of work have

---

* Editor's note: Portions of Dr. Bloomfield's essay appeared as an article titled "Linguistics and Reading," in The Elementary English Review XIX, no. 4 (April 1942), 125–30, and XIX, no. 5 (May 1942), 183–86. Bloomfield's article was abstracted from this essay, which was written well before 1942 (and clearly with the expectation that Bloomfield's "system" would eventually see publication). A reference to the essay is in Bloomfield's letter of Nov. 7, 1937 to C. L. Barnhart and quoted in the new introduction to this edition of *Let's Read*. The essay provided guidance for many editorial decisions made by Barnhart as the original *Let's Read* manuscript was being written. The process of development itself—long after Bloomfield's death—was in essence a completion of Bloomfield's early and far less encompassing design.

been spent upon this subject, and many useful and interesting facts have been brought to light.[1] No one, not even the cleverest person, could hope, by his unaided efforts, to duplicate these results. Our schools will continue to waste time and energy and to reap meager success unless and until the teacher in the early grades knows the main linguistic facts and principles that play a part in the act of reading.

This essay is planned to present—in a practically useful arrangement—these facts and principles.

2. Speech and Writing

To understand reading, one must understand *the relation of written (or printed) words to speech.*

Compared to speech, the use of writing is something artificial and relatively modern. To be sure, writing was used thousands of years ago in Egypt and in Mesopotamia, and the art of writing has never since then been lost. Our own alphabet is probably a descendant of the ancient Egyptian hieroglyphs. However, until recently, the art of writing was confined to a very few nations, and within these nations to a very few persons. It is only within the last two hundred years that literacy has become widespread in a few countries. Most languages have never been represented in writing; it may be that less than half of the people alive today know how to read and write.*

Written notations in the English language began to be made only some centuries after the beginning of the Christian Era. For several centuries these notations were confined to words or brief phrases; they were made in the clumsy alphabet known as Runes, and only a few pagan priests or magicians were able to read them. It is only around the year 800 or so that we get connected texts written in English in the ordinary Latin alphabet. Even then the art of reading and writing was confined to the priesthood. Slowly this art spread to wider and wider classes, but anything like general popular literacy has arrived only within the last hundred years; It is well to recall also that in the Middle Ages the few persons who knew how to read and write did most of their reading and writing in Latin rather than in their native language.

To the present-day literate person it seems almost incredible that people could get along without reading and writing, and that even today many savage tribes are in this position, and many civilized nations contain a great proportion of illiterates. What happens to a language if the people who speak it have no books—no dictionaries, grammars, spelling

---

1. This history is very interestingly presented in H. Pedersen's *Linguistic Science in the Nineteenth Century*, translated by J. Spargo (Cambridge, MA: 1931).

* Editor's note: Based on estimates contemporary with this essay (1937).

books, and so on? The answer to this question was one of the first and most surprising results of linguistic study: unwritten languages function and develop in the same way as languages that have been reduced to writing. In fact, taking the great mass of human history, the non-use of writing is the normal state of affairs, and the use of writing is a special case and, until very recent times, a most unusual case. The effect of writing on language, where there is no popular literacy, is practically nothing, and where there is popular literacy, as among us, the effect of writing is merely to introduce a few small *irregularities* into the process of linguistic development. This, of course, is the opposite of the popular view, but it is the result of every investigation that has been undertaken and is today firmly accepted by every student of language.

Writing is merely a device for recording speech. A person is much the same and looks the same, whether he has ever had his picture taken or not. Only a vain beauty who sits for many photographs and carefully studies them may end by slightly changing her pose and expression. It is much the same with languages and their written recording.

For our present purpose we need only understand *how speech is recorded by means of written or printed signs*.

Language consists of sounds—musical sounds and noises. These sounds are produced by movements of the speaker's vocal organs (larynx, tongue, and so on). These movements produce sound waves in the air, and these sound waves strike the hearer's eardrums. In this way we signal to one another, and the signals are what we call language.

Suppose we want to signal to someone who cannot be reached by the sound of our voice—to someone far away, or to coming generations. Nowadays we could use the radio or make a phonograph record. These are modern inventions, and writing is only a somewhat less modern invention of much the same kind.

There have been many systems of writing, but all of them seem to consist of three devices or of various mixtures of these three devices: *picture writing, word writing*, and *alphabetic writing*.

3. Picture Writing

First, there is *picture writing*, in which you simply draw a picture that represents the story you would tell your reader if you could reach him by the sound of your voice. Some tribes of American Indians were great picture writers.[2] Here is an American Indian's picture message:[3]

---

2. The best examples are to be found in G. Mallery's study, published in the 4th and 10th *Annual Reports* of the Bureau of American Ethnology, Smithsonian Institution (Washington, DC: 1886 and 1893).

3. Ibid., 4th *Annual Report* (1886), p. 220.

At the center are two crossed lines; at one side of these there is a gun and a beaver with thirty little strokes above it; at the other side are sketches of a fisher, an otter, and a buffalo.

This means: "I will trade you a fisher-skin, an otter-skin, and a buffalo-hide for a gun and thirty beaver pelts."

A message like this is effective, provided the writer and reader are in accord as to the meaning of the pictures. They must agree that the crossed lines mean an act of trading, and that the set of strokes means a number, and that the animals are a beaver, an otter, a fisher, and so on. These things are determined by convention: the beaver is always drawn in one way, the otter in another, and so on for every animal, so that even a poor draughtsman can show which animal he means.

The important feature of picture writing is that it is not based upon language at all. A reader who knows the conventions by which the pictures are drawn, can read the message even if he does not understand the language which the writer speaks. If the reader knows that the picture of an animal with a big tail means a beaver, he can get this part of the message, even though he does not know how the word for beaver would sound in the writer's language. In fact, he can read the picture correctly, even if he does not know what language the writer speaks. Without going too far into the psychology of the thing, we may say that the reader does not get the speech sounds (the words or sentences) which the writer might use in conversation, but he gets the practical content (the "idea") which in conversation he would have got from hearing those speech sounds.

4. WORD WRITING

The second main type of writing is *word writing*. In word writing each word is represented by a conventional sign, and these signs are arranged in the same order as the words in speech. Chinese writing is the most perfect system of this kind. There is a conventional character for every word in the language. To write a message you put the character which represents the first word into the upper right hand corner of the paper, below it you write the character for the second word, and so on; when you have reached the bottom of the page you start again at the top, to the left of the first word, and form a second column down to the bottom of the paper, and so on. Each character represents some one Chinese word. As the vocabulary of a literate person runs to about twenty thousand words, this means that in order to read even moderately well, one must know thousands of characters. Learning to read Chinese is a difficult task, and if the Chinese reader does not keep in practice, he is likely to lose his fluency.

It is probable that word writing grew out of picture writing; at any rate, in the system known to us, some of the characters resemble conventionalized pictures. However, the difference between these two kinds of writing is far more important for our purpose than any historical connection. The characters of word writing are attached to words, and not to "ideas." In picture writing you could not distinguish such near symbols as, say, *horse*, *nag*, *steed*; but in word writing each one of these words would be represented by a different character. In picture writing very many words cannot be represented at all—words like *and, or, but, if, because, is, was*, and abstract words like *kindness, knowledge, please, care*—but in word writing each such word has a conventional symbol of its own.

We ourselves use word writing in a very limited way in our numerals, 1, 2, 3, 4, 5, 6, 7, 8, 9, 0 and in signs like $, +, −, =, × (in arithmetic, representing the word *times*). The symbol 5, for instance, by an arbitrary convention, represents the word *five*, and the symbol 7 represents the word *seven*. There is no question of spelling or sound involved here; the symbol is arbitrarily assigned to the word. The characteristic feature of word writing, from the point of view of people who are used to alphabetic writing, is that the characters, like our 5 and 7, do not indicate the separate sounds which make up the word, but that each character as a whole indicates a word as a whole. Viewing it practically, from the standpoint of the teacher and pupil, we may say that there is no spelling: the written sign for each of the words (*four, seven*, etc.) has to be learned by itself. You either know that the character 7 represents the word *seven* or you don't know it; there is no way of figuring it out on the basis of sounds or letters, and there is no way of figuring out the value of an unfamiliar character.

Word writing has one great advantage: since a character says nothing about the sound of the word, the same character can be used for writing different languages. For instance, our numeral digits (which, as we have seen, form a small system of word writing) are used by many nations, although the corresponding words have entirely different sounds. The following table shows the words which are represented by the characters 1 to 9 in English, German, French, and Finnish.

Character	1	2	3	4	5
English	one	two	three	four	five
German	eins	zwei	drei	vier	fünf
French	un	deux	trois	quatre	cinq
Finnish	yksi	kaksi	kolme	neljä	viisi

	6	7	8	9
English	six	seven	eight	nine
German	sechs	sieben	acht	neun
French	six	sept	huit	neuf
Finnish	kuusi	seitsemän	kahdeksan	yhdeksän

The advantage of this is that we can all read each other's numbers. Different regions of China speak different dialects which in part are mutually unintelligible, for the extreme differences are perhaps as great as between English, Dutch, and German. But thanks to a system of conventions like that of our numeral digits, a piece of Chinese writing is readable in all parts of China, regardless of the different-sounding words, just as the digit *4* is readable all over Europe, although the words of the various languages sound very differently.

5. ALPHABETIC WRITING

The third main type of writing is *alphabetic writing*. In alphabetic writing each character represents a *unit speech sound*. The literate Chinese, with his system of word writing, has to memorize thousands of characters—one for every word in his language—whereas, with an alphabetic system, the literate person needs to know only a few dozen characters—one for each unit speech sound of his language. In order to understand the nature of alphabetic writing we need to know only what is meant by the term unit speech sound, or, as the linguist calls it, by the term *phoneme*.

The existence of unit speech sounds, or phonemes, is one of the discoveries of the language study of the last hundred years. A short speech—say, a sentence—in any language consists of an unbroken succession of all sorts of sounds. When we hear speech in our own language, the sounds are so familiar and the meaning is so obvious that we do not notice the mere noise effect, but when we hear an entirely strange language, we wonder if there can be any system in such a gibberish of queer noises, and we may question whether it could ever be reduced to alphabetic writing. Systematic study has shown, however, that in every language the meaning of words is attached to certain characteristic features of sound. These features are very stable and their number ranges anywhere from around fifteen to around fifty, differing for different languages. These features are the unit speech sounds or phonemes. Each word consists of a fixed combination of phonemes. Therefore, if we have a written character for each phoneme of a language, the sum total of characters will range anywhere from fifteen to fifty and with these characters we shall be able to write down any word of that language.

The existence of phonemes and the identity of each individual phoneme are by no means obvious: it took several generations of study before linguists became fully aware of this important feature of human speech. It is remarkable that long before scientific students of language had made this discovery, there had arisen a system of alphabetic writing—a system in which each character represented a phoneme. It seems that alphabetic writing has developed out of word writing, and that this remarkable development has taken place only once in the history of mankind—somewhere between 2000 and 1000 B.C. at the eastern end of the Mediterranean, with the Egyptians, the Semitic-speaking peoples (such as the Phoenicians), and the Greeks successively playing the principal role.

All forms of alphabetical writing, then, are offshoots of a single original system. The details of this origin and of the later history, so far as we can get at them, are of great interest but would carry us too far afield. It is important for us to know that alphabetic writing was not invented at one stroke, as a finished system, but that it grew gradually and, one could almost say, by a series of accidents, out of a system of word writing. Neither then nor at any time since was there any body of experts who understood the system of phonemes and regulated the habits of writing.

Accordingly we find many ups and downs in the perfection of the system. The ancient Greeks seem at some times and places to have reached an almost perfect application of the alphabetic principle and then to have lapsed from it: in medieval and modern Greek writing the alphabetic principle is very poorly carried out. A similar story could be told of the ancient Romans. Among modern nations, some have almost perfect alphabetic systems (such as the Spanish, Bohemian, and Finnish systems of writing), but others have relatively imperfect systems (such as the Italian, Dutch, or German), and still others have extremely imperfect and arbitrary systems (such as the modern Greek, and French, and the English).

6. ENGLISH WRITING IS ALPHABETIC

We can illustrate the nature of alphabetic writing by means of English examples, for, in spite of its many imperfections, our system of writing is in origin and in its main features alphabetic. This is proved by the simple fact that we can write every English word by means of only twenty-six characters, whereas a system of word writing would demand many thousands. As an illustration we may take the written representation of the word *pin:*

p i n

It consists of three characters, and each of these three represents a single phoneme. If anyone told us to use these three characters to represent the word *needle*, we should find the suggestion absurd, because these characters do not *fit the sound* of the word *needle*. That is, each of the three characters *p, i, n* is used conventionally to represent a unit *sound* of our language. This appears plainly if we compare the written symbol for other words, such as *pig* and *pit*, or *bin* and *din*, or *pan* and *pun*; or if we reverse the order of the letters and read *nip*, or if we place the letter *p* at both ends and read *pip*.

The alphabetic nature of our writing appears most plainly of all, however, when we put together a combination of letters that does not make a word and yet find ourselves clearly guided to the utterance of English speech sounds; thus, nobody will have trouble in reading such nonsense syllables as *nin, mip, lib*. Alphabetic writing differs entirely from picture writing in that the visible marks do not represent things or stories or "ideas." As a picture of a pin, the marks

p i n

are simply no good at all. Alphabetic writing differs from word writing in that the characters are not assigned, one by one, in an arbitrary, take-it-or-leave-it system, to words, but represent unit speech sounds, so that the way of writing each word bears a close relation to the speech sounds which make up that word.

If our system of writing were perfectly alphabetic, then anyone who knew the value of each letter could read or write any word. In reading, he would simply pronounce the phonemes indicated by the letters, and in writing he would put down the appropriate letter for each phoneme. The fact that we actually can do both of these things in the case of nonsense words, such as *nin* or *mip*, shows that our system of writing is alphabetic.

In order to read alphabetic writing one must have an ingrained habit of producing the phonemes of one's language when one sees the written marks which conventionally represent these phonemes. A well-trained reader, of course, for the most part reads silently, but we shall do better for the present to ignore this fact, as we know that the child learns first to read aloud.

The accomplished reader of English, then, has an overpracticed and ingrained habit of uttering one phoneme of the English language when he sees the letter *p*, another phoneme when he sees the letter *i*, another when he sees the letter *n*, still another when he sees the letter *m*, still another when he sees the letter *d*, and so on. In this way, he utters the conventionally accepted word when he sees a combination of letters like *pin, nip, pit, tip, tin, nit, dip, din, dim, mid*. What is more, all readers will agree as to the sounds they utter when they see unconventional combinations, such as *pid, nin, pim, mip, nid, nim, mim*. It is this habit which we must set up in the child who is to acquire the art of reading. If we pursue any other course, we are merely delaying him until he acquires this habit in spite of our bad guidance.

7. Irregular Spellings

English writing is alphabetic, but not perfectly so. For many words we have a conventional rule of writing which does not agree with the sound of the word. Take, for instance, the two words which are pronounced *nit*. One is actually spelled *nit*, but the other is spelled *knit*, with an extra letter *k* at the beginning, a letter which ordinarily represents one of the phonemes of our language, as in *kin, kit, kid*.

When we study the history of our language—and this, again, is a branch of the study of linguistics—we learn that up to about two hundred years ago the word *knit* (along with other words like *knee, knife, knave*) was actually spoken with a "*k*-sound" (that is, with the initial phoneme of words like *kin, kit, kid*) before the *n*-sound. In fact, we are told that in some places in England the country people still speak in this older way. About two hundred years ago the prevalent manner of speaking English changed: the initial *k*-sound before *n* was dropped. However, the old tradition of writing persisted, all the books one read spelled the word with this letter *k*, and people simply kept on writing it as they had always seen it written. So far as reading is concerned, this extra letter *k* makes no difference at all, for (owing to the above-mentioned change in pronunciation) no English word now begins with sounds *k* plus *n*, and when we see a word written with the initial letters *kn*, we have the habit of not trying to pronounce the *k*.

Now someone may ask whether the spelling of *knit* with *k* does not serve to distinguish this word from *nit* "the egg of a louse." Of course it does, and this is exactly where our writing lapses from the alphabetic principle back into the older scheme of word writing. Alphabetic writing, which indicates all the significant speech sounds of each word, is just as clear as actual speech, which means that it is clear enough. Word writing, on the other hand, provides a separate character for each and every word, regardless of its sound, and at the cost of tremendous labor to everyone who learns to read and write. Our spelling the verb *knit* with an extra *k* (and the noun *nit* without this extra *k*) is a step in the direction of word writing. This convention goes a little way toward giving us a special picture for the verb *knit* (as opposed to its homonym, the noun *nit*) and it does this at the cost of a certain amount of labor, since the reader must learn to ignore initial *k* before *n*, and the writer must learn where to place it (as in *knit, knight, knave*) and where not to place it (as in *nit, night, nave*). However, we shall have enough to do later with the irregularities of our spelling; for the present it is far more important to see that in its basic character, in its bones, blood, and marrow, our system of writing is alphabetic—witness merely the fact that we get along with twenty-six characters instead of twenty-six thousand.

8. PHONIC METHODS

The letters of the alphabet are signs which direct us to produce sounds of our language. A confused and vague appreciation of this fact has given rise to the so-called "phonic" methods of teaching children to read. These methods suffer from several serious faults.

The inventors of these methods confuse writing with speech. They plan the work as though the child were being taught to pronounce—that is, as if the child were being taught to speak. They give advice about phonetics, about clear utterance, and other matters of this sort. This confuses the issue. Alphabetic writing merely directs the reader to produce certain speech sounds. A person who cannot produce these sounds cannot get the message of a piece of alphabetic writing. If a child has not learned to utter the speech sounds of our language, the only sensible course is to postpone reading until he has learned to speak. As a matter of fact, nearly all six-year-old children have long ago learned to speak their native language; they have no need whatever of the drill which is given by phonic methods.

In exceptional cases, children get into school before they have thoroughly learned to speak. A child may replace the *r*-sound by the *w*-sound, saying *wed* instead of *red,* or he may replace the *th*-sound by the *f*-sound, saying *fin* instead of *thin*, or his speech may be altogether indistinct and blurred. Conditions like these may be due to gross anatomical defects, such as a cleft palate; or to a deep-seated deficiency of the nervous system, such as idiocy; or to minor nervous faults, as is the case in stuttering; or to social maladjustment, which will prompt a child to seek advantage in such things as baby talk; or they may be due simply to the fact that he speaks some language other than English, so that English speech sounds are foreign to him. In all such cases, the economical course and the course that is best for the child, is to remove the defect of speech before trying to make the child read. In some cases, to be sure, this cannot be done. The extreme and typical case of this kind is that of deaf-and-dumb children. Such cases demand very elaborate care and training; they must be dealt with in a manner very different from ordinary reading instruction. In short, the problem of teaching children to speak is entirely different from that of teaching children to read. In all normal cases, the child has learned to speak before we are called upon to teach him to read, and our task is merely to give him the habit of uttering the familiar speech sounds at the sight of the printed or written letters. To ignore this distinction, as the phonic methods do, is to befuddle the whole process.

The second error of the phonic methods is that of isolating the speech sounds. The authors of these methods tell us to show the child a letter, for instance *t*, and to make him react by uttering the *t*-sound; that is, the English speech sound which occurs at the beginning of a word like *two* or *ten*. This sound is to be uttered either all by itself or else with an obscure vowel sound after it. Now, English-speaking people, children or adults, are not accustomed to making that kind of noise. The phoneme [t] does not occur alone in English utterance; neither does the phoneme [t] followed by an obscure vowel sound. If we insist on making the child perform unaccustomed feats with his vocal organs, we are bound to confuse his response to the printed signs. In any language, most phonemes do not occur by themselves, in isolated utterance, and even most of the successions of phonemes which one could theoretically devise, are never so uttered. English speakers do not separately pronounce the sound of [t] or [p] or of [u] as in *put*, and a succession like [s p], for instance, as in *spin*, does not occur alone, as a separate utterance. Learning to pronounce such things is something in the nature of a stunt, and has nothing to do with learning to read. We must not complicate our task by unusual demands on the child's power of pronouncing. We intend to apply phonetics to our reading instruction; this does not mean that we are going to try to teach phonetics to young children. In this absurdity lies the greatest fault of the so-called phonic methods.

9. THE WORD METHOD

In spite of the special methods, such as the "phonic" method, which have been advocated at various times, the actual instruction in our schools consists almost entirely of something much simpler, which we may call the *word method.* The word method teaches the child to utter a word when he sees the printed symbols for this word; it does not pretend to any phonetic breaking-up of the word. The child learns the printed symbols, to be sure, by "spelling" the word—that is, by naming, in proper succession, the letters which make up the written representation of the word, as *see-aye-tee: cat,* and so on. No attempt is made, however, to take advantage of the alphabetic principle. If one examines the primers and first readers which exemplify the various methods that have been advocated, one is struck by the fact that the differences are very slight: the great bulk of the work is word learning. The authors are so saturated with this, the conventional method, that they carry their innovations only a very short way; they evidently lack the linguistic knowledge that would enable them to grade the matter according to relations between sound and spelling. It is safe to say that nearly all of us were taught to read by the word method.

The word method proceeds as though our writing were word writing. Every word has to be learned as an arbitrary unit; this task is simplified only by the fact that all these word characters are made up out of twenty-six constituent units, the letters. In order to read a new word, the child must learn the new word character; he can best do this by memorizing the letters which make up this new word character, but these letters are arbitrarily presented and have nothing to do with the sound of the word.

If this plan could be consistently carried out, our children would be in much the same position as the Chinese child who has to acquire a system of word writing. Like him, they would have to learn thousands of complex symbols, one for each word in the language. Learning to read would be the task of years, and any serious interruption of practice would result in wholesale forgetting. Actually, the child's nervous system is wiser than we are: in spite of our not telling him the values of the letters and in spite of our confusing hodgepodge, the child does acquire, unknowingly, a habit of connecting letters with speech sounds. This appears from the fact that he learns to read in less time than would be required by a genuine system of word writing; it appears also in some of the child's mistakes, such as trying to read *debt* with a *b*-sound or *walk* with an *l*-sound—mistakes which show that the child is operating, however imperfectly, on an alphabetic principle.

The most serious drawback of all the English reading instruction known to me, regardless of the special method that is in each case advocated, is the drawback of the word method. The written forms for words are presented to the child in an order which conceals the alphabetic principle. For instance, if near the beginning of instruction, we present the words *get* and *gem*, we cannot expect the child to develop any fixed or fluent response to the sight of the letter *g*. If we talk to him about the "hard" and "soft" sounds of the letter *g*, we shall only confuse him the more. The irregularities of our spelling—that is, its deviation from the alphabetic principle—demand careful handling if they are not to confuse the child and to delay his acquisition of the alphabetic habit.

Our teaching ought to distinguish, then, between *regular* spellings, which involve only the alphabetic principle, and *irregular* spellings, which depart from this principle, and it ought to classify the irregular spellings according to the various types of deviation from the alphabetic principle. We must train the child to respond vocally to the sight of letters, and this can be done by presenting regular spellings; we must train him, also, to make exceptional vocal responses to irregular spellings, and this can be done by presenting systematically the various types of irregular spelling. For instance, we must train the child to respond by the *k*-sound to the sight of the letter *k* in words like *kiss, kid, kin, kit*, but we must also train him not to try pronouncing a *k*-sound when he sees the written *k* in the words like *knit, knife, knee, knight*.

The material in existing primers and readers is not thus graded, because the authors of these books lacked the linguistic training necessary for such a classification. The knowledge required to make this classification is not very profound. In fact, the teacher who reads over the list in this book will soon grasp the principles that are involved, and in doing so will have acquired all the phonetics needed for ordinary instruction in reading. Although this knowledge is easily gained, persons who lack it are likely to make troublesome mistakes. For instance, the author of a treatise on reading methods asks how we ought to teach children to read the word *of*. He does not know whether we ought to read it with the sound of *f* as in *if* or with the sound of *v* as in *have*; the latter pronunciation he thinks is "careless" and imprecise. This author is to be blamed not so much for his ignorance of phonetics as for his failure to consult a book or a person who could tell him the answer. He is in the position of a writer on chemistry who at this day and age deliberated in print as to whether diamonds were or were not a form of crystallized water. As a matter of fact, a glance into *The New English Dictionary*[4] shows that the word *of* was pronounced with the sound of *f* (as in *if*) up to about the time of Shakespeare. At that time there occurred a change which resulted in two forms of the word: as a preposition (unstressed) it received the sound of *v* (as in *have*) and in this use it is now spelled *of* and pronounced *ov*, but as an adverb (stressed) it kept the old *f*-sound, and in this use it is now spelled *off*. The pronunciation which this author prefers, then, has been out of existence for more than three hundred years.

The author of a textbook or the classroom teacher does not need a profound knowledge of phonetics; he needs only to realize that information on this subject is available and that he need not grope about in the dark.

10. Ideational Methods

Although the various methods that have been advanced are in practice only slight adaptations of the universal method of word reading, it will be worth our while to glance at another method, which has some vogue, namely, the *sentence method* or *ideational reading*. This method attempts to train the child to get the "idea" or content directly from the printed page.

---

4. Reprinted as *The Oxford English Dictionary*, 13 vols. (Oxford, England: 1933).

When a literate adult reads, he passes his eyes rapidly over the printed text and, scarcely noticing the individual words or letters, grasps the content of what he has read. This appears plainly in the fact that we do not often notice the misprints on the page we are reading. The literate adult now observes the laborious reading of the child, who stumbles along and spells out the words and in the end fails to grasp the content of what he has read. The adult concludes that the child is going at the thing in a wrong way and should be taught to seize the "ideas" instead of watching the individual letters.

The trouble with the child, however, is simply that he lacks the long practice which enables the adult to read rapidly; the child puzzles out the words so slowly that he has forgotten the beginning of the sentence before he reaches the end; consequently he cannot grasp the content. The adult's reading is so highly practiced and so free from difficulty that he does not realize any transition between his glance at the page and his acceptance of the content. Therefore he makes the mistake of thinking that no such transition takes place—that he gets the "ideas" directly from the printed signs.

This mistake is all the more natural because the adult reads silently; since he does not utter any speech sounds, he concludes that speech sounds play no part in the process of reading and that the printed marks lead directly to "ideas." Nothing could be further from the truth.

The child does his first reading out loud. Then, under the instruction or example of his elders, he economizes by reading in a whisper. Soon he reduces this to scarcely audible movements of speech; later these become entirely inaudible. Many adults who are not very literate move their lips while reading. The fully literate person has succeeded in reducing these speech movements to the point where they are not even visible. That is, he has developed a system of internal substitute movements which serve him, for private purposes, such as thinking and silent reading, in place of audible speech sounds. When the literate adult reads very carefully—as when he is reading poetry or difficult scientific matter or a text in a foreign language—he actually goes through this process of internal speech; his conventional way of reporting this is that he internally pronounces or "hears himself say" the words of the text. The highly-skilled reader has trained himself beyond this: he can actually shut out some of the internal speech movements and respond to a text without seeing every word. If you ask him to read aloud, he will often replace words or phrases of the printed text by equivalent ones; he has seized only the high spots of the printed text. Now this highly skilled adult has forgotten the earlier stages of his own development and wants the child to jump directly from an illiterate state to that of an overtrained reader.

The marks in a piece of American Indian picture writing represent *things*, or, if you prefer, *ideas*. The characters in a piece of Chinese writing do not represent things (or ideas) but words. The letters in a piece of English writing do not represent things, or even words, but *sounds.* The task of the reader is to get the sounds from the written or printed page. When he has done this, he must still, of course, perform a second task: he must understand the meaning of these sounds. This second task, however, is not peculiar to reading, but concerns all use of language; when we are not reading, but hearing spoken words, we have the same task of appreciating the content of what is said. The ideational methods, in short, show us the age-old confusion between the use of writing and the ordinary processes of speech.

It is true, of course, that many children in the upper grades—and even, for that matter, many postgraduate students in the university—fail to seize the content of what they read. It was this unfortunate situation which led to the invention of ideational methods in reading instruction. This, however, meant confusing two entirely different things. A person who can read aloud a text that is before his eyes, but cannot reproduce the content or otherwise show his grasp of it, lacks something other than reading power, and needs to be taught the proper response to language, be it presented in writing or in actual speech. The marks on the page offer only sounds of speech and words, not things or ideas.

So much can be said, however: the child who fails to grasp the content of what he reads is usually a poor reader also in the mechanical sense. He fails to grasp the content because he is too busy with the letters. The cure for this is not to be sought in ideational methods, but in better training at the stage where the letters are being associated with sounds.

The extreme type of ideational method is the so-called "non-oral" method, where children are not required to pronounce words, but to respond directly to the content. They are shown a printed sentence such as *Skip around the room,* and the correct answer is not to say anything, but to perform the indicated act. Nothing could be less in accord with the nature of our system of writing or with the reading process such as, in the end, it must be acquired.

It is not easy for a student of language to speak patiently of such vagaries, in which educationalists indulge at great cost to thousands of helpless children. It is exactly as if these same educationalists should invent their own guesswork system of chemistry and introduce it into our schools.

Even the most elementary understanding of systems of writing suffices to show the fallacy of "ideational" reading. The kind of writing which can be read ideationally is picture writing. There the visible marks directly represent the content and do not presuppose any particular wording. In word writing and in alphabetic writing, the visible marks are tokens for speech forms and not for "ideas." The visible word marks tell the Chinese reader to speak (out loud or internally) such and such words of his language. The visible letters of alphabetic writing tell us to speak (out loud or internally) such and such phonemes of our language. If the Chinese reader or we choose to skip the less important of these directions and to notice only the high spots, we can go all the faster, but we do not accurately reproduce the author's words; as soon as the exact wording is important, as in a poem or a difficult exposition, we do in fact accurately follow the visible signals to speech. In short, the black marks on paper which represent an English word, say,

h o r s e

do not represent the shape or smell or any other characteristics of a horse, or even the "idea" (whatever that may be) of a horse; they merely direct us to utter the speech sounds which make up the English word horse. These speech sounds, in turn, are connected for us as a kind of signal, with the animal, and it is only through these speech sounds that the black marks

h o r s e

on the paper have any connection with the animal, or, if you will, with the "idea" of the animal. The adult's instantaneous step from the black marks to the "idea" is the result of long training. To expect to give this facility directly and without intermediate steps to the child is exactly as though we should try to teach the child higher mathematics (which solves complicated problems with power and speed) before we taught him elementary arithmetic. If we insisted on doing this, the child would merely learn elementary arithmetic in spite of us, from our inappropriate examples, and he would not get his higher mathematics until he had, in this irksome way, acquired his elementary arithmetic. Moreover, his mathematics, arithmetic and all, would remain shaky, unless and until, again in spite of us, he had by a vast amount of repetition, gained sureness in the elements which we had neglected to teach him. In practice, the ideational and sentence reading methods are so overwhelmingly diluted with the word method that the children taught in this way are but slightly less sure of themselves than are the pupils of less modern practice.

11. The Content

The circumstances which lead the more intelligent but linguistically untrained school man to seek an "ideational" method is the distressing fact that many older students and adults are unable to get the content from a printed text. We have all heard of the devastating results of experiments in which pupils or adults are given a paragraph to read, and then are asked to reproduce the content; a large proportion of the persons tested are unable to make anything like a correct statement of what the author was trying to tell them. The schoolman concludes that these people were not properly taught to read, and therefore seeks to make elementary reading instruction bear more directly on the content. In this, however, he confuses two entirely different things—the ability to respond to visible marks by uttering speech sounds and the ability to respond correctly to speech. The child who is laboring to find out what words or phrases he must utter when he sees certain printed marks cannot be expected at the same time to respond correctly to the meaning of these words or phrases. If he has spelled out the words *Bill hit John*, we need not be surprised that we can trap him with the question "Whom did John hit?" His problem is to say the correct word or phrase when he sees the black marks, and, indeed, this is enough of a problem; it takes a sophisticated but linguistically untrained adult to underestimate its difficulty. The other problem, which the schoolman confuses with ours, is the problem of responding correctly to speech, and it concerns actual speech just as much as reading. When one tests graduate university students by making a simple oral statement and asking them to reproduce it, the result is just as discouraging as that of similar reading tests. This is a problem which our schools have to face, and the beginning will doubtless have to be made in the earliest grades, but the one place where this problem most certainly cannot be solved is in the elementary instruction in reading, where the child has all he can do to pass from the visual symbols to the spoken words.

In fact, an understanding of the latter difficulty will lead us to see our problem in its simplest terms. Aside from their silliness, the stories in a child's first reader are of little use, because the child is too busy with the mechanics of reading to get anything of the content. He gets the content when the teacher reads the story out loud, and later on, when he has mastered all the words in the story, he can get it for himself, but during the actual process of learning to read the words he does not concern himself with the content. This does not mean that we must forego the use of sentences and connected stories, but it does mean that these are not essential to the first steps. We need not fear to use disconnected words and even senseless syllables, and, above all, we must not, for the sake of a story, upset the child's scarcely formed habits by presenting him with irregularities of spelling for which he is not prepared. Purely formal exercises that would be irksome to an adult are not irksome to a child, provided he sees himself gaining in power. In the early stages of reading, a nonsense syllable like *nin* will give pleasure to the child who finds himself able to read it, whereas at the same stage a word of irregular spelling, such as *gem*, even if introduced in a story, will discourage the child and delay the sureness of his reactions.

There is always something artificial about reducing a problem to simple mechanical terms, but the whole history of science shows that simple mechanical terms are the only terms in which our limited human capacity can solve a problem. The lesser variables have to wait until the main outline has been ascertained, and this is true even when these lesser variables are the very thing that makes our problem worth solving. The authors of books on reading methods devote much space to telling why reading is worth while. The authors of these books would have done far better to stress the fact that the practical and cultural values of reading can play no part in the elementary stages. The only practical value of mathematics lies in its application in commerce and science, but we do not try to teach economics and physics in connection with first-grade arithmetic. The only practical value of responding correctly to the letters of the alphabet lies in the messages which reach us through the written or printed page, but we cannot expect the child to listen to these messages when he has only begun to respond correctly to the sight of the letters. If we insist upon his listening, we merely delay the fundamental response.

If you want to play the piano with feeling and expression, you must master the keyboard and learn to use your fingers on it. When you have mastered the keyboard and the fingering, you may still fail for other reasons, but certain it is that if you have not the mechanical control, you will not be able to play.

12. BEFORE READING

The first step, which may be divorced from all subsequent ones, is the recognition of the letters. We say that the child *recognizes* a letter when he can, upon request, make some response to it. One could, for instance, train him to whistle when he saw an A, to clap his hands when he saw a B, to stamp his foot when he saw a C, and so on. The conventional responses to the sight of the letters are their names, *aye, bee, see, dee, ee, eff,* and so on, down to *zee* (which in England is called *zed*). There is not the slightest reason for using any other responses.

The letters have queer and interesting shapes; their interest is enhanced if they are presented in colors. Begin with the printed capitals in their ordinary simple form. When these have been mastered, take up the small printed letters. The written forms of the letters should not be taught until reading habits are well established; the early introduction of writing is a cause of delay.

The child should be familiar with all the letters, capital and small, of the printed alphabet before reading is begun. Not all of them will be used in the first reading work, but we do not want the reading work, at any stage, to be upset by the appearance of unfamiliar shapes.

Every teacher knows, of course, that the pairs *b* and *d* or *p* and *q* involve a fairly abstract geometrical distinction and have to be carefully presented and practiced. Another feature of the same kind is that of the left-to-right order of our writing and printing. This presents difficulty to some children. The left-to-right order of printed marks corresponds to a sooner-to-later order of spoken sounds and forms. That is, the letters are arranged from left to right in a succession that corresponds to the succession in time of the corresponding phonemes (e.g., *p-i-n* corresponding to the spoken sound of the word *pin*), and the words, also, are arranged from left to right in a succession that corresponds to the succession in time of the spoken words (e.g., *Give me a pin*). This seems simple to us only because of our long practice; in reality it involves considerable abstraction and demands careful teaching. The beginning should be made before reading is begun, in connection with the letters; the letters are presented in alphabetic order and their names read off from left to right. Then other combinations of letters should be presented, including actual words. The child need not even be told that the combinations are words; and he should certainly not be required to recognize or read the words. All he needs to do is read off the names of the successive letters, *from left to right.*

All this belongs to the stage before the child starts to read. Before the child reads we present the letters, capital and lower-case, the numeral digits, and exercises in the lef-to-right and top-to-bottom orders. The work should go on until the child can name each letter when it is shown to him and can name in the proper (left-to-right) order a sequence of letters shown to him. The pictures in the before-reading stage show objects which move from left to right.

If the children do not have printed material for the before-reading stage, the teacher must exhibit the letters on the blackboard. In drawing pictures or diagrams to show the left-to-right order, one must be careful to avoid ambiguous subjects. For instance, a railway train is not a good subject. When a train passes us, we see first the locomotive, then the tender, then the baggage car, and so on, but if we draw the train accordingly with the locomotive at the left-hand end, our picture will represent a train which is moving from right to left; the picture is ambiguous. The type of correct picture or diagram is a man shooting an arrow, which in the picture is flying from the left-hand part of the surface toward the right.

When the letters and the left-to-right order have been thoroughly mastered, we are ready to begin reading. In the words to be read during the first stage every letter must represent only and always one single phoneme. The great task of learning to read—one of the major intellectual feats in anyone's life—consists in learning the very abstract equation: *printed letter = speech sound to be spoken.* This equation is all the more difficult because it never occurs in simple form, but only in the complex shape where several letters in left-to-right order serve as the signal for several speech sounds in the corresponding soon-to-later order. If we try to simplify this by presenting single letters as signals for single speech sounds, we only make matters worse, since the isolated speech sounds are foreign to our language. This task is sufficiently difficult; we must not make it even more difficult by introducing irregular spellings before the basic habit is set up, or by asking the child to attend to the meaning of what he reads.

13. DIFFERENCES OF PRONUNCIATION

Before we begin reading we must settle a question which troubles many teachers. How are we to pronounce our words? The sound of English speech differs greatly in different parts of the English-speaking countries. Almost everyone is diffident about the sound of speech—especially the teacher, who is used to reflecting about such matters.

Our first impulse is to follow some authority who will tell us what is proper. If this were possible, our problem would long ago have been settled, and all of us—or, at any rate, all educated people—would be using the same pronunciation. At various times various men have set themselves up as authorities on how English should be pronounced, but none of them has succeeded in getting people to follow his prescriptions. The man who sets himself up as an authority prescribes the style of pronunciation which he happens to use, and the great majority of people, who are used to pronouncing otherwise, object to his prescriptions and in the end ignore them. The reason for this is plain enough. English is spoken differently in different places. It would be very hard to make London teachers talk like Chicagoans. If we decided to make some one local pronunciation the standard for the whole English-speaking world, then all teachers would have to be natives of the favored place, or would have to go through a long and severe training until they acquired the favored pronunciation. Few things are harder to do than changing one's pronunciation in one's native language. There would remain the more difficult task of making the children use this pronunciation. Accordingly, the present-day phonetician who writes about the pronunciation of English does not set himself up as an authority; he tells us whose pronunciation he is describing (usually it is his own) and tries to tell what other people use the same pronunciation; even thus he lists many variant pronunciations; compare, for instance, Daniel Jones, *Outline of English Phonetics* (Third ed., Leipzig, 1932), p. 12. In short, there is no authority, and if there were we should probably find his prescriptions too difficult to follow.

In the theater, our actors are trained to use the type of pronunciation that prevails among the upper classes in southern England. It would be an enormous task, and doubtless in many cases beyond our power, to teach our pupils to pronounce in this fashion. There would be no time left in which to teach reading.

So far as the general style of pronunciation is concerned, then, the teacher of reading need not worry about her own habits. Of course she should speak distinctly and in a style of pronunciation which she herself accepts as polite. Above all, she ought to avoid affectation. Affected and prissy speech is not good for the children and, since one cannot keep up a pose at all times, it leads to inconsistency.

If the teacher comes from a very distant part of the country, there may be noticeable differences between the pronunciation of the teacher and that of the pupils. Even if the teacher does not adapt her pronunciation to theirs, it is well to remember that the most we can ask of our pupils in this respect is that they speak like *the educated people in their own part of the country.*

For instance, if a teacher from New England comes to Chicago, she would be wrong if she tried to train her pupils to speak the so-called "broad" sound of *a* (as in *father, jar*) in words like *laugh, grass, aunt.* The attempt would consume a vast amount of time and energy, the pupils would fail to follow consistently, and outside of the classroom they would in any event lapse back into the pronunciation which they hear from everybody else.

The greatest mistake of all, however, is when a teacher, say in Chicago, who does not come from New England and does not naturally use the "broad *a*," tries to affect it in the classroom. She uses it inconsistently, often forgetting to put it into the words to which (in London or New England) it belongs, and sometimes putting it into words where it does not belong (even in London or New England)—words such as *lass, bass,* or *fancy.*

The "broad *a*" has been here mentioned as an example. There are many other differences of pronunciation between different parts of the country. They do no harm, and the teacher need not worry about them. The only kind of practice, in this matter, that will do harm is priggishness and affectation. One sometimes hears teachers use outlandish varieties of pronunciation which no one else, and not even they when they speak plainly and naturally, would ever think of using.

Among the geographical differences in the pronunciation of Standard English there are a very few which we must consider in this book. One of these is the "broad *a*": a word like *class*, for instance, is spoken in England and in eastern New England with the vowel sound of *father, far,* and in most of the United States with the vowel sound of *hat, lass.* We give these words in separate lists; for each of these lists the teacher must decide upon the choice in accordance with the pronunciation that prevails in the part of the country where she is teaching.

The only pronunciations that are not acceptable are those which are not current among educated people in the pupils' locality. In Chicago, for instance, *git* for *get, ketch* for *catch, wrastle* for *wrestle* are widespread, and so, some time back, was *bile* for *boil,* but these forms are not used by educated adult speakers. It would be a mistake to make a fuss when a pupil uses these forms, but the teacher, of course, should use the Standard English forms and should consider only these forms in the reading instruction.

The pupil who uses such forms as *git* or *I seen it* or *I ain't got none* is not making "mistakes in English" or talking "bad English." There is a widespread superstition which attributes the use of forms like these to "carelessness" or some other sort of depravity. The forms just cited, and others like them, are forms of *substandard English* or of local dialects. They are perfectly good English, but they do not belong to the dialect which we call Standard English. Since Standard English is, to all practical purposes, the only type of English that is represented in print and writing, our instruction will naturally ignore all other dialects and consider only the standard forms.

It is another matter, and in the main quite separate from reading instruction, that we want our pupils to learn to speak and write Standard English. So much may be said here, that this can be attained not by instruction in theoretical grammar, such as sentence analysis and the like, but only by a vast amount of drill in the use of the Standard English forms that differ from the pupil's substandard or local dialect. Practice of this kind should cover also the forms which are likely to be confused with the form that is foreign to the pupil. If we merely train a child to substitute *saw* for *seen*, we may find him saying *I have saw it*. We must train him, then, in pairs and sets or phrases:

> *I saw it.*
>
> *I've seen it.*
>
> *I have some.*
>
> *I've got some.*
>
> *I have none.*
>
> *I haven't any.*
>
> *I haven't got any.*

All this, however, is by way of digression, for the teaching of Standard English to pupils who speak some other type is a matter quite different from teaching them to read. There is only this connection, that since the texts are in Standard English, reading helps the pupil to acquire the use of this more favored form of our language.

In sum, then, the teacher should use a polite but natural type of pronunciation and should base the reading instruction upon pronunciations which are current among educated speakers in the pupils' own community. The main thing is to avoid affectation in one's own classroom language; above all, one should never make the mistake of introducing pronunciations that are foreign to the pupils' community (for instance, in the Middle and Far West, *class* with "broad *a*") or outlandish and fantastic forms that are not used anywhere in the English-speaking world (for instance, *lass* with "broad *a*," or *pre-see-us* instead of *preshus* for the word that is written *precious*).

14. FIRST MATERIALS

Our first material must show each letter in only one phonetic value; thus, if we have words with *g* in the value that it has in *get, got, gun*, our first material must not contain words like *gem*, where the same letter has different value; similarly, if we have words like *cat, can, cot*, our first material must not contain words like *cent*. Our first material should contain no words with silent letters (such as *knit* or *gnat*) and none with double letters, either in the value of single sounds (as in *add, bell*) or in special values (as in *see, too*), and none with combinations of letters having a special value (as *th* in *thin* or *ea* in *bean*). The letter *x* cannot be used, because it represents two phonemes (*ks* or *gz*), and the letter *q* cannot be used, because it occurs only in connection with an unusual value of the letter *u* (for *w*).

The best selection of value of letters to be used in the first materials for reading is the following:

Vowel Letters

a as in *cat*	o as in *hot*
e as in *pet*	u as in *cut*
i as in *pin*	

Consonant Letters

b as in *bit*	n as in *net*
c as in *cat*	p as in *peg*
d as in *dig*	r as in *red*
f as in *fan*	s as in *sat*
g as in *get*	t as in *tan*
h as in *hen*	v as in *van*
j as in *jam*	w as in *wet*
k as in *keg*	y as in *yes*
l as in *let*	z as in *zip*
m as in *man*	

Note that this list contains one duplication: *c* and *k* both designate one and the same English phoneme. This will be a difficulty later, when the child learns to write, but it need not trouble us now, since he has merely to read the words as they are presented to him.

Our first reading material will consist of two-letter and three-letter words in which the letters have the sound values given in the above list. Since the vowel letters *a, e, i, o, u* are the ones which, later on, will present the greatest difficulty, we shall do best to divide this material into five groups, according to the vowel letter contained in each word. Within each of these five groups, two arrangements are possible; we can form groups by final consonants (e.g. *bat, cat, fat,* etc.) or by initial consonants (e.g. *bad, bag, bat,* etc.). We begin with the former because it is easier to watch the first letter than the last, and because rhyme is familiar to the child.

The parent or teacher points to the word

c a n

in small printed letters in Lesson 1 in this book, or shows the word either on the blackboard or on a card. The child knows the names of the letters, and is now asked to read off those names in their order: *see, aye, en.* The parent or teacher says, "Now we have spelled the word. Now we are going to *read* it. This word is *can.* Read it: *can.*"

The parent or teacher now shows another word with the same vowel and final consonant, but with a different initial, for instance *fan,* and goes through the same procedure.

The aim is now to make the child distinguish between the two words—that is, to get him to read each of the words correctly when it is shown by itself, and, when the two words are shown together, to say the right one when the parent or the teacher points to it, and to point to the right one when the parent or the teacher pronounces it.

We should not, at this stage ask the child to write or print the words: that comes much later.

The early reading lessons should not be very long, for they demand a severe intellectual effort. It may be well to take up only two words in the first lesson.

In the second lesson, after review, add two or three more words of the same group, say *pan, ran, man.*

The drill should continue until the child can read correctly anyone of the words when the parent or teacher points to it. Then the words should be shown in various orders, and separately, until the child can easily read all of them. The other words of the group should be added, one by one (*Dan, tan, Nan, van, ban,* and finally, *an*). This may take quite a few lessons: it is all-important to have a firm foundation. Some of the words will be strange to the child. In fact, a familiar word, such as an, when presented alone, is likely to convey no meaning. There is no harm in telling the child that "a van is a big covered truck for moving furniture," or that "Nan is a girl's name."

If the child has learned the pattern in the list of actual words, he should be able to read nonsense syllables using the same pattern. The nonsense syllables are a test of the child's mastery of the phoneme. Tell the child that the nonsense syllables are parts of real words which he will find in the books that he reads. For example, the child will know *han* in *handle* and *jan* in *January* and *mag* in *magnet* or *magpie.* The acquisition of nonsense syllables is an important part of the task of mastering the reading process. The child will learn the patterns of the language more rapidly if you use the nonsense syllables in teaching. However, the lessons may be taught without teaching the nonsense syllables, if you so desire.

Reading is so familiar to us that we are likely to forget how difficult it is for the beginner. The child has so hard a time forming a connection between visual marks and speech sounds that he cannot attend to the meaning of what he reads. We must help him to establish this connection, and we must not bother him, for the present, with anything else. We can best help him by giving him the most suitable words to read, and these are short words in which the letters have uniform values. We present as many as possible of these, without regard to their meanings. The child will get the meanings only when he has solved the mechanical problem of reading.

When we present a pair of words like *can* and *fan*, a child may have no notion that these words are similar in sound, or that the similar spelling indicates a similar sound. It would be a waste of time to try, as do the advocates of "phonic" methods, to explain this to him. All we do is to present such words together; the resemblance of sound and spelling will do its work without any explanation from us. Only, we must remember that this takes a great deal of time and repetition. Above all, we must not upset the habit by presenting words in which the letters have different values.

When the *an* group has been learned, we may go on to another final-group, such as *bat, fat, hat, mat, Nat, Pat, rat, sat, tat, vat*. In doing this we also present pairs like *bat ban, cat can, fat fan, mat man, Nat Nan, pat pan*.

Let's Look

The pictures on these pages are designed as exercises in looking carefully. The images are arranged in sequence and each implies a "story" with a conclusion. The first and second groups begin at the left and move to the right. The third group of images on pages 50–52 is arranged vertically, from top to bottom. The pupil can explain what is happening or might be more interested in details, either of which will indicate close attention.

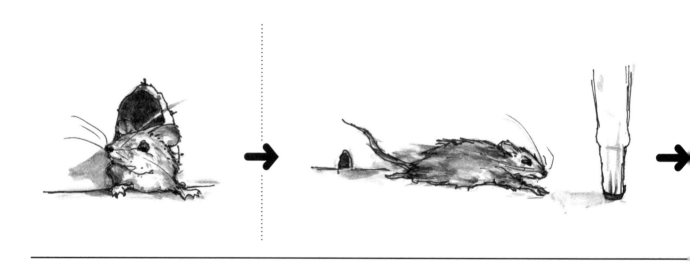

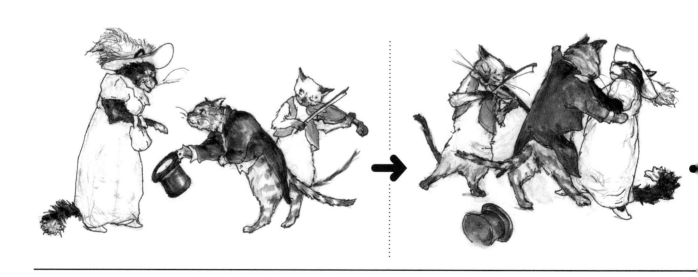

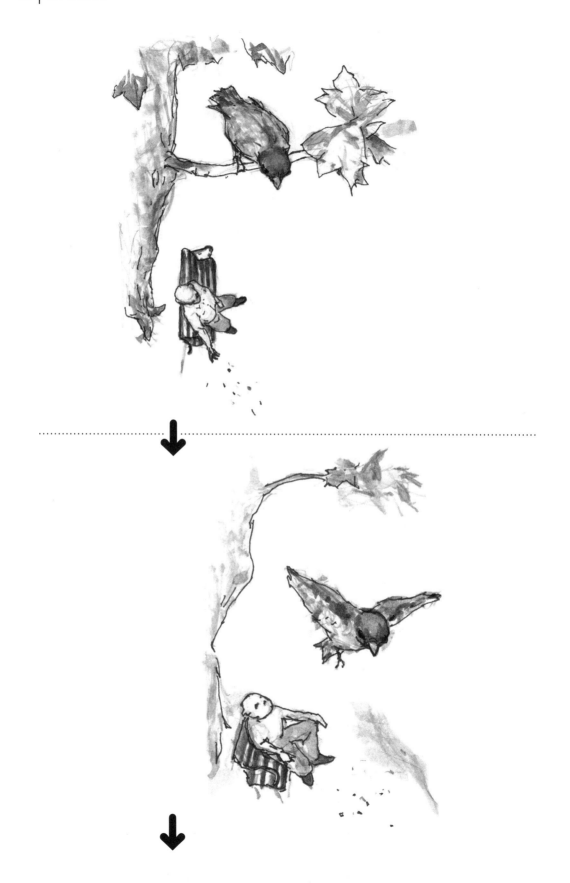

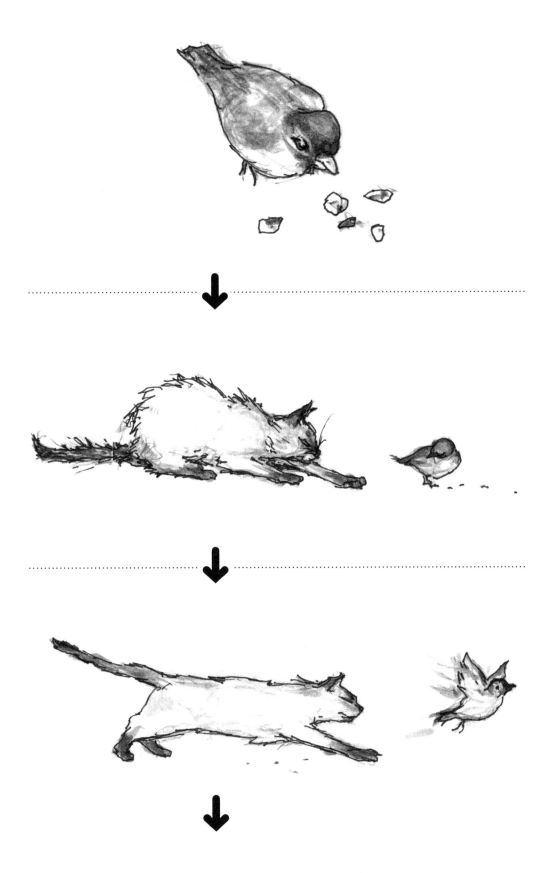

ALIKE AND DIFFERENT: EASY DISCRIMINATION

1. Which shape in each row is different?
2. Which shapes are the same?

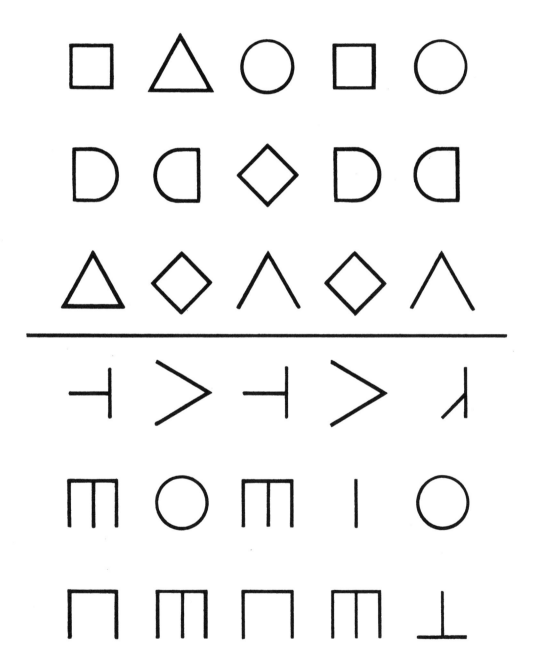

THE ALPHABET

Can the pupil recognize and name each of the capital letters?

A   I   Q   B   M

R   C   K   O   S

D   L   P   T   Z

Y   U   E   J   N

V   W   H   X   G

F

Can the pupil recognize and name each of the small letters?

c   i   x   u   y

e   k   q   w   d

j   p   v   z   o

b   h   n   t   m

g   a   s   l   r

g   f   *a*

PART I

First Reading

Guide to Part I, Lessons 1–36

Part I lays the foundation of all later reading lessons and perhaps, because of the habits established in this beginning work, is most likely the most important part of all. These lessons introduce the basic spelling patterns of consonant-short vowel-consonant (C-V-C) words—*bad, pin, set, nut, not,* for example—which occur most frequently in written English. The words in these patterns teach the pupil the most common and regular sound equivalents for the letters that make up these words; in part I, the pupil discovers that letters are used in predictable arrangements to make up words that are predictable in their sound.

Only regular sound-letter correlations are taught in part I: *c* invariably has the value of the *c* in *cat, g* as in *get, s* as in *sat,* along with the short-vowel values that are relatively standard in American English. Because of their variable sound values in written English, use of *w* is limited in part I, and *x* and *q* are avoided altogether. By limiting vocabulary to those word patterns that express unvarying sound values (with a few exceptions as explained below), the pupil can concentrate on decoding and reading without the distraction or confusion of irregular sound-letter correlations, which are introduced later in *Let's Read.*

The choice of both vocabulary and the sound system it exemplifies is not arbitrary or whimsical. These C-V-C words are the phonemic basis of written English; they constitute its alphabetic foundation.

Learning to read is a rigorous intellectual exercise and an enormous accomplishment for any individual. While some youngsters do teach themselves to read, most need instruction, and most like learning. In the school setting, of course, youngsters expect to be taught to read and do classroom work, but a child might very well be completely puzzled by a parent's decision to teach him or her to read at home. There are, of course, countless variants to the experience and great differences between children even within a family. For the parents and others who teach children at home, it is important to be, above all, patient, encouraging, and persevering, because as the lessons progress the pupil will begin to discover for him- or herself the thrill that comes from doing something well and will thus find learning not difficult and very rewarding.

SCOPE OF PART I

Short-vowel monosyllables with:

- *a* as in *can*
- *i* as in *big*
- *u* as in *bun*
- *e* as in *bet*
- *o* as in *cot*

Lessons are arranged with new word patterns at the top of each lesson page, followed by connected reading (short phrases and sentences), which is in turn often followed by pairs of words at the bottom of the page. Both the connected reading and the contrasting pairs of words are designed to reinforce the new vocabulary patterns, each element drawing upon what is new and reviewing what has been previously taught. In part I we have also included a selection of two-syllable words, such as *sunset* and *gallop*. These are words made from the familiar C-V-C monosyllables and can be easily decoded by the fledgling reader.

This is the very early first work; the vocabulary is not sophisticated, and the message of the connected reading is likewise uncomplicated and direct. The goal at this stage is simply to teach the most common elements of written English; the long-term goal is, of course, to enable the pupil to decode so automatically that all his or her concentration can be focused on the message in the reading. These lessons are a critical first step toward that goal. Review pages, which include no new vocabulary, are provided throughout part I.

SUGGESTIONS FOR THE TEACHER

- Have the pupil use an index card or other stiff paper as a marker to help focus on each word or group of words. Alternatively, the pupil may choose to use his or her finger as a marker. In either case, as the pupil's comfort level rises, using a marker or pointing will become less and less important.

- Keep each lesson short, perhaps a maximum of fifteen to twenty minutes.
- Allow the pupil to work on the same material until he or she has mastered it and is ready to move on to the next list. Avoid setting a particular goal for what the pupil should accomplish during a lesson. However, be sure to accomplish *something* during each session—even on a bad day.

1. Begin by having the pupil spell and say each word in the vocabulary list. Point to each letter of the word, moving left to right, and have the pupil identify each one—for example *c-a-t.* Then say, "That spells *cat.*" Once the pupil understands what to do, have him or her point to each letter and spell the word, the teacher providing the word, the pupil repeating it. In part I, a lesson begins by reading the word lists by columns from left to right. Next repeat reading the vocabulary words in any order until the pupil can read them all easily, spelling only those words that are a problem. The connected reading also serves this purpose.

   After a few lessons, it is not unusual for a pupil to be able to spell a word in a new pattern and read it without any cue from the teacher.

2. The pupil next reads the phrases or sentences aloud without spelling each word and spelling only those words he or she cannot read. The pupil should be asked to read the sentences until reading them comes relatively easily. The connected reading serves as review of vocabulary previously learned.

   Note that the first lesson introduces the article *a,* as in "a cat." In lesson 2, the pronoun *I* is introduced. Simply tell the pupil what *a* is (or any of the other sight words gradually presented) until the pupil recognizes it.

   Note: Remember that learning spelling patterns is the goal of these early lessons. The pupil's fluency and comprehension will improve with progress and practice. In the simple sentences and phrases of the first connected reading, meaning is a fairly straightforward matter and serves mainly as an introduction to what reading is, but it is also another way of reinforcing pattern by contrast. If you feel compelled to check comprehension, it is fairly easy to do so by asking the pupil a question.

   At lesson 9 in part I, the pupil encounters the first significant change in the alphabetic patterns with introduction of the medial vowel *i.* For some pupils, this new fact is completely unremarkable; for others, it can pose a challenge. As with all challenges, patience, repetition, perseverance, and pattern will assure success in overcoming difficulty.

It is also important to remember that most beginning readers do not read with good expression, but with practice and growing confidence, they gradually read aloud in a manner that more closely reflects their natural speech.

3. Lastly, the pupil reads the pairs of words that sometimes appear at the bottom of the page. These pairs of words have only one letter that is different between them and are meant to help the pupil establish a firmer grasp of the sound-letter correlations of the C-V-C spelling patterns. The word pairs can be read in any order.

4. Move on to the next lesson as soon as the pupil seems comfortable with the present lesson.

NOTES

1. *Vocabulary and Punctuation.* The vocabulary lists may contain words unfamiliar to a pupil, such as *nag* ("old horse," also "find fault with again and again") or *vat* ("huge barrel"). Keep in mind that many pupils enjoy learning new words and meanings and adding them to their vocabularies. Answer any questions a student might have about the meanings of the words. Having a dictionary handy may be helpful.

   The connected reading uses the period, the question mark, and the exclamation mark for complete sentences, while the simple phrases generally have no punctuation. It is up to the teacher to decide what the pupil needs to know about the punctuation marks, although sometimes knowing what they are makes reading easier. Throughout the program a teacher should follow the pupil's cues. If the pupil is curious to know what the punctuation marks are and what they mean, explanation is essential.

2. *Irregular words.* Part I includes a selection of sight words (*a, I, the, of, to, do, into,* and *onto*). Sight words are arbitrary in their spellings and in general do not conform to phonic rules, but they appear so frequently in writing that they come to be recognized without analysis, hence their name. Because it is nearly impossible to function without such words in ordinary speech and writing, a few have been added to make the connected reading flow more easily. They are inserted into the sentences and not introduced as regular vocabulary. The teacher can simply identify each word for the pupil as it is encountered, until such ordinary collocations as *a bit of* or *do it* become as familiar as they are common constructions in spoken English. Other irregularities are taught as sight words in later lessons.

3. *Multisyllable words.* A full list of multisyllable words made of the regular monosyllables already taught in part I can be found on pages 113–22. As they become more confident readers, many students like trying to read longer words, and the list contains words selected specifically for them. The list begins with less challenging words and

moves on to the more difficult words. Use of this list is left entirely to the discretion of the teacher.

4. *Index cards.* Make a set of index cards for each pattern. The pupil can arrange the cards to make sentences or phrases, substitute words to make different sentences, etc. If you already have a set of cards for the alphabet, they can be similarly used in word games/exercises.

5. *Word games.* Using vocabulary from a lesson, ask the pupil to find a describing word (adjective) or a doing word (verb) or a name of someone or something (noun). Or have the pupil insert modifiers in phrases and sentences (for example, *A man had a nag. A man had a sad nag.*). Without comment from the teacher, the pupil is indirectly or inductively learning about word function while practicing reading.

6. *Small books.* Make up short stories that will interest the pupil, putting one sentence on each page. To personalize the stories, include details about the pupil, for example, the pupil's name.

cat

bat   fat   hat   rat   at

a hat   a bat   a rat   a cat

at bat   a fat rat   a fat cat

1

A cat.

A bat.

A hat.

A cat at bat.

cat   mat   at

bat   fat   hat

mat   Nat   pat   sat

tat   vat

1

a mat   a pat   a vat

A rat sat.

A cat sat.

A bat.

A fat bat.

A fat bat sat.

Pat a cat.

Pat a bat.

Pat a rat.

Nat   rat   hat   sat   vat

mat   cat   fat   bat   tat

can   man   Dan   fan   Nan

a can   a man   a fan

2

A man sat.

Can Dan fan Nan?

Dan can.

A fan.

Can Nan fan a cat?

Nan can.

Nat at bat.

Nan at bat.

Dan at bat.

can	Nat	fat	man
cat	Nan	fan	mat

pan   ran   tan   an

ban   van   Lan   Jan

2   Nat ran.

Pat ran.

I ran.

Pat can bat.

Nan can bat.

I can bat.

A van.

A tan van.

A man ran a van.

an   rat   van   ban   pat

at   ran   vat   bat   pan

Nat at bat.

Pat at bat.

2

A fat cat.

A tan cat.

A fat tan cat ran.

I ran. I sat.

Jan ran. Jan sat.

Van ran. Van sat.

I can bat.

Jan can bat.

Can Van bat?

Rat-a-tat-tat! A cat can bat at a rat.

Rat-a-tat-tan! A rat ran at a can.

bad   dad   had   lad   mad

A cat.

3 A bad cat.

I had a bad cat.

Dad had a van.

Van had a tan hat.

Nan had a cat.

Nan had a fat tan cat.

A fat tan cat ran at a rat.

Bad cat! Mad rat!

A lad had a bat.

A lad ran.

Dad ran. I ran.

ban   mad   hat   man

bad   mat   had   mad

pad   sad   Tad   ad

cad   fad   gad

a pad   a lad   a sad lad

3

Dad had a van.

Dad ran a van.

A cat had a mat.

A rat had a pad.

A sad man sat.

I sat.

A cat had a pan.

A bat had a hat.

A rat had a fan.

pad   sat   fad   pad   ad

pan   sad   fat   pat   at

cap	gap	lap	map
rap	nap	sap	tap
pap	yap	Hap	

4

A sad man sat.

The sad man had a map.

Hap can yap.

Hap ran. Hap sat. Hap had a nap.

Can a cat nap? The cat had a catnap!

Van can tap a can. Rat-a-tat-tat!

A man at bat.

The man had a tan cap.

a can	a map	a rap
a cap	a mat	a rat

A fat rat sat.

A tan cat had a nap.

The rat can bat at the cat.

The cat ran at the rat.

Bad cat! Sad rat!

4

Van had a bat.

Can Van bat?

Van can bat.

Can Tad bat?

Tad can.

Can I bat? I can bat!

bag	gag	lag	nag
sag	tag	wag	rag
		jag	hag

5

Can Tad tag Jan?

Tad ran. Jan ran.

Tad can tag Jan.

Tad, tag Jan!

A sad nag had a bag.

The nag had a ragbag.

Wag had a rag.

Wag ran. Wag sat.

Wag had a nap.

a bag	a nag	a rag	a fat nag
a bat	a nap	a rat	a sad man

dam	ham	jam	Pam	am
Sam	ram	cam	yam	tam

a ram   a yam   a ham   a dam   a tam   6

Sam had a nag.

Pam had a cat.

Pat had a ram.

A fat rat had a yam.

The fat rat had ham.

I am Sam.

I had jam.

I had ham.

rag	Pat	jag	yap	I am
ram	Pam	jam	yam	an ad

cab   dab   jab   nab   Rab

tab   lab   gab   Bab

7

A man ran a cab.

Can Dad nab the cab?

A mad cat. A bad cat.

A sad rat.

The sad rat had a nap.

The bad, mad cat ran at the rat.

Bab had a Lab.

Can I pat the Lab?

Rab had a cap.

Bab had a hat.

Wag had a tam.

can   dab   jam   nap   tab

cab   dam   jab   nab   tap

Cal   Al   Hal   gal   Mal

pal   Val   Sal   gas

a gas can   a gas cap   **8**

I am a pal.

I had a pal, Val.

Val had a van.

Al had a cap.

Sal had a hat.

Mal had a tam.

Sam ran. Sal ran.

Can Sam tag Sal?

Sam can!

Sam   Van   pal   gab

Sal   Val   pan   gas

A tag.

The cap had a tag.

8

A tab.

The can had a tab.

A gap.

A bad gap.

Tad had a tan ram.

The ram sat in a pan.

Sad ram!

Al ran a cab.

The cab had a gas cap.

Al had a gas can.

Sal had jam.

Sal had a pal, Al.

Al had jam.

Rab had a ram.

Nan had a nag.

Pam had a pan.

Bab had a bag.

Pat had a pan.

A man had a vat.

Val ran a van.

Jan had a jam can.

I had a dab.

A bad rat ran at a ham.

Can the rat nab the ham?

The bad rat did nab ham.

8

big	dig	jig	pig
wig	fig	gig	rig

9

a rig	a pig	a wig	a can
a big rig	a fat pig	a tan wig	a can of jam

Jan had a can.

Jan had a can of jam.

Jan had a big can of fig jam.

Pam had a big pig.

Rab had a big nag.

A man ran a big rig.

I ran a big van.

a big man   a big fat pig   a big fig

bin	din	fin	pin	Min
tin	win	kin	in	sin

Nan had a big pin.

Nan had a hatpin.

Did Nan jab a pin in a hat?

A ram ran in a zigzag.

The ram had a nap in a bin.

A pig had jam.

The pig had a napkin!

10

a tin can	a pig in a bin	in a zigzag
a can of gas	a man in a rig	in a ragbag

bid   did   hid   kid

lid   rid   Sid   mid

11

the lid of a can   A can had a lid.

a tin of ham   Sal had ham in a tin can.

a dab of jam   Did Wag nab a dab of jam?

I am a kid. I ran. I hid.

I hid in a big bag.

A man had a gig.

The gig ran in a zigzag.

Sam had a big rig.

Sam ran the rig.

wig   mid   tin   gig

wag   mad   tan   gag

bit   fit   hit   kit   lit

pit   sit   wit   it

12

Wag had a big yam.

Wag hid it in a can.

Simkin Cat hid.

Simkin hid in a big tin can.

Can Mal bat?

Can Mal hit?

Can Mal do it? Mal did it!

A cat can sit in the hat.

The cat sat in the hat.

The cat had a nap in the hat.

| a bit of jam | hit at it | in a pit | lit it up |
| a bit of ham | hid in it | in a pan | Wag bit it |

bib   fib   rib   nib   jib

a jab in the rib

13 a bib

Did Sal jab Jan in the rib?

A pig had a big bib.

Did Sal do it?

Hit a pan.

Jab a pin.

Nab a bad man.

Did Nan fib? Nan did it.

Bad Nan! Sad Nan!

I can bat it.

Can Van bat?

Van did. Van did it!

dim   him   Jim   rim

Tim   Kim   vim

the rim of a cup   the lid of a pan   **14**

I hit it to him.

I hit it to Jim.

I ran. Tim ran.

I ran to the dam. Did I win?

Kim had a kit to tap sap.

The kit had a tin pan.

The pan had a big lid.

It had sap in it.

A fat cat sat at the rim of a bin.

A rat hid in the bin.

Can the cat nab him?

to hit   to fib   to win   to dig   to do a jig

dip	hip	lip	nip
rip	sip	tip	zip
Kip	Jip	yip	pip

15

a hip	a lip	to dip	to yip
a rip	a sip	to tip	to zip

The lip of the pan had a gap in it.

Nan had a cap. It had a rip in it.
Can Nan pin it?

A cab hit a pit.
Did it tip?

A bag had a zip.
Can I zip it?

Kip had a dip.
Kip had a dip in a big vat!

if   Sis   Vic   Lil   Liz

I can hit it. I can win.

If I can do it, I can win.

I am Sinbad. I am a big rat.

I am Simkin. I am a big, big cat.

16

A can had sap in it.

Sam Rat had a sip.

Sam had a big sip of it.

Vic hit a rib.

Vic had to sit.

Pigwig can dig a big pit.

Did Pigwig do it?

Pigwig sat in it.

16

Liz had a tam. Did Jip nab it?

Jip did. Jip ran in a zigzag.

Did Jip rip the tam?

Jip did. Bad Jip.

Did Liz nab him?

Simkin had a bag.

Simkin had a bag of catnip.

Simkin had a tidbit.

Simkin ran. Simkin hid the catnip!

A fat rat sat on the rim of a can.

Did the tin can tip?

The rat ran. The rat hid in the attic.

bun   fun   sun   run

gun   pun   nun   dun

A bad bandit had a gun.

17

The bandit hid the gun in a bag.

Can Vic run? Can Vic win?

Vic ran. Vic had fun.

A fat pig sat in the sun.

The pig had a nap in the sun.

The pig had a suntan!

I had a big bun. I had jam in the bun.

bun   dun   fun   run

ban   din   fan   ran

bus   us   Gus   pus

bun   Gus   pun

18   ban   gun   pan

bin   pus

Gus ran a bus.

Gus ran the bus into a pit. Bam!

Did it tip?

Pal can run.

Run to us, Pal! Pal ran to us.

a tidbit of ham

a dab of jam

a bit of a bun

fig jam in a can

cup   pup   sup   up

a tin cup   do a situp   run at sunup

a hiccup   the rim of a cup

19

I ran up to Jim.

I can tag him.

A pup sat up.

The pup had a bit of ham in a bun.

The pup had a hiccup.

Can a fat man do a situp?

The fat man can do a situp.

Can a fat man run?

The fat man can run.

cup   pip   sap   us

cap   pup   sup   up

but	cut	nut	hut	rut
	gut		jut	

20

Dad cut up a ham.

Wag had a bit of it.

Sam ran to tag Jim, but Jim hid.

Jim hid in a hut. Sam did not tag Jim.

Kim ran a cab.

The cab ran into a rut.

The cab sat in mud.

Can Sam get it up?

A pig hid a nut in a pan.

The pig had a nut, a fig, a bun.

The pig had a big nap.

but	cat	gut	rat	nun
bun	cut	gun	rut	nut
bug	dug	lug	jug	hug

a big hug   a fat pug   lug a big jug

21

A bug had a mug.

It had sap in it.

The bug had a sip of the sap.

At sunset, Pigwig dug a big pit.

Did Pigwig lug a big rug to it?

Pigwig had a nap on the rug in the pit.

A tug had a gap in it.

Did it tip?

bun	dug	run	pup	hag
bug	dun	rut	pug	hug

cub   hub   rub   sub

dub   nub   tub

22

Kit Cat dug up a bug.

Kit Cat hid it in a cup.

A fat cub sat in a tub.

The cub had a can.

The can had sap in it.

The cub had a sip of the sap.

The cub had a picnic in the tub!

Rub-a-dub-dub, a pup in a tub.

Rig-a-jig-jig, a pig did a jig.

cub   nib   tab   dab   rib

cab   nub   tub   dub   rub

gum   hum   sum   yum

bum   mum   rum

A bandit had a jug.

The bandit hid it in a bag.

23

Gus had gum. I had a bit of it.

Yum! Yum!

Sis can tap.

Hal can hum a bit.

Wag can yap.

The cat can sit mum.

bud   Jud   mud   cud   dud

24

A pig sat in mud.

The pig dug up the mud.

It ran in the mud.

The pig had fun.

Jud had a big ram.

The ram ran. Jud ran.

The ram hid in a tub.

A bug sat in a fat bud.

The bud had sap on it.

The bug had a sip of it.

a tin cup	do a situp	run at sunup
a jug of sap	a hiccup	the rim of a cup
a tub of mud	a big hug	a bad cut

24

Cal had a sub.

Cal ran it in a tub.

Vic had a picnic.

Vic had ham in a bun.

Bud Bug had a nap in the sun.

Bud Bug had a suntan.

A bus hit a rut.

The rut had mud in it.

bet	get	let	met	net
pet	set	wet	yet	vet

25

Jim had a bet.

Did Sal let Jim win?

Did Jim win the bet?

A man had a big net.

It had a rip in it.

It had a big gap in it.

The man can do it up.

I had a pet pup.

The pet had a vet.

Did the pup let the vet pet him?

bet	let	vet	set	wet
but	lit	vat	sit	wit

Ben	den	hen	Ken	Len
men	pen	ten	fen	yen

26

Pigwig has a pigpen.

Pigwig can get up at sunup.

Pigwig can get in a bed of mud at sunset.

A man ran a bus. Ten men sat in a bus.

Ten men had a nap in the bus.

A cub hid in a den.

It had a nap in the den.

Len met Ken.

Len met Ken at the bus.

bin	man	fun	pan	ten
Ben	men	fin	pin	tan

bed   fed   led   red   Ned

Ted   Jed   wed   Ed

27

Ted led the pig into the pigpen.

Ted fed it in the pigpen.

Ed had a red cap.

Al hid it.

Can Ed get the cap?

Jed fed Ned a red fig.

Ned fed Ed ham in a bun.

Wag had a tidbit of the ham,

    but the cat had a dab of jam.

fed   lid   wet   rid   bed

fen   led   wed   red   bad

beg   keg   leg   Meg   peg

A bad man had a bad leg.

The man hid in a hut.

28

Can Dan tap a peg into a keg?

Hit it, Dan! Hit the peg into the keg!

Dan did it.

Meg can get a pet.

Did Meg get a cat?

Did Meg get a pup?

Meg did get a pup.

The pup can sit up. The pup can beg.

Les	yes	pep	Lem
Wes		hep	hem

29

Did Les get Lem a pet pug?

Yes, Les did.

Can Wes get the big keg

    into the van?

Pigwig had pep.

Pigwig did a jig.

The hem of a bag had a rip in it.

Can Meg get a pin into it?

Can Meg hem up the rip?

Les	yet	pip	hem	wet
Lem	yes	pep	him	Wes

web   Deb   Jeb   Zeb   Mel

Mel met the bus at sunset.

Mel met Deb at the bus.

30

Zeb had a bad leg.

Zeb had cut it.

Get up, Jeb!

Get up! Let us in!

Did Jeb get up?

Yes. Jeb let us in.

Jeb	jib	jab	jam	jet
jab	Jim	jag	Jem	jut

Jim had a red tin sub.

Jim set the tin sub in the tub.

30

It ran in the tub.

Did the sub get wet?

Did Jim get wet yet?

Did the cat get up at sunup?

Yes, it had to get up to nab a rat.

Did the cat get the rat?

The rat ran. The cat ran.

The cat had pep, but the rat hid in a den.

| cot | dot | got | hot | lot |
| not | pot | rot | tot | jot |

31

cannot	I cannot run. I got a bad cut.
rotten	A rotten vat sat in mud.
gotten	The vat had gotten wet.

A dot of red got on a rug.

Not a lot, but a dot.

A tot can run a bit, but a lad

    can run a lot.

Pip had a pad.

Peg got a pen.

Can Pip jot a lot on the pad?

Hal had a nap in the sun. Hal got hot.

lob	sob	job	mob	hob
Bob	gob		cob	rob

32

bobcat	A bobcat sat in a pen.
goblin	A goblin hid in a pot.
hobgoblin	A hobgoblin got into the pot.
cobweb	A bug had a nap in a cobweb.
robin	A robin got wet in a vat. It had a dip in it.

Dot had a pet cub.

It got into a can of jam.

Jam got into a hat. It got into the rug!

The cub sat in a big gob of jam!

Dot let the cub lap up the jam.

hop   mop   sop   lop   pop

cop   fop   top   gallop   popgun

at the top   at the tiptop

33

Get a pan! Get a mop!

Get up the wet mud! Mop it up!

Meg got a bad cut.

Meg had a cut leg.

Meg cannot run, but Meg can hop.

Sam had a popgun.

Pop! Pop! It did pop a lot.

Did the cop get the bandit?

The cop got the bandit into a van.

A tot has a top.

Can the tot get it to run?

cod   God   nod   pod   rod

hod   sod

34

A bug got into a pod.

It had a nap in it.

Bob ran a big red tug.

Bob got a lot of cod in a net.

Bob cut up a cod.

Bob fed the cat a bit of cod.

A man had a sod hut.

The man had a bed in it.

Sis got a rod.

Sis got a big cod.

cog   jog   tog   mom   Tom

A man had a gig. Can the nag lug it?

The nag can lug it,

> but the nag cannot run.

It cannot gallop.

35

Mom got Tom a red cap.

It did not fit him,

> but it did fit Dan.

Mom had a cap. Dan had a cap.

Tom did not!

cog   jug   tog   mum   Tim
cot   jog   tug   mug   Tom

Don   on   con   Lon   Doc

Ron   yon

36

Don got onto a bus.

Did Ron don a hat?

Did Lon dab at a cut?

Did Mom let in Pom, the pup?

Wag got a bad cut.

A big pup bit him.

Doc can dab at the cut.

Doc can do it up.

A fat rat sat on a rug.

The rat got mud on it.

a gob of jam

a big sob

a bad job

a big mob

a hot hob

36

Doc ran a big van.

A big van can lug a lot.

Doc had a lot in the van.

Doc got gas.

Doc ran the van up, up, up.

Doc ran the van on, on, on.

Doc ran the van until sunset.

Word-attack: A List of Multisyllable Words

To expand upon the consonant-vowel-consonant foundation so carefully laid as the pupil progresses through the first lessons, the following list of multisyllable words, whose syllables are recognizably composed of the patterns of part I, is provided to sharpen word-attack skills, increase awareness of vocabulary, or as an interesting way to apply this new skill. (Some of these multisyllable words have been introduced in the connected reading for lessons 1–36.) Including them in the lessons is an optional matter; they are intended as a supplement.

Older pupils, in particular, can significantly benefit from these lists of longer words by reading them to expand their reading horizons beyond the C-V-C monosyllables just learned. They can see for themselves that it is possible to unlock much longer, more sophisticated words. Success engenders confidence.

The lists conform to the patterns as they are introduced in part I. However, some words require adjustment to pronunciation (such as *panda* or *cabinet*) and follow groups of words that are pronounced with level stress (such as *ragbag* or *sunset*).

I. WORDS WITH THE MEDIAL VOWEL *a*, LESSONS 1–8

–an	Man dan	Can a da
	Man hat tan	ban dan na
	rat tan	At lan ta
	pan da	ba nan a

Ja pan   san dal

cat a ma ran   van dal

Sa van na   vas sal

An na   mam mal

San ta   al fal fa

                       Al a bam a

–ap cat nap   Gal a had

mad cap   ca nal

Kap lan

                       –as can vas

–am sam pan   ras cal

                       pam pas

mad am

Ad am   NAS A

ban tam   Dal las

ma cad am   at las

Tam pa   a las

                       A las ka

–al Al lan

bal lad   **–ac** mac

sal ad   al ma nac

II. WORDS WITH THE MEDIAL VOWEL *i*, LESSONS 9–16

–ig zig zag   Lin da

wig wag   Sin bad

sig nal   a kin

                       A lad din

–in nap kin   as sas sin

cat kin

                       –id kid nap

cab in   can did

sat in   pal lid

Lat in

gam in   ac rid

                       a mid

	rap id		tac tic
	val id		fab ric
	in val id		pic nic
	av id		Mic mac
	rab id		at tic
			an tic
–it	ban dit		fan tas tic
	rab bit		At lan tic
	tid bit		pan ic
	nit wit		mim ic
	gam bit		fan at ic
	gas lit		sa dis tic
	ad mit		
	pit a pat	*–il*	an vil
	hab it		pis til
	in hab it		
			Wil ma
–ib	in hib it		Wil da
			vil la
–im	dim wit		va nil la
	lim pid		Ma nil a
	lim it		sil i ca
	tim id		
		–iv	viv id
–ip	cat nip		liv id
	Pip pin		
		–i	*(recommended for the*
–is	mis fit		*more advanced pupil)*
	mis hap		Af ri ca
	fis cal		Af ri can
	His pan ic		ad mi ral
	bal lis tic		bib li cal
			can ni bal
	vis ta		
	tal is man		an i mal
			cap i tal
–ic	vic tim		hab i tat

rad i cal

Vat i can

tac ti cal

i tal ic

Mis sis sip pi

III. WORDS WITH THE MEDIAL VOWEL *u*, LESSONS 17–24

–un   sun tan

sun lit

pun dit

un til

un did

un fit

un pin

un cap

un zip

–us   rus tic

cac tus

cam pus

cal lus

lit mus

nim bus

ab a cus

–up   hic cup

cat sup

pin up

sit up

–ut   cat gut

tut-tut

un cut

hal i but

–ub   hub bub

pub lic

sub mit

nub bin

–um   hum bug

sum mit

yum-yum

rum pus

pab lum

al bum

min i mum

um bil i cal

–uf   muf fin

puf fin

rag a muf fin

–ul   sul tan

cup ful

man ful

sin ful

fit ful

pit i ful

Tul sa

sul fa

–uc   yuc ca

IV. WORDS WITH THE MEDIAL VOWEL *e*, LESSONS 25–30

–et				
	in let			mag net ic
	up set			met ri cal
	sun set			cab i net
	let up			min a ret
	in set			cas ta net
	fan jet			tet a nus
	set up			ret i na
	met al			riv u let
	pet al			Ti bet an
	ca det			val et
	be set			riv et
	met ric			
	Ti bet	*–en*		pig pen
	fet id			den tal
				ten nis
	bas ket			men tal
	tab let			pen man
	pup pet			len til
	mag net			den im
	mus ket			ten et
	nug get			
	mal let			Al len
	ham let			fat ten
	cask et			hap pen
	cut let			kit ten
	pal let			mit ten
	gas ket			got ten
	gob let			bit ten
	mil let			hid den
	gul let			sud den
	mul let			red den
				mad den
	lin net			sad den
	sig net			rid den
	rus set			lin den
	as set			bid den

sul len

bat ten

sod den

giv en

lin en

un bid den

fun da men tal

sen ti men tal

pen in su la

an ten na

ben e fit

u ten sil

pa ren tal

–ed   med al

ped al

mis led

ed it

bed lam

red-hot

bed bug

em bed

med ic

med i cal

jag ged

bet ted

fit ted

mat ted

un lim it ed

un in hab it ed

un in hib it ed

–eg   nut meg

Peg a sus

Win ni peg

–el   hel met

vel vet

vel lum

pel vic

pel vis

pel let

El lis

rel ic

del ta

Mel ba

dis pel

im pel

la pel

re pel

pas tel

run nel

fun nel

ken nel

tas sel

dam sel

man tel

pum mel

mus sel

pet ral

tin sel

lin tel

sen ti nel

cam el

pan el

gav el

rav el

reb el

pel i can

hel i pad

e nam el

un ravel

el lip tic
el lip ti cal

–es   ves sel
des pot
fes tal

ma jes tic
in tes tin al
fes ti val
pes si mis tic

–eb   deb it

–ev   sev en
dev il
lev el
rev el
bev el
e lev en

–ec   hec tic
Mec ca
Az tec

–em   lem on
em bed
a hem
di lem ma
tan dem

–ep   pep sin
tep id

ep ic
sep tic
zep pe lin
ep i dem ic
an ti sep tic
rep li ca

–ez   Ez ra

–e   *(recommended for the*
more advanced pupil)
se dan
be gan
be gin
be gun
be fit
re mit
re but

Ne vad a
ve ran da
me rid i an
me tal lic
re pub lic
re pub li can
re but tal
imp e tus
Se mi tic
e mit
e las tic
e nig ma

V. WORDS WITH THE MEDIAL VOWEL *O*, LESSONS 31–36

–ot
can not
mas cot
hot bed
got ten
rot ten
bal lot
mag got
ab bot
cab ot
piv ot
piv ot al
al lot
Cam e lot

–ob
cob web
bob cat
gob lin
hob gob lin
gob let
dob bin
rob in

–op
a top
tip top
pop gun
mop pet
top ic
gal lop
de vel op
en vel op

pop lin
op tic
op ti mis tic
op ti cal
top i cal

–od
ram rod
mod el

–og
nog gin

–om
tom cat
tom-tom
com et
com bat
pom pon
om let
com ma
vom it
com ic
com i cal
nom i nal
ab dom i nal

ven om
at om
a tom ic
com pel
com mit
com mit ted
wom bat
bot tom
ran som
sel dom
ran dom
cus tom
ac cus tom

–on
bon net
sun bon net
ton sil
con sul

ton ic

son ic

Con rad

on set

up on

ba ton

a non

sa lon

son net

Mon tan a

Wis con sin

an a con da

Am a zon

pen ta gon

San ta Mon i ca

con i cal

con tin en tal

non com mitt al

non sen si cal

lem on

mel on

wag on

can on

tal on

com mon

un com mon

sum mon

can non

can yon

les son

Nel son

Han son

Sam son

Wil son

Mil ton

cot ton

but ton

un but ton

mut ton

rib bon

gib bon

ten don

pis ton

gal lon

Leb a non

Mad i son

ven i son

Ham il ton

a ban don

bad min ton

–oc

moc ca sin

oc ta gon

oc to pus

oc tet

hav oc

–og

cat a log

to bog gan

–ol

pol len

sol id

pol i tic

vol can ic

Sol o mon

al co hol

Col o rad o

pis tol

gam bol

cap i tol

–os

gos sip

pos sum

fos sil

gos pel

host el

hos pi tal

co los sal

as bes tos

—o *(recommended for the
more advanced reader)*

to bog gan

do mes tic

po lit i cal

Co lum bus

Mo ham med

bo tan i cal

go ril la

ab do men

ac ro bat

daf fo dil

dip lo mat

dip lo mat ic

un dip lo mat ic

gon do la

man do lin

hip po pot a mus

met ro pol i tan

ec o nom ic

ec o nom i cal

kil o met ric

lan o lin

an tag o nis tic

o pos sum

pan o ram a

pan o ram ic

mem o ran dum

oc tag o nal

mon op o lis tic

PART II

Easy Reading

Guide to Part II, Lessons 37–71

The lessons in part II introduce words like *split*, *lisp*, *milk*, and *scram*, which are made up of consonant clusters or blends that are regular, or alphabetically consistent with those sound-letter correlations taught in part I. These combinations of consonants, and in fact all the patterns of part II, expand on the sound-letter correlations already established in part I but do not materially alter them. Part II also introduces the pupil to doubled consonants, some plurals, possessives, and contractions.

As always, it is important for the teacher to step back and allow the pupil's own speech patterns to dictate how a word or pattern is pronounced. Some young pupils may still retain favored pronunciations from their early speech. These idiosyncrasies do not necessarily get in the way of learning to read with *Let's Read*, and the teacher should be cautious about reordering an individual's speech patterns, which, in any event, can be an exercise in futility. Many youngsters do not hear subtle (to them) differences between various sounds and so create their own sound systems that in the main serve them well enough. Oftentimes, parents are a little sad when these remnants from early childhood drop out of use.

With pronunciation problems—as with other problems—patience, practice, and the sheer volume of patterns will prevail in overcoming them. These elements are a far more effective prescription than focusing on the pronunciation (or repronunciation) of sounds the pupil may or may not discern.

Scope of Part II

- Group I
  - regular consonant clusters, *sl-, sk-, fl-, tw-*, etc., as in *sled, skin, flop, twig*
  - *-st, -lf, -pt*, etc., as in *best, dusk, self, kept*
- Group II
  - simple plural nouns with *s*, as in *caps, mats, locks, duffs*
  - third-person singular of verbs formed by adding *s* (with the value of *s* as in *sit*), as in *hops, sits, cranks*
  - possessives and contractions, such as *its, Beth's; it's, let's*
- Group III
  - digraphs *wh-, -ng*, as in *which, sing*
  - doubled consonants, as in *egg, fuzz, bill*
  - *qu-* as in *quick, squid*
  - *-x* as in *fox, box*

The words in the patterns of part II, despite being composed of combinations of two or more consonants, are consistently alphabetic in their spelling—or regular in their sound-letter correlations—and common in their use. In the case of the digraphs, they have a consistent single-sound value, as does final *x*, and they constitute the last of the most alphabetic spelling patterns in the *Let's Read* sequence of lessons.

Suggestions for the Teacher

Part II builds on part I and does not require much alteration of method for the teacher.

1. In part II, new vocabulary is listed at the top of the page, usually in columns. The lists are to be read from the top to the bottom of each column to emphasize the significant differences between the words within a column and between columns. Significant differences are evident vertically—between the words in a column—and are often also evident horizontally—between words in adjacent columns, which provides plenty of opportunity for review.

2. Have the pupil spell and say the words in a pattern. If the pupil seems comfortable with a new pattern, it is not necessary to spell each new word before saying it. In fact, the pupil has made a giant stride if he or she is able to read the words in a new list without spelling them first. Far from being an indication of good guesswork, this

flicker of independence is a demonstration of the pupil's internalization of sound-letter correlation even in these new multiletter combinations.

3. Repeat groups of words that cause difficulty. Especially in the first lessons of part II, the pupil is dealing with many variables in both the patterns and the connected reading.

When a pupil stumbles, it is sometimes enough to simply tell or remind him or her what a word is after it has been spelled. However, it is often more helpful to show the pupil how to read a troublesome word by the process of analogy, by presenting the pupil with a familiar C-V-C word and then using that word to discover by pairing how to unlock the unfamiliar one.

For example, by contrasting *cat* and *scat*, or *lad* and *glad*, or *lit* and *split*, the pupil can independently discern their relationships and will by this process understand and respond correctly.

This technique can be used quite inventively: the teacher, by alteration of *only one letter at a time*, shows the pupil how to proceed—or advance by analogy—comparing what is known to what is not recognized.

4. Once the pupil can read the pattern of words at the beginning of a lesson, move on to the connected reading that follows. This reading can be challenging, because the pupil must read not only familiar three-letter words but also much less familiar words of four or five letters that contain, as well, any of the five vowels. These first lessons can go very slowly, and for this reason the patterns are initially introduced over several lesson pages.

5. As was the case with connected reading in part I, the sentences in part II are not complex and not open to much interpretation. It is a good idea and a fairly simple matter to establish that the pupil has understood the sentence or group of related sentences by asking him or her a simple question about what has just been read.

6. Move ahead to the next lesson as the last is completed. Review or repeat any lessons that seem to mystify the pupil. Frequently, the learning curve for part II is initially fairly steep but should level out as the pupil progresses through the first lessons and gains confidence—and momentum.

NOTES

1. *Phonic cues.* It is perhaps worth remarking that attempts by the teacher to explain consonant blends to the pupil in the hope of giving help are most likely doomed to failure. In English, these blends are not separated in pronunciation (i.e., the *sp-* of *split* is neither divisible nor explainable in that way, rather it is the same as the *sp-* of

spot or *spin* or *lisp* and a prolific pattern in English). The repetition within patterns will be the means by which the pupil assigns sounds to particular pairs or groups of letters in words.

2. *The apostrophe.* As practiced readers and writers know, the apostrophe is a signal of the writer's intention in written English, but it will help the learner if the teacher explains that the apostrophe tells the reader something important about a word (something belongs to someone or something, or that a letter is omitted).

3. *Irregular words.* As in part I, irregular or sight words are included in the connected reading. In part II they are *be, he, she, we, her, were, has,* and *is,* all of which defy alphabetic explanation but are as common to English usage as pits are to cherries. Pupils will recognize these words through repetition and context rather than through any analysis a teacher might offer. Continue as before to read the word for the pupil if he or she cannot read it or until the pupil recognizes it through context or practice.

4. *Writing.* Writing words can be a powerful incentive to a pupil who is anxious to use the skills he or she has learned. However, for the pupil who is not quite ready to write, it can be a very troublesome chore. As has been observed earlier, writing is an entirely individual matter, dependent upon the maturity and interest of the pupil and the teacher's desire to pursue written exercises. Certainly making words and sentences by writing them is one way to supplement the oral reading lessons. Younger pupils may find a chalkboard with its larger scope easier to write on than paper. And for the artistically inclined pupil, drawing a picture about something that has been read can be a very satisfactory activity.

5. *Dictation.* Many teachers find that dictating pairs of words (as *nap, snap* or *lip, slip,* etc.) and having pupils spell them is an effective and satisfying activity. It can be done with cutout letters or by writing, if the pupil is so inclined.

6. *Reinforcements.* The teacher should continue to draw upon the arsenal of reinforcements used in part I that appealed to the pupil and/or seemed especially effective. However, as the pupil becomes more practiced and comfortable with learning to read, the need for special reinforcement diminishes fairly dramatically.

led	sled	lab	slab	lob	slob
lid	slid	lag	slag	lug	slug
lop	slop	lip	slip	lap	slap
lit	slit		slat	lot	slot
	slim		slam		slum

37

Mom Cat had a pot of jam.

Tom Cat got a bit on a bun.

Slim Jim Cat got a big gob of jam.

Did it slop? It did.

The jam slid onto the rug.

Slim Jim can be a slob!

Nat had a nag. The nag sat.

She did not get up.

Nat had to slap the nag on her leg to get her up!

nag   snag   nip   snip   snit

nap   snap   nub   snub

37

Sam slid on a big red sled.

The sled hit a snag. He slid into a pit.

Can Pam slam a bat?

Can she get a run? She did!

Pat can slug a hit. He did it!

Pat got a hit.

I cut a slit in the rug.

Mom got upset.

Did Wag snap at Kit Cat?

He did. Scat, Cat!

Kit Cat got into a snit. She hid.

cab	scab	kid	skid
can	scan	Kim	skim
cat	scat	kin	skin
cot	Scot	kip	skip
	scum	kit	skit

37

I can hop! I can skip! I can run!

We did a skit.

Meg had a big red wig.

I had a big, big hat.

We had to snag a big bad hen.

In the skit, Meg got the hen.

Scot had a red cap.

It got into a fan. It got a rip in it.

Can he hem up the slit in the cap?

mug   smug   wag   swag   swim

      smut   wig   swig   swam

                              swum

37

I had a can of pop.

Jim had a swig of it.

Simkin, the tan cat, hid in a bin.

It had mud in it. It had smut in it.

He got smut on him.

Who can swim?

Can a hen swim?

Can a cat swim?

Can Tim swim? Yes, Tim can.

Tim swam.

Smug Ben can skip.

Nan cannot skip yet.

But Ben cannot be smug.

pan	span	pit	spit	pot	spot
pin	spin	lit	split		sped
pun	spun		splat		spud

38

Sam hit a jam pot. Splat!

Jam got on the rug. Jam got on Sam.

A spot got on the pup.

A big blob got on a pen.

Sam sped to get a rag.

He got the rag wet to mop up the jam.

Can Kim swim yet? She can swim.

Can Deb skip? Deb can run but she cannot skip.

Dad got Tom a big red top.

Can Tom spin it?

Can Tom spin the top?

Spin it, Tom, spin it!

Tom spun the big red top.

tab	stab	top	stop	stem
tag	stag	tub	stub	step
tan	Stan		stud	stun

39

Who can tag Stan? He can run in a zigzag.

But Stan cannot stop! Stop, Stan! Stop!

Do not slam into the pigpen!

But Stan did not stop. He sped into the pigpen.

It had a lot of mud in it. It had the pig, Pigwig, in it.

Stan slid in the mud. Pigwig got up.

Who can tag Stan? Pigwig can.

A man got a stag.

He got a big, big stag.

A big rut! Can the bus stop?

It cannot! It slid! It spun! It did not stop!

Slam! The bus slid into the rut!

Scot had a sled. Meg had a pan.

Stan had a big red sled.

Scot slid on the sled. Stan slid on the red sled.

39

Meg slid on the pan.

Stan sped on the red sled. It slid!

It hit a snag.

A slat split in the sled.

Stan got a cut on the leg. Sad Stan!

Meg got Stan to sit on the pan.

Scot let Meg get on the sled.

The sled sped. The sled slid.

Stan slid. Stan sped on the pan.

He did not hit a snag.

He sped on, on, on.

rag	brag	rig	brig	ran	Fran	rib	crib
ran	bran	rim	brim	red	Fred	ram	cram
rat	brat				fret	rag	crag
					from		crab
							crop

40

Ten men sat in the brig.

The men in the brig were bad!

Fran had a red hat.

The hat had a big brim.

The hen sat in a pan.

The pan had bran in it.

The hen sat in the bran.

The hen had the bran from the pan.

The hen had a nap in the bran in the pan.

Dad got a big crop. He did not brag.

A rat can be a brat.

A rat can be a crab! Can a rat be a crab?

rab	drab	rub	drub	ram	pram	prom
rag	drag	rug	drug	rig	prig	
ram	dram	rum	drum	rim	prim	
rip	drip		drop	rod	prod	prop

40

A bus ran into a pit. Did it drop into it?

It did. Ten men had to prop up the bus.

Ten men got a van to drag it from the pit.

Fred had a pup in a pram.

The pram ran into a spot of mud.

Mud got on the pram. Mud got on the pup.

Can Fred drag the pram from the mud?

I am in bed to nap.

But Tim has a drum.

Bam! Bam! Rat-a-tat-tat!

Stop it, Tim. I cannot nap!

But Tim cannot stop.

ram	tram	ram	gram	grab
rap	trap	rid	grid	grin
rim	trim	rim	grim	grit
rip	trip	rip	grip	grog
rod	trod	rub	grub	
rot	trot			

41

Fred had a nag.

The nag can trot.

She can drag a trap.

Trit-trot! Trit-trot! The nag can trot a lot.

Mal ran a tram.

He ran the tram from sunup to sunset.

A big bad man got a cup of grog.

He had a big swig of it.

The man had a pan of grub.

He had a lot of grub.

ram	scram	rap	strap
rap	scrap	rip	strip
rip	scrip	rum	strum
rub	scrub	rut	strut

41

A man set a big rat trap.

A big rat got into the trap.

He cannot scram. He cannot strut.

He had a nap in the trap.

Stan got a strap onto a rig.

Can he grab the strap?

Can he drag the rig up from the mud?

Cut it up! Snip! Snip!

Trim it! Snip! Snap!

Fit it! Pin it up!

Zip it up! Zip-zip!

Snap it up! Snap! Snap!

Do it up! Zip! Snap!

I won but I did not brag. To brag is bad.

I am a grub. I am a bug.

42 I cannot skip but I can run. I do not strut.

I can sit on a stem. I sit in mud.

Can I step on a spot? Yes, step on it.

Can I spin on it? I cannot.

Brad fed Tom Cat a scrap of ham.

Did Wag beg? Did Wag grab it from Tom?

Tom Cat got mad at Wag, but Wag got the ham.

Tom ran at Wag. He hit Wag on the leg!

Bad Wag! Sad Wag.

Brad got Tom a scrap of ham.

Wag did not grab it from him.

lad	clad	lip	clip	lad	glad
lap	clap	lot	clot	Len	Glen
	clan		clod		glib
	clam		clog		glum
	Clem		club		glut
	clef				

43

Glen had a club.

The club met in a hut.

Grab the bat, Clem! Grip it!

Slug it! Slam a hit!

She did it! Clem got a big hit!

I am glad Clem got to bat.

Mom, drop a clam into a hot pot.

Nan, clap a lid on it.

A Scot from a clan had on a red tam.

The Scot clad in the red tam did a jig!

lag	flag	flog	lab	blab	lot	plot	wig	twig
lap	flap	flop	led	bled		plan	win	twin
	flat	fled		blob		plod	wit	twit
	flit			blot		plum		
	flip			blat		plus		
	flip-flop					plug		
						plat		

43

Did a bug flop from a stem to a bud?

He sat up on the flat top of the bud.

The bug did a flip. It did a flip-flop onto a twig.

A bug can flit from spot to spot.

Ned had a flag. Flip! Flap!

Fred had a drum. Rum-a-tum-tum!

Pigwig had a big red plum.

I am glad. I am not glum.

I am not grim. I am not mad.

I am not sad.

I grin. I can grin a big grin.

44

Glen got a cut from a brad.

It bled a lot. We can stop it.

Get a strip of rag!

Blot it. Dab it.

Brad had a nag.

Brad got on the nag.

But Nan, the nag, did not trot.

Brad did not jab her, but she got a slap from him.

Did Nan Nag run! She sped at a clip.

A flag can flap.

A cut bled.

Clip-clop. A nag can run.

45

A flat clam sat in the sun.

A kid did a flip.

A bug sat on a twig.

The pig ran at a clip.

A blob of plum got on a flip-flop.

The club met at sunset.

A bad man fled in a bus.

Did Ben plan a skit?

Clap a bit.

Grin a lot.

an	and	hand	end	send	bond
	band	handbag	bend	tend	fond
	land		mend	rend	pond
	sand		lend	vend	wind
	sandbag		wend	intend	fund

46

A fat clam had a nap in the sand.

The fat clam did not intend to nap.

It got up. It slid into the pond.

Sam did not intend to hit Al and Hal.

But he hit Al on the leg and Hal on the hand!

Hap got hot.

He had a swim in the pond.

Nan had a red handbag and a red hat.

Ten men can lend a hand to mend the
    split in the dam.

an	ant	tin	tint	ten	tent	rent	bun	bunt
	pant		hint		bent	sent		hunt
	rant		lint		dent	vent		punt
			mint		lent	pent		runt
	font		dint		went			Lunt

47

Tim went to the pond.

Tim and Tom went to swim.

A crab in the pond bit Tim.

Tim and Tom went to get the bad crab.

Tom got it. He sent it onto the sand.

Pal ran and ran and ran.

Pal got hot from the run.

Did he pant? He did. A lot.

Fred can hit, but Bud can bunt.

best	pest	must	mist	dusk	desk
nest	west	just	list	husk	disk
rest	vest	gust	fist	tusk	risk
test	zest	rust		musk	lisp
lest	jest	bust		rusk	wisp
		dust			

48

At dusk, just a wisp of mist on the pond.

    Just a hint.

A man went west in a van.

An ant had the best nest in a desk!

Sal had a list. She got a blob of jam on it.

A gust of wind got dust on the flag.

Len Lunt won the bet.
He did grin at the rest of us.

belt	gilt	silt	elf	elk	bulk	help
felt	hilt	tilt	self	ilk	hulk	yelp
melt	jilt	wilt	itself	silk	sulk	kelp
pelt	kilt		himself	milk		pulp
welt	lilt		gulf			gulp

49

held	weld	elm	helm
gild	bulb		film

An elf got himself onto a twig.

He sat on the twig. He had a sip of milk.

Kim had a kilt, a silk belt, and a red hat.

She felt best in the kilt.

Yelp! Yap! Pal got into the pigpen.

Help him! He got into the mud.

He cannot get himself up from it.

Tad had a big gulp of milk.

bump	camp	gift	act	kept
dump	damp	rift	fact	wept
hump	ramp	sift	pact	tempt
jump	tamp	lift	tact	hemp
lump	vamp	left	duct	
pump	lamp	deft	sect	apt
rump	limp	tuft	insect	rapt
romp	imp			

50

At dusk, Mom lit the lamp on the desk.

Do not tempt Fred into the pond.
Fred cannot swim.

An insect bit Sis on the hand.
She felt a welt from it.

A man ran a van up a ramp.

A hemp strap held the top on a bin.

Hot milk in a pot,

    Hot milk in a jug,

Hot milk in a cup,

    Hot milk in a mug.

50

Do not be smug. Do not brag.

Do not prod. Do not grab.

Do not scrap. Do not slap.

Do not fret.

Do not gulp. Do not slop.

Do not slump.

Do not jump.

Do not skip. Do not flip.

Do not! Do not! Do not!

I cannot just sit! Can I grin?

cat	get	mop	tent	nest	limp
cats	gets	mops	tents	nests	limps

The plump pups slept in tents.

bats	jets	fits	cots	cuts	caps
hats	lets	hits	dots	huts	naps

A ram tramps up the ramp into the van.

pants	rests	gifts	bulks	camps	bumps
dents	facts	fists	sulks	lamps	jumps

A man sets up a tent on the sand and camps.

The ham in a pan tempts Tip.

He jumps up. He gets it!

Bad Tip!

Hal sips milk from a cup.

Tomcat laps milk from a pan.

But Tip, the pup, gulps milk.

He slops it.

Pat	the cat	it
Pat's bat	the cat's leg	its leg

52 Pat's bat got dents in it.

The cat cut its leg.

The cat's leg got cut.

Pat's hot.	The cat's sad.
It's hot.	It's bad.

Let's run.	Let's jump.
Let us run.	Let us jump.

It's hot. We can swim.

Let's swim. It's fun.

Ted must not lift the desks himself.

Scot, Pam, and Brad are to help him.

Brad mops the desks. Pam and Scot dust.

Ted sets lamps on the desks.

skim   stun   plum   wept   rust   lamp

skimp   stunt   plump   swept   crust   clamp

53

tract   strict   cleft   drift   swift   runt

smelt   spelt   spilt   skulk   cramp   grunt

scamp   stamp   tramp   blimp   crimp

prompt   clump   frump   slump   stump

A limp blimp slumps on the sand.

trump   brand   grand   stand   strand

blend   spend   trend   blond   scant

spent   print   splint   sprint   stint

blunt   crept   slept   brisk   frisk

crest   twist   trust

We sat in the grandstand.

The band sat in the bandstand.

Ben had on flip-flops. He ran in them and slid.

Jen did a handstand.

stamp	grunt	twist	trust	drift	print
stamps	grunts	twists	trusts	drifts	prints

54 A tug drifts and twists in the wind.

Sid prints on a pad.

A pig stamps and grunts.

tracts	clefts	tramps	smelts	skulks
cramps	scamps	frumps	blimps	crimps
prompts	clumps	splints	slumps	stumps
trumps	frisks	crests	sprints	stints

The pup frisks and jumps.

A flag twists in the brisk wind.

Tim sprints and gets cramps.

Fred and Tom did stunts.

Fred and Tom did twists and jumps.

Tom did a handstand. Fred had a rest from stunts.

A rat sat on a pot. The cat crept up on it.

The rat sat up. Run, rat, run! Scram!

Pat's pup can do stunts.

She sits up and can beg.

She jumps into a bag.

Pat's pup's the best!

54

It's a brisk wind.

The wind drifts sand into the tent.

It dumps sand on the pots, the cots, and the lamps.

It's in a clump on the stump we sit on.

We are in a lot of sand!

king	bang	hung	clang	cling	clung
ring	rang	rung	slang	fling	flung
sing	sang	sung	twang	sling	slung
wing	hang	lung	sprang	sting	stung

55

The king has a big ring. It was a gift from his dad.

An insect clung to a twig. He hung on and
stung an ant.

ding	gang	swing	swung
ping	pang	spring	sprung
ting	fang	bring	strung
zing	tang		

The gang had a band.

Zeb had a drum. Bam! Bang!

Fran had a lid from a pot.

Clang! Clang! Jed had a trumpet. Tat-a-tat-tat!

A clang and a twang and a bang.

A big din rang from the band.

The band was bad, but the gang had fun.

ink	rink	bank	rank	bunk	punk
link	sink	dank	sank	funk	sunk
mink	wink	hank	tank	hunk	
pink		lank	yank	junk	

56

Kit had a tug in the tub. It got wet.

Did it sink? Yes, Kit's tug sank in the tub.

Fran had a cab. It ran on gas.

She got a tank of gas.

The bus is just a hunk of junk.

It's got rust on it. It has gaps in it. It has dents in it.

A cat had a nap on the rim of a tank.

The tank had ink in it.

The cat sang and slept and hung from the rim.

It sprang from the rim and flung itself into the tank!

It got into the ink. The ink was wet.

But the cat got up onto the rim.

It can rub the ink from itself.

blink   brink   blank   crank   drunk   flunk

clink   drink   clank   drank   trunk

slink   flank   frank   skunk

stink   plank   Frank   slunk

spank   prank   spunk

stank   swank   stunk

56

Vic had to get help. He sent Sis to get it.

She ran and got Dad and ten men.

She and Dad and the men got ten planks.

Vic had to get the help and the planks to prop up
the rotten hut.

Vic helps the men set up the planks.

Vic and Sis and Dad and the ten men prop up
the hut.

shed	shot	sham	shrub	shrimp
shelf	shotgun	shag	shrug	shrift
Shep	shop	shad	shred	
	shod			

57

A man shot a shotgun. It went bang-bang!

ship	shut	shank	shrink
shift	shun	shaft	shrank
shin	shunt	shrunk	

Shep got shut in the shed. He yelps. He yaps
  until Hap gets him.

Fran had a grand trip on a big ship.

A hen had a nest on a shelf in the shed. She sat in it.

Frank cannot shut the big trunk. If he jumps on
  it, Frank can get it to shut.

Bob got a bad bump on the shin.

57

A skunk slunk into the pigpen. It hid.

The pig sat on the skunk. The skunk got mad.

The pig stinks of skunk!

The cats were shut up in the shed and got into a bag of shrimp.

Mac's a Scotsman.

Mac's tam got wet and shrank. It can fit an elf!

In the tent, Tom and Frank had just a cup and a mug to drink from.

Tom drank from the cup, and Frank drank from the mug.

ash bash cash dash gash

lash mash rash sash hash

Bob got a gash on his shin. It bled.

A bad man had cash in a bag.

58

clash flash slash splash

brash crash trash stash smash

Frank Pig has a pan of mash. In a flash he gulps

it up.

mesh flesh fresh dish fish wish

bosh gosh josh slosh swish

Men fish in the gulf. The men get shrimp in nets.

gush hush lush mush rush tush

brush crush blush flush plush slush

a mish-mash   a catfish   ten codfish

a dishpan   a dishrag

58   A catfish and ten codfish swam in a pond.

If I flush, I get red. If I blush I get red.

Do not crush Pat's hat. But Pal did sit on it,
and he did crush it.

A hen had a dish of mush. It's a mish-mash of mush.

Tad flung the trash into the trash can.

Has Scot's belt shrunk?
It's not the belt; the belt did not shrink.
It's Scot. Scot's just gotten plump!

Peg is hot. I am hot.

We had a big swim in the pond.

It was the best swim. We are not hot.

58

Splash! Men on a ship drop a net into the gulf.

Shrimp get hung up in the mesh of the net.

In a flash, the men yank the shrimp up to the
ship in the net.

Ed went to get gas in his van.

He began to pump gas into the tank.

The gas spilt and sprang from the tank in a gush.

Nan had a lush plum in a bag.

Shep sat on it! Did Shep crush it?

It was mush! Shep got plum mush on his pants
and on the plush rug.

And Shep cannot brush the mush from his pants.

chin	chap	chug	chop	chipmunk
chip	chat	chum	chest	
chink	champ	chump	Chet	
chit	Chad	chunk		

59

Pat kept a pet chipmunk in a pen. Pat fed it nuts and milk. The pen had a chink in it. The chipmunk fled.

Did Ted chop up an elm? He did not. Ted just cut a twig from a shrub.

Chet can run the best. In a flash, he can dash to the pond and jump in. He sprints to the pond. He jumps in. Chet's a champ!

Chad had ham and a yam. His chum, Chet, had hash. I had a chops and a spud.

rich	inch	bench	bunch	filch
much	finch	drench	lunch	belch
such	pinch	French	munch	mulch
	winch	trench	punch	gulch
	clinch	ranch	crunch	sandwich

60

It's such a big chest. Can Stan lift it?
He did not lift it much. Not an inch! Stan must
get help. If he can get a chap and a winch, Stan
and the chap and the winch can lift the chest.

Pam sat on a bench and had lunch.
She had a ham sandwich and milk. She fed
scraps of ham to her pup.

Did a bunch of chipmunks filch nuts
from a chap's bag? The scamps did!

Pat went to a big ranch in the West. Pat
slept on a bunk in a cabin. She did not get much
rest. Pat had a big job on the ranch.

thin	thank	thresh	thrust	thrift
thing	thump	thrash	thrum	
think		thrush		

61

The thin thrush thinks of a big lunch. It's the best thing to do.

Bob thumps on the drum. I bang on pots.

Beth	depth	length	tenth
Seth	width	strength	fifth
Smith			twelfth

Beth and Seth cannot lift Frank's trunk.

It's such a big thing!

Seth thinks Frank must lend his strength to lift it.

Beth thinks Frank must get a winch to do the job.

Tom Smith went on a trip on the tenth.

Jan Finch went to camp on the twelfth.

I get on a bus to go west on the fifth.

A finch and a chipmunk had a chit-chat on
    a branch.

A thrush lit on the branch.

61

The finch, the chipmunk, and the thrush chat.

In a bit, the thrush flits up to nab insects.

The finch gets a bug sandwich from his bag.

The chipmunk has a dish of nuts.

The chipmunk, the thrush, and the finch had a
    grand lunch.

Chet's pup got shut in a chest.

Chet cannot get the chest's lid up.

He chops at it and chips a chunk from the lid.

The pup jumps from the chest.

Beth thinks it's hot. "Let's swim, Fran."

"Yes, let's. I cannot stand the sun."

Beth and Fran swim the length of the pond and
    its width.

biff	cliff	cuff	buff	scuff	fluff
tiff	skiff	puff	ruff	stuff	snuff
Jeff	sniff	muff	gruff	bluff	
	stiff	huff	scruff		

62

Biff and Cliff had a tiff. Biff got into a huff.

Cliff thinks Biff's a bit of a chump.

Biff thinks Cliff's gruff.

Jeff and Vic and I went up the cliff. Vic huffs and
puffs a lot.

We had to stop and rest. And Jeff got a stiff leg.

But we got to the top of the cliff.

We sat and felt a stiff wind.

Nat's pup got into the mud on the bank of the pond.

Nat must get a stiff brush to scrub the mud from
the pup.

Sniff! Snuff! The pig thinks he can sniff nuts in
the mud.

He sniffs until he gets a pan of mush from Dan.

kiss	Bess	dress	undress	lass	fuss
miss	Jess	press	unless	mass	muss
hiss	Tess	cress		bass	truss
bliss	less	tress	bless	crass	
Swiss	mess	stress	chess		

63

Pam got a muff from the trunk in the shed. It has ants on it, but Pam can get rid of the ants. Clem got a dress from the trunk. Mom says we must get rid of the trunk. It has a lot of stuff in it. But Clem and Pam think the trunk must be kept. The stuff in it is fun to dress up in.

Jess got a gift from his dad. It's a grand chess set.

Such a fuss. Bess got a dress. She had to press it.

Yum-yum. A lass had a cress sandwich!

bill	Jill	will	frill	
fill	chill	dill	grill	a windmill
hill	skill	gill	trill	a hilltop
kill	spill	rill	shrill	a millpond
mill	still	drill	thrill	

64

A windmill sat on a hilltop.

It's still on the millpond.

bell	yell	shell	shall	mull	hull
fell	Nell	spell	doll	dull	cull
sell	dell	smell	loll	gull	null
tell	hell	swell	Moll	lull	
well	ell	dwell			

Chet will sell his swell shell to Bill.

Nell fell into the millpond. Did she yell!

The big bell had a dull ring. Not shrill, just dull.

A gull sat on a stump. It had a lunch of a fat fish.

Jill got a doll. She can dress and undress it.

mitt	fizz	Ann	add	egg
butt	buzz	inn	odd	ebb
mutt	fuzz	jinn		
putt	jazz			

65

Frank Hunt had a mutt, Spot.

Spot's an odd mutt. He drinks pop. He laps up
  the fizz on it!

Ann had an egg. It had a crack in its shell.

Ann got egg on her pants. Such a mess!

Jill had an odd jug. It had a jinn in it.

Jill thinks if she can rub the jug, the jinn can flit
  from the jug.

Bill and Nell had lunch at the inn.

Bill had an egg sandwich. Nell had a crab from
  the grill.

A finch had a nest. It had fluff in it and an egg.

The finch sat on the egg.

which	whiff	whish	whisk
which	whiff	whish	whisk
whip	whiz	whim	whit
when	whet	whelp	whang

66

Chet's sled went whiz on the big hill. Whish! Swish!

When Shep trots in, the cat whisks onto its bed.

On a whim, Fred Cat hid on a ship, which went on a big trip.

Tom whisks an egg in a dish.
The whisk whips up the egg.

Wind whips the skiff into the bank.
It splits up and sinks.

Just a whiff of skunk sent Bess into the shed.

Jeff and his dad went into a shop to get lunch.
Jeff felt bad. He did not wish to get a sandwich.
Dad got Jeff milk. When Jeff drank the milk, he felt well.

Ann has lunch in a bag. When she sits on a bench, a mutt trots up to Ann. It can smell the sandwich in the bag. The mutt sits up to beg.

66

An odd hen sits on Hap's mitt. The hen thinks the mitt's a nest! When the hen flaps from the mitt, she has left an egg in it!

Insects buzz.

A bell will clang. It will ring.

A nag can trot.

A pig will grub.

A man will scrub and mop up the mess.

A wind will whip a flag.

Pop has fizz.

A lad had a whim. He had a wish.

A fish swam in the pond. It went swish, swish.

back   pack   lack   crack   track   thwack

hack   rack   black smack   shack

Jack   sack   clack   snack   whack

Mack   tack   slack   stack   blacksmith

67

Jack's a blacksmith. Jack's shop's in a shed.

Jack whacks and thwacks and smacks and

     bangs hot metal.

It's a red-hot job.

Dick   pick   brick   flick   thick

kick   sick   prick   slick   Rick

lick   tick   trick   stick

Nick   wick   click   chick   a pickup

Dick and Nick went to get a pickup.

It's a trick to back it up.

Mack's hat fell into the pond.

Rick went and got a stick.

Mack must lift it up on the stick.

deck	buck	puck	cluck	chuck
neck	duck	suck	pluck	shuck
peck	luck	tuck	truck	
check	muck	stuck	struck	

68

A hen had an egg in a nest.

The hen sat and sat on it.

Cluck! Cluck! Crack! Crack!

When the shell split, the hen had a chick.

cock	rock	block	crock	smock
dock	sock	clock	frock	stock
lock	hock	flock	shock	

A skunk sat on the sack of socks, and it stinks.

The lock sticks.

A hen pecks at a sack of bran.

When a truck struck the shed,

    the shed split up into bits.

patch	snatch	itch	witch	botch	splotch
catch	scratch	ditch	switch	notch	Dutch
hatch	thatch	hitch	twitch	blotch	hutch
latch	fetch	pitch	snitch	crotch	clutch
match	stretch	Fitch	stitch	Scotch	crutch

69

Will the skiff catch the puff of wind?

The pig had in itch on its back. It must scratch it.

Ann got a rip in her pants.
She can patch it and stitch it up.

Jack will sketch the ship. It's a big ketch.

The hen has an egg. In the egg is a chick.
If she sits on it in her nest,
    the chick will hatch from the egg.
It will peck at the shell and drag itself
    from the egg.

Did the rat snitch the bag of nuts?
It did. Such a brat!

quack	quip	quell	squid	squint
quick	quit	quest	squib	squelch
quilt	quiz	quench	squish	
quill				

70

A flock of ducks swam in the pond. Ducks can
    quack a lot.

Ducks do not cluck, but a hen clucks a lot.

A squid shot ink onto a crab. The squid hid in
    its ink.

The crab hid in back of a rock.

A witch had a crash. She went into a branch.

The witch limps. She has a black crutch.

Pat dips the quill pen in the ink.

It drips ink on Pat's hand. Pat's a mess!

ax	fix	Rex	next	ox	tux
lax	mix	sex	text	box	flux
Max	six	Tex		Cox	crux
tax	sixth	vex		fox	
wax	jinx	flex			
	minx			sandbox	

71

A branch fell on the shed in the wind.

Quick, Jack, fetch an ax.

Let's chop up the branch and fix the shed.

Max got a rip in his pants. He can mend it.

A patch will fix it. Max will stitch
    a patch on his pants.

To fix a mud bun, dip mud into a tin can and mix
    it well. Get six cups.

Drop the mud in the cups and add ink—just a
    dash of it. Set the cups in the sun.

A red fox sits on a stump. He thinks of lunch.

Tex had a grand red cab. A bus hit it in the back and sent it into a ditch. Tex had to fetch a truck to drag the cab from the ditch. The trunk got dents in it and a big scratch from the crash. Tex will fix it up and scrub and wax the cab.

71

Did Tess miss the bus at six? Yes, but she got the
   next bus.
The next bus got a flat! Such bad, bad luck!

Lift up the box, Jack, and set it on the bench.
Shut the lid and lock it and get the box up on
   the bench.

Jill and Jack's cat is ill. She went to the vet.
The vet says the cat must be still but will get well.
Jill gets a thick quilt. Jack gets hot milk.
The cat naps on the quilt. Next she gets up.
She frisks up the hill. She is well!
She will catch herself a big fish from the pond.

More Easy Reading

Guide to Part III, Lessons 72–97

P art III marks the point where the pupil is prepared to master patterns in English that are still regular within the *Let's Read* scheme but are a departure from the patterns in part II. In part II, the pupil learned consonant blends or clusters that were still rooted in the alphabetic sound-letter correlations taught in Part I. Part III, by contrast, turns the pupil's attention to two-vowel combinations, such as *ee*, *ea*, *oo* and *oi*, as well as *r* and *y* in the final position, patterns that are exceedingly prolific in English. For the pupil, these are different vowels embedded in familiar vocabulary; in terms of *Let's Read*, they represent regular alphabetic sound-letter correlations and are taught in the same way as in parts I and II.

Part III can be viewed as an expansion stage for the learner. There is a marked expansion of both pattern and vocabulary as the pupil leaves the familiar world of C-V-C monosyllables and the slightly more complex territory of consonant blends and clusters for these new vowel patterns. Part III, although it expands on vowel patterns, does not depart from the single-sound principle of sound-letter correlations. However, the teacher should be aware that within these patterns, variations of pronunciation are likely, depending upon both regional and personal pronunciation. As usual, we do not advocate tweaking individual pronunciation systems to conform to the patterns of letters and, as usual, remind the instructor that variant pronunciations tend to conform to pattern (and vice versa). Variance may be most obvious in words that end with *r*, which affects pronunciation of the preceding vowel (for example, the difference between the pronunciation of *ou-* in *out* and *our*). For this reason, patterns where pronunciations tend to vary are given in separate lessons. Likewise, final *y*, which also affects pronunciation, is taught near the end of part III. Similarly, words that end with the so-called "silent *e*" are included in the last lessons. These patterns are limited to those like *goose*, *else*, and *give* that do not affect already-established sound-letter correlations.

Scope of Part III

- *ee* as in *see; eer* as in *deer*
- *ea* as in *eat; ear* as in *dear*
- *oo* as in *moon; oor* as in *poor*
- *ai* as in *sail; air* as in *pair*
- *ay* as in *day*
- *oa* as in *boat; oar* as in *board*
- *ou* as in *loud; our* as in *sour*
- *ow* as in *cow*
- *aw* as in *saw*
- *au* as in *haul*
- *oy* as in *boy*
- *oi* as in *boil*
- words ending in silent *e*, as in *house, sneeze*

Suggestions for the Teacher

Part III does not require much alteration of method for the teacher, with lessons organized in the familiar format of new vocabulary arranged in columns at the top of the page, followed by practice reading.

1. Introduce the pupil to new patterns by reading the columns vertically. If the pupil seems to need additional practice, the new vocabulary can be read across the page—or in any order. Of course, such random reinforcement is one of the purposes of the connected reading.

2. Have the pupil spell and say the words in a pattern. If the pupil is looking carefully at each word, it will most likely be unnecessary to spell and say more than one or two words in a pattern by this point. If the pupil is not looking carefully, of course, the remedy of spelling each new word before reading it is easily applied.

3. The connected reading of part III has somewhat more content than in part II, but by this time the pupil should be able to handle the connected reading with some ease.

Have the pupil spell any word that is puzzling and reread aloud any sentences that seem difficult.

4. Move ahead to the next lesson when it is clear that the pupil has grasped the material in a lesson. Review or repeat any patterns or lessons that seem to trouble the pupil. If a pupil seems to falter more often than the teacher expects, consider that it is possible a pupil's hesitancy does not mean that new material has not been assimilated but rather that he or she is paying closer attention to the more complex reading.

NOTES

1. *Connnected reading.* The reading in part III more nearly reflects ordinary speech and writing by virtue of the accumulated wealth of patterns from earlier lessons. The first purpose of the connected reading remains, however, practice.

   While the connected reading is still largely composed of short sentences, some is in paragraph form, and some of the sentences create small stories with titles. It is up to the teacher to determine whether or not the pupil will benefit from discussion of these conventions of writing, although it is generally better to provide more information as the pupil either asks for it or seems ready to accept it.

2. *Comprehension.* The goal of learning to read is to be able to read easily and, more importantly, to understand the message. In respect to comprehension, by this time, the teacher should regularly ask the pupil if he or she knows the meaning of a vocabulary word. The teacher should also try to elicit from the pupil some kind of reaction to a sentence or story and, as appropriate to the text, ask questions such as, "Do you think that is silly?" or "Do you think that is true?" or "Why do you think that happened?" These should not be extended psychological explorations, but this device does highlight the fact that words convey information, and discovering that message is what reading is about.

3. *Review pages.* Review pages appear at regular intervals after groups of patterns.

4. *Semi-irregularities.* In the last lessons of part III, the pupil encounters the first irregular pattern in *Let's Read.* While we have introduced irregular vocabulary earlier as sight vocabulary, in these last lessons, the irregularity of words with a final *e* are introduced as a pattern. They are considered semi-irregular because the presence of the final *e* (or silent letter) does not affect the regular value of the vowel in the word: *have* is pronounced as *hav*, *give* as *giv*, etc.

5. *Supplementary activities.* It is not necessary to have the pupil do supplementary work in order to progress satisfactorily in *Let's Read*, but it is wise to be sensitive to how well a pupil seems to be learning new patterns and how easily or how much difficulty a pupil has when reading the sentences and stories. The teacher should provide reinforcement that seems useful. For the pupil who enjoys writing (either from dictation or by invention), drawing, puzzles, word games, etc., such activities are a necessity.

bee	free	beet	sheet	feed	bleed
see	tree	feet	sleet	seed	freed
fee	three	meet	fleet	weed	speed
wee	flee		sweet	need	breed
lee	glee		street	heed	creed
tee	spree		greet	deed	greed
	treetop		tweet	indeed	tweed

72

A bee sat on Pat's neck. Pat felt it.

When Pat hit the bee with a smack, it stung her.

Al fell from a tree and did not land on his feet.

Did he bleed? He did not, but he did limp.

Did you see the robin land in the treetop?

It had to flee from quick Frank Fox.

The streets are full of sleet.

Lots of trucks slip and get stuck.

They cannot get free of the sleet

    and skid to a stop.

deep	creep	peek	feel	seen	reef
keep	sheep	seek	heel	keen	beef
peep	sleep	week	peel	teen	seem
seep	steep	leek	keel	green	deem
weep	sweep	meek	reel	queen	teeth
	reek			beech	

73

Jack and Jill went up a steep hill to fetch ten sheep.

Jack did not feel well. Jill had to get the sheep herself.

steel	sheen	leech	beechnut	fifteen
wheel	screen	speech	weekend	sixteen
cheek	creek	screech		

Chet had fifteen beechnuts in a dish.

He will feed them to his pet pig.

Creep into the shed to see Pat's sixteen pet chicks.

The chicks peep and peck at a pan of bran.

The queen had a green silk dress.

It had a big red sash.

It must feel grand to be a queen!

jer peer queer steer deer

veer leer cheer sheer deerskin

The men on a ship peer into the mist.

They see a reef. The ship must veer left

    to clear the reef.

The ship must steer to the left. The men cheer

    when they see the ship will not crash into the reef.

Can a cat sneer?

Can a rat leer?

Can a duck jer at a fox?

A deer did a queer thing.

The deer fell into a deep vat of muck! Yuck!

Ted got a grand gift.

Ted got deerskin mocs.

Meg got a deep cut on her heel.

Doc Smith had to stitch it up.

We need to cheer up Meg.

74

Dick's Cat

This week Dick Smith got a sleek cat.

74

It's a grand cat, but it's a scamp.

It jumps at Dick's pup. It sits on the pup's back.

It can run up a tree in a wink.

When the cat hid in the tree next to the shed,

Dick went to get it. But he did not see it in the big
   beech tree.

Dick went to the street. But he did not see the cat in
   the street.

Dick felt sad.

Dick's dad asks Dick to fetch the ax from the shed.

Dick went into the shed to get his dad the ax.

The ax was on a shelf. And on the shelf sat his cat!

Dick's dad got the ax, and Dick got his cat.

sea	bean	wean	tea bag
tea	dean	lean	peanut
pea	Jean	clean	seaweed
flea	mean		

75

Dean and Jean had a swim in the sea.

Jean swam into a mess of seaweed. Yuck!

eat	heat	peat	treat	bleat
beat	meat	seat	wheat	cleat
feat	neat	cheat		

Did Jim see the pup scratch a flea on its back?

Yes, and next the pup fell onto his back!

Dean sits on a bench. He has a bag of peanuts.

He eats six peanuts. Dean can see a chipmunk.

He sets three peanuts on the seat of the bench.

The chipmunk hops up.

He cracks the nuts and eats just the meat, not the shell.

Dean has a treat and the chipmunk has a treat.

bead	beak	weak	bleak
lead	leak	creak	freak
read	peak	sneak	squeak
	teak	speak	streak

76

Tom got sick. Jill got him a mug of weak tea.

Will Tom drink it?

A cat sleeps in the sun. A pup sneaks up on him.

The cat jumps up. The pup streaks into the shed.

I can read. I read from *Let's Read.*

A bad man hid a black box in the sand.

Can Shep lead us to the box? We will dig it up.

Next Shep and I will be rich!

A sheep bleats. A duck quacks.

A hen clucks. A pig grunts.

deal	real	steal	each	teach
heal	seal	squeal	beach	bleach
meal	veal		peach	breach
peal			reach	preach

76

We went to the beach. We swam and swam.

We had lunch. Next we dug in the sand.

The wind whips the big beech tree.

The beech creaks in the wind, but it will not snap.

A seal sat on a big flat rock. He had a meal of fish

and a nap in the sun.

Ring the bell! Let it peal!

Jack Smith plants crops. He plants beets and wheat.

If it's hot, the heat can kill the crops, but rain helps

Jack get a big crop of beets and wheat.

Fred and Mack each had a peach. It's a real treat.

Miss Cox can teach Jill to read. Jill thinks she can read,

but she cannot, not yet.

beam	cream	steam	steam heat
seam	dream	stream	sunbeam
team	gleam	scream	upstream

77

Did Jean scream when she had a bad dream?

Nell had to stitch up a dress. It had a rip in the seam.

heap	leaf	east	least	leash
leap	sheaf	beast	yeast	heath
cheap		feast		sheath

a green leaf   east and west   a sheaf of wheat

Pal can fetch his leash and bring it.

Pal leaps up to get the leash.

He will bring the leash to me.

Beth whips the cream. Fran and Max each peel a peach.

A grand treat. A feast!

Peach and cream! Yum-yum.

ear	fear	hear	rear	tear
dear	gear	near	sear	year
spear	shear	clear	beard	smear

78

Next year I will help shear the sheep.

A man got on the bus and sat near us in the rear.

He had a big beard and a queer black bag.

When we got near the beach, we ran and ran.

Each year Mal and Seth weed and clear up trash.

Hear the pig squeal! Hear the sheep bleat!

Hear the hen cluck! Hear the pup yap!

Hear the ducks quack! Hear the chicks cheep!

I will not weep. I will not shed a tear.

I will not scream. I will not squeal.

But I did get a mean cut from a stick.

Bess will drink milk. Dick will get pop.

Jean and Mom will drink tea.

boo	woo	moon	loon	teaspoon
coo	zoo	noon	spoon	moonbeam
moo	shoo	soon	croon	
too		boon	swoon	

79

Run, Seth! Sprint to catch the bus to the zoo!

The cat got into the trash. Shoo, cat, shoo!

boot	shoot	loop	stoop	cool	spool
hoot	scoot	poop	swoop	fool	stool
loot		scoop		pool	
		sloop	troop	tool	
		snoop	droop	drool	

Quick! Scoop up the mess.

A loon swoops to the pond to catch a fish.

A troop of chimps hid in the brush.
Will the chimps fool the big cat near them?
The big cat snoops and sniffs the air.
The chimps must be still. Soon the big cat
        trots to the pond to get a drink.

boom	food	goof	tooth	toothbrush
doom	mood	woof	booth	toothpick
loom	brood	poof	boost	
zoom		proof	spook	
bloom				

80

A Tramp and Spooks

A big shed and a tree stand in the gloom of the hill.

A tramp sneaks up. He seeks a spot to sleep.

Will the squeaks and creaks of the shed spook him?

Not a bit. The tramp can stand the gloom.

The wind shifts. Poof! It snuffs the tramp's lamp.

Bang! Boom! The tramp jumps up. The split planks on
the shed swing and bang in the wind.

It's not a spook. It's just the wind.

But the squeaks and gloom and wind spook the tramp.

He cannot get back to sleep in the big shed. It's got
spooks in it!

poor   boor   moor   spoor

An east wind whips the tree. The tree creaks.

81

The wind sent the tree into the shed. Crash! It fell on

the shed.

The tree did not crack the top beam of the shed in

the least.

We cannot fix the tree, but we can fix the shed.

Poor Jean and the Chill

Poor Jean! She fell into the pond and got a bad

chill. She must stay in bed and sleep a lot. She must

sleep with ten quilts! And Jean must eat just hot mush

and cream.

Poor thing! If Jean can heat herself up, she can eat

lunch. Will Jean eat the mush? Will poor Jean eat a

sandwich? Will Jean get too hot from ten quilts?

I think Jean will get too hot, and I think Jean will

not eat mush! Yuck!

Fluff and Kit

Can Kit lift Fluff? Yes, Kit grips Fluff's neck. Kit lifts and drags Fluff. Fluff will squeak and squeal, but Kit will get him back into the box in the shed. Poor Fluff!

When Fluff gets big, Kit cannot keep him in the box. Fluff will steal scraps from Shep's food dish. Fluff will jump on Shep's back. Fluff will fool Shep.

Next Shep will grab Fluff's neck and drag him back to the shed and the box. But Shep cannot lock the shed. Poor pup. He cannot keep Fluff in the shed!

gain	brain	train	faint	aid
main	chain	strain	paint	laid
pain	drain	Spain	saint	maid
rain	grain	sprain	taint	paid
lain	plain	swain	quaint	raid
vain	stain			braid
	maintain			staid

82

Ann fell from a tree. She got a bad bump and felt faint. Bill ran to her aid.

Pat got green stain at the shop on Main Street. Pat and Dick must fix the big box and paint it green. They will be paid to do the job.

Pat's Truck

We had a big rain.

Pat's truck slid into a deep drain on Main Street. Pat got a chain to drag the truck from the drain. Next he had to clean the mud from his truck and hang up the chain in the shed.

fail	rail	tail	frail
pail	wail	mail	flail
bail	nail	mailbox	snail
ail	jail		quail
hail	sail		trail

83

Tom hit a nail into the plank.

The mail truck will bring the mail, and I can fetch it from the mailbox.

aim	wait	trait	waist	faith
claim	bait		waif	

See the split in the rail? If a rail has a split in it, a train can crash.

The trackmen peer at the crack in the rail and fix it.

Fred went to catch fish with a rod and bait.

Jeff gets too mad too much. It's a bad trait.

Wag stuck his tail into a pail of paint.

Let's get Wag to help us paint the mailbox!

air   fair   pair   hair

chair   stair   lair

84 Jed got on an airship. He got airsick on the trip.

Jen had a hairpin to keep her hair back.

Jock must get a haircut soon!

A snail cannot run and jump. A snail just creeps.

I have pair of pants, a pair of gray pants.

And pair of socks, a pair of red socks.

The man has a pair of trunks, a pair of swim trunks.

Can you say a pair of sheep, cats, and chicks?

A pair of chicks sat in the nest.

A pair of sheep is in the shed.

And a pair of cats sleeps on the chair.

bay	may	bray	clay	away
day	nay	fray	play	plaything
hay	pay	gray	slay	railway
jay	say	pray	flay	haystack
lay	ray	tray	stay	
Fay	way	dray	spray	
gay	sway		stray	

85

The big fox had on a gay vest of black and red and
   green fabric.

The fox had on gray pants, too.

Jim and Tad slid down the hill on a tray.

Chet points the way to the bus stop. I may get a bus soon.

A jay sits on its nest. A cat creeps up to it.
The jay will send the cat away from its nest. Caw-caw!
Screech-screech! Get away! Run away, bad cat!

The pup had a flea. He will scratch and scratch it.

A man slept in a haystack. The man had a grand sleep
   in it.

I can fix the bed.

I can lay a sheet on the bed.

Next I can stretch it and tuck it in.

85

Next I can nap on the clean sheets.

Dick and the Stray

Dick had a tramp on the trail. He met a stray pup. Dick did not pick him up. But, in a way, the pup did pick up Dick. The pup went up to Dick. The pup's tail went wag-wag.

Dick thinks the pup may need a drink. Dick thinks the pup may need food.

Next Dick thinks the pup will need a pal. Next Dick thinks the pup must stay. The pup will not stray away from Dick. The pup's got a pal. Dick's got a pal, too.

It's a cool day. It's a hot day.

It's a grand day. It's a sad day.

It's a gay day. It's a gray day.

Well, it's just a day!

85

The Codfish Men

A ketch drifts from its fleet in the mist on the sea.

The men on the ketch catch cod in nets.

A stiff wind flaps the sails. The planks of the deck creak.

Each codfish man squints and can see land. It's near.

A swell lifts the ketch. It sweeps the ketch onto the rocks.

The rocks split the hull. It's split into bits!

The gush of the sea into the hull sinks the ketch.

The men must leap into the sea.

The men cling to planks from the ketch.

The codfish men drift on the planks to a beach.

oat	float	goad	boast	coal
boat	shoat	load	coast	goal
coat	stoat	road	roast	foal
goat	throat	toad	toast	
moat		soap		

86

A toad and a stoat got into a sailboat. The boat had a

leak in its hull.

The toad and the stoat had to swim. The boat sank.

coach	oak	Joan	foam	coax
poach	soak	loan	loam	hoax
roach	cloak	moan	roam	oath
	croak	roan		oaf
		groan		loaf

A cockroach sat on a toadstool and had lunch.

A frog croaks. A goat bleats. A toad says jug-a-rum.

A chipmunk sits in an oak tree and cracks nuts.

Joan got a loan from the Coast Bank. Joan must pay it

back.

I can hear a jay in the tree. It jumps to catch an insect.

Fay had a clay pot. The pot's gray.
Fay set a big green plant in it.

A sailboat will swing and sway on the swell of the sea.

I will pay Ned to paint the bench. He can paint it gray.
He can paint green and red spots on it—a gay bench,
    indeed.

Seth's Goat

Seth's dad got him a goat. Seth thinks the goat's a
pet. Seth pats the goat, but the goat jumps and butts
him. Seth picks himself up and thinks, "The goat did
not mean it." Seth pets the goat on its neck, but the
goat jumps back. Seth hops away and thinks, "The
goat did not mean it." Seth steps up and pats the goat
on its back, and the goat jumps and stamps in the mud.
Seth thinks, "A goat butts and kicks and stamps. A
goat just cannot play. A goat is a goat, not a pet!"

oar   board   roar   hoard

boar   aboard   soar

87   a nail in a board   a big blackboard   a billboard

Get aboard the boat, Sal, and hand Jan an oar.

Bang the nail into the board. It sticks up.

A boar grunts. It's a pig.

Joan can read well.

Joan can read from the blackboard.

Joan can read the print on a billboard, too.

Did Joan teach herself to read? I think Joan did!

Just hear the wind roar!

See the treetops sway in the wind!

Soon it will rain. It may rain a lot!

The chipmunks hoard nuts.

out   scout   stout   ouch   grouch

bout   shout   trout   couch   slouch

lout   snout   sprout   pouch

rout   spout   crouch   foul

88

I got a fish! It's a trout! I will shout about it!

Sis got a grand outfit—a red coat and hat.

Ouch! A bee stung Jeff. Hear him shout!

bound   pound   ground   shroud

found   round   loud   count

hound   sound   cloud   mount

mound   wound   proud

Jean got a pound of ground beef. The pup can smell it.
Can the pup get it out of the bag?

Jim wound the clock and set it at three.

Let's run down to the playground.

our   sour   flour   scour

89

Our hound pup got into a bag of flour. The pup got flour on himself and on the cat and on the rug.

Bill left the milk in the sun. It went sour. Yuck!

Scour the pan and get it clean.

Biff, help us! We need help!

Help us get the big board up onto the top of the shed.

Biff will help Frank and Al and me.

We can nail the board to the top of the shed and keep the rain out.

Can you hear the sound of the wind in the treetops?

Now hear the sheep bleat!

Hear the pig grunt!

Hear the pups yip and yap!

Hear the chicks peep!

Hear the hen cluck!

Hear the ducks quack!

Hear the owl hoot!

bow	brow	owl	down	clown
cow	plow	fowl	gown	brown
how	prow	howl	town	crown
now	scow	jowl		drown
sow	scowl	prowl		frown
vow		growl		

90

I went uptown and downtown. I ran around the town.

Bett says moo and sleeps in a cowshed. Bett's a cow!

A fox is on the prowl.

Bow-wow! Bow-wow! Hear Shep howl and growl
    at the fox near the cowshed.

The fox is on the prowl to catch a fowl. How can a
    poor fox eat if Shep sets up such a row?

The Rain Cloud

See the big black cloud in the south!

Feel the wind! Soon it will rain.

Quick! Let's run and get out of the wind.

Now I can feel rain. Let's not get wet.

Let's not stay out in the rain.

Let's play in the shed.

The Pup and the Toad

Our hound pup found a toad on the ground. Our hound pup did not snap at the toad. He did not pick it up. Our pup just sat still and let the toad hop about. The pup just let the toad hop around on the ground. When the toad hops away, the pup sniffs the ground. The pup thinks the toad is an odd thing indeed.

90

jaw	claw	awl	dawn	hawk
law	craw	bawl	fawn	squawk
paw	draw	brawl	lawn	outlaw
raw	flaw	shawl	pawn	seesaw
saw	slaw	crawl	brawn	
caw	thaw	scrawl	drawn	
	straw	sprawl		

91

Frank can draw well. Frank will draw the sea.

Next he will draw a big ship. It will sail on the sea.

See the hawk! It swoops. It streaks! It can sail on the air.

It can grab its food in its claws and swoop back to a crag.

It will sit on the rocks and eat its food.

A fox crept up on the shed. I can see it.

A fox will crawl into the shed if it can.

I run near the fox. The fox lifts its paw.

It sniffs the air. It thinks about its meal in the shed.

But it will not stay. It streaks away from the shed.

haul   fault   launch   jaunt   taut

Paul   haunch   taunt

Saul   paunch   flaunt

92

Nan and Jess must fix a box. Jess gets string.
Nan yanks on it until it's taut around the box.

Jill thinks she can print and draw. But it's just a scrawl.

Paul and Jock sprawl on the couch. Mom thinks Paul
and Jock cannot sit.

A Deer Hunt

Saul and Max are on a deer hunt and sleep in a
tent. At dawn, Saul and Max get up and tramp out into
the brush. Max points to the brush near them. "Look,
Saul! Look in the brush! I think it's a deer!" Saul and
Max creep up on the deer. It's not a deer. It's a fawn.
And it just sits still. It lets Saul and Max catch it. Saul
and Max pick it up and bring it back to camp.

The next day Max and Saul bring the fawn back
to the house. When it gets big, Max and Sam will set it
free.

boy   Roy   coy   cloy   cowboy

joy   toy   soy   Troy

Roy got a gift of a toy train. The train ran on a round track. It ran round and round and round. Toot-toot! Hoot-hoot! It can whiz and speed and swish around the track.

93

Joy can see Troy snatch Jack's cowboy hat. Troy keeps the hat and streaks away.

Skip, Jack's hound pup, looks up to see Troy run with Jack's hat. When a pup spots a boy on the run, the pup thinks he must run, too. He must catch up and play.

Skip jumps up to snatch Jack's hat from Troy. And Troy lets him get the hat.

Thanks to Skip, Jack gets back his cowboy hat. Joy thinks Skip must get a treat.

oil	toil	coin	moist	topsoil
boil	foil	join	foist	uncoil
soil	spoil	joint	hoist	pinpoint
broil		point	joist	standpoint

94

The shed walls are held up by joists.

If the joists rot, the shed will crash to the ground.

The Owl

"See the big owl up in the tree!"

Fran can see the owl, and Sal can, too, but Tom and Bill do not see it.

"Point at it, Fran. Point it out to Tom and Bill. Maybe Tom and Bill will see it, too." Fran points to the owl. Bill and Tom still cannot see the owl. Sal thinks a boy cannot see well.

The owl still sits up in the tree. "Hoot, hoot, hoot," says the owl. Tom and Bill hear the owl and think it says, "See me!"

When Tom and Bill hear the owl, they see it, too. Tom and Bill think it's a neat owl.

Joan and May went on a jaunt in a launch.

Joan and May had lunch on the boat.

The jaunt in the launch went on until dusk.

94

Mom and Jean and Will left at dawn on a hunt to see deer and hawks and muskrats and maybe an owl.

Jean found a muskrat's den in a bank near the stream. But the muskrat hid in its den.

Now, a hawk swoops in the air. A jay taunts it. The jay has a loud caw. The hawk sits in a treetop and waits. It is on a hunt, too.

An owl hoots from a tree near to the stream.

On the way back from the hunt, Jean and Will spot a deer and its fawn. Mom can see it, too. Such a grand hunt!

| goose | loose | geese | grease | hoarse |
| moose | noose | lease | crease | coarse |

95

A goose got loose from its pen. It met a moose.

The goose got a lift from the moose on its back.

The cat stuck its paw in a pool of grease.

Will it lick its paw clean?

house	blouse	rinse	apse
mouse	grouse	manse	lapse
douse		sense	copse
souse		pulse	glimpse
louse		else	

Val got a dollhouse. The cat slept in it!

Ten men stay in the bunkhouse.

The chicks got out of the henhouse. Did Sam lock it up?

Dad got plants from the hothouse.

Max helps Mac fix a clubhouse in an oak tree.

If it's cool, Jill cannot sleep in the playhouse.

breeze   sneeze   wheeze   gauze   adze

freeze   squeeze   axe

How can I spell ax?

96

"A" plus "x." And "a" plus "x" plus "e."

Hear Tom sneeze! He must not stay out in the cool

breeze.

Tom will get sick. He will get hoarse. He will sneeze

and wheeze.

Dick got up at dawn and went out to feed the

chicks. He saw a deer and a fawn. They saw Dick and

ran away and hid in the copse.

Next Dick saw a hawk. Hawks steal chicks. Dick

had to run. He had to keep the hawk from the chicks.

Dick ran around them and led them into the

henhouse and shut it up. The chicks hid in the straw.

The hen sat on top of her chicks! And the hawk went

away.

have	sleeve	leave	solve	shelve
give	peeve	weave	twelve	delve
live		groove		

97

Ann can weave. Ann has a loom.

Each board had a groove in it.

A cow can give a big pail of milk.

Let's have lunch at twelve. Let's have a big lunch!

Jeb saw a bug weave a web.

Stan and Jean live in the manse on the hill. It's a big house.
It's a neat house to play in.

Six plus ten is sixteen.
Can I solve six plus three? Yes, it's a snap!

A seal sits on a rock with its pup. It waits to catch a fish.
It will give the fish to its pup.

Pam can pick up the cat but she must not squeeze it.
The cat will squeal if you squeeze him.

Seal Tricks

Did you see the seal at the zoo?

The seal did tricks.

97

Did a man train the seal? Yes, he did. He fed the seal

a fish when the seal did a trick.

Did the man fling a fish at the seal?

Yes, and the seal can catch it in its mouth.

The seal can snatch the fish out of the air!

A seal can catch fish well!

Goat Tricks

A man had a goat. He had to load his goat into a van.

But the goat had a fear of trucks.

The man got a stick to goad the goat. The goat got the

stick in his mouth and had a meal of it.

How can the man get the goat into his truck?

The way to get the goat into the truck is to feed it grain

and hay.

If the man sets oats and hay on a ramp into the truck,

the goat will eat his way up the ramp.

And the man can get the goat into his van!

A cat will catch a mouse.

A fox will steal a goose.

A bat will swoop down to catch insects in the air.

97

A Wet Cat

Sis spots a cat in a tree near the pond.
The cat sits on a branch. It hits at a bug.

Flip-flop! The cat and the bug fall into the pond!
The poor cat cannot swim. Can Sis fish him out on a
stick? Sis must get Paul to help do it. Can Paul help
haul him out?

If the cat can just grab the end of the stick and
stay on, Paul and Sis can hoist it from the pond. But
will the cat stay still and hang on to the stick?

Yes, the cat will! Paul and Sis lift the cat from the
pond.

When the cat's on land, it jumps from the stick. It's
a wet cat! And it's a mad, mad cat!

The cat slinks away. It is too mad to say thanks.

The Commonest Irregular Words

Guide to Part IV, Lessons 98–151

Part IV embarks on new patterns that depart from the one-to-one sound-letter correlations that have been the subject and unifying principle of parts I–III. For the remaining 148 lessons of parts IV–VI of *Let's Read*, the pupil will be introduced to irregular sound-letter correlations for vowels and consonants. Unlike the earlier lessons, the lessons of part IV advance through increasingly less-alphabetic patterns of written English. These patterns represent large chunks of common vocabulary. Some of this vocabulary has already been introduced as sight vocabulary in previous lessons but is more fully covered here, in particular as an integral part of idiomatic English.

Despite the different character of the patterns, the organization and procedures for teaching in part IV remain the same. For the most part, many of the irregular spelling patterns taught in these lessons represent sizable groups of words in English. Even though they are irregular, or nonalphabetic in their spelling by *Let's Read*'s standards, they will appear logical and regular to the pupil by virtue of the predictability of the sound-letter correlations within a pattern.

SCOPE OF PART IV

- Group I
  - *th* as in *then, breathe*
  - *s* as *z*, as in *his, eggs, elves, Jill's*
  - *-es* or *-'s*, suffix adding a syllable, as in *dishes, Gus's*

- *-d* or *-ed*, suffix as in *played, pleased, rubbed*
- *-ed*, suffix adding a syllable, as in *lifted, crowded*
- *-ed* as *t*, as in *slipped, kissed*
- Group II
  - pronoun contractions, such as *I'll, you'll, we've*
  - two-syllable contractions with *not*, such as *hasn't, isn't*
- Group III
  - two-, three-, and four-syllable words, such as *haircut, benefit, Thanksgiving, delivery*
- Group IV
  - *-ing*, suffix as in *acting, grabbing, living*
  - words ending with *r*, such as *temper, hammer, doctor*
  - words ending with *l*, such as *ramble, apple, metal*
  - words ending in *n*, such as *kitten, button, robin*
  - words ending in *m*, such as *atom, problem*
  - *-y, -ey, -ie, -ly*, endings, suffixes, and inflected forms, as in *history, carry/carries, Annie, Willy, softly*

The word lists in many of the lessons of part IV do not contain all available vocabulary in each pattern and are, rather, representative of a class of English words.

The following paragraphs explain in more detail the thrust or intention of the lessons. Some of the discussion is relatively technical, and, although interesting, none of it is essential for the teacher to know in order to teach the lessons or for the pupil in order to learn.

Lessons in Group I deal with words whose spellings are the same as regular, alphabetic patterns taught earlier but whose pronunciations differ: for example, the value of *s* as in *sit* is now expanded to include *s* with the value of *z* as in *duds or sheds;* and *th* is expanded to encompass the sound in *then* or *smooth.*

Group II is concerned with forms of pronouns that occur so frequently in idiomatic English, their use and meanings are understood, but how they are made is not so obvious. Thus, lesson 116 deals with both pronoun combinations (*my, myself*) and pronoun-plus-verb contractions (*I/I'll; they/they've*). The reading exercises reinforce the meanings and use of these forms.

Group III teaches examples of words that are regular in spelling but are pronounced with different stress on one syllable or another, depending upon meaning (*content, conduct*) or have neutral vowels within them (as in the case of *benefit*, where the middle *e* is unaccented).

Group IV explores patterns of words with endings that are widely used in English. These groups are so large that a case could be made for considering them regular, if different, patterns formed by the addition of a suffix. These lessons also include doubled consonants, syllabic consonants (as in the *-al* in *metal*, *-le* in *apple*), as well as the titles *Mr.*, *Mrs.*, and *Ms.*

Suggestions for the Teacher

At this point, both teaching technique and habits for the pupil are well established; what works for a teacher and a pupil should be the way lessons continue to be done.

1. Continue to spell and say new vocabulary until the pupil can respond accurately. By repetition of pattern, these new irregularities will become familiar regularities. Consistency and pattern will work their magic here as they have in all earlier parts of *Let's Read*.

2. New vocabulary is listed at the top of each lesson page with connected reading following. The connected reading differs markedly from the earlier reading. Primarily it is much more idiomatic by virtue of the kind and amount of vocabulary now available. There is also more content in the reading, not only because more vocabulary is available but also for perhaps the more compelling reason that the pupil, by now a fairly fluent reader, is able to pay increasing attention to meaning. From the increase in content should flow a proportional interest in it.

Notes

1. *Shifting sound-letter correlations.* It would be counterproductive to introduce into the lessons explanations of how the patterns in this section of *Let's Read* differ from those in earlier sections. The pupil has already a firm grasp of the reliability and regularity of spelling patterns; while part IV's patterns represent variants in value, stress, or accent, patterns that deviate from the familiar, even in variation there is pattern. And, as both teacher and pupil know, it is pattern, above all else, that helps the pupil learn and retain new facts.

2. *The reading.* The intention of the connected reading is to apply decoding skill to narrative, to practice the skill of reading. The sentences and stories are varied according to the lesson. Some reading, such as the anthropomorphic stories in part IV, will strike different youngsters differently, appealing to some more than to others. Some of the short sentences that employ wordplay may require explanation, but many youngsters

find quirks of usage and meaning interesting or amusing. Depending upon the reaction of any particular pupil, the teacher can judge how deeply to delve into comprehension and stylistic devices in any given story or passage.

Part IV also employs some print conventions that the pupil might notice and be curious about. Often the stories have titles. The dash, colon, quotation mark, and italic type are also used. It is absolutely a matter to be decided between the teacher and the pupil when and how much to call attention to such conventions. For some pupils, these elements signal the transition to "real, grown-up reading," and for others, they are unremarkable. It is not the intention to teach the learner how to write standard narrative. Rather, the goal is to raise awareness of the special vocabulary of language in print.

Pupils may also notice that the type size has been reduced. This is a signal that the reader has progressed well beyond the bounds of the novice and is capable of exploring more advanced reading.

3. *Comprehension.* While it is important to find out if the pupil understands the reading, it is not necessary for the teacher to dwell on it. It is enough if the pupil can give a short description or summary of the story (describing setting, plot, and characters). More subtle aspects of the story (such as motivation and possible outcome) do not have to be explored in depth. However, if the pupil wants to ponder why or how something happened or was done or said, the teacher should take full advantage of the pupil's interest.

4. *Pace.* By part IV, some pupils move so quickly through the lessons that the teacher may wonder how much learning is taking place. Pace is an individual matter, but it does tend to accelerate with the pupil's growing confidence and mastery. It is as counterproductive to hold a pupil back as it is to push him or her forward. Often longer lessons (ones with longer reading passages) will take several sessions to complete. Assimilation of vocabulary patterns, though, appears to be almost automatic for the pupil, which, in fact, it is.

5. *Ancillary activities.* With an exponential growth in vocabulary comes the opportunity to begin to focus on categories of words, such as things, colors, feelings, actions, etc. At this stage, some pupils want to make their own dictionaries; others want to write stories; others simply want to get to the next lesson and thence to the end of *Let's Read.* These kinds of activities are entirely an individual matter. While they are not necessary to becoming a proficient reader, they do, in all likelihood, add a great deal to the pupil's appreciation of words as powerful and flexible tools.

the	then	with	smooth
this	them	without	breathe
that			
that's			

98

Ann and Joan went out on a sailboat, and Wag, the pup, went, too.

Did Ann and Joan have a smooth trip? Well, the wind did huff and puff. And the boat went up and down. And they went up and down on the boat. This was not smooth at all! But Ann and Joan can sail that boat without help in a big wind.

Wag just got down in the boat and slept.

When the wind let up, Ann and Joan had a rest on the boat. Without a lot of wind, they can sit in the sun and breathe the fresh air. And they did just that, with Wag, too.

Grab this end, Jack, and I can grab that end. Then we can lift this big branch without strain.

is	as	'tis	tease	choose	noise
his	has	ours	please	cheese	cause

99

Frank's Noise

Frank's loud. His noise is as loud as a train in the house!

Frank has a popgun. He pops it from sunup till sundown. That's the popgun noise. And Frank has a pair of boots that clump and cause a lot of noise. And that's the boot noise.

Will Frank choose not to cause noise? Frank will not choose to be still, but when Frank gets into bed, the noise stops. Our house is as still as can be. Frank's noise has us in a fix. It's fun to be with Frank, but if you choose to play with him, you need earmuffs.

Ed Black's Pup

Ed Black feeds his pup an egg on toast. Ed has an egg on toast, too. Ed Black's pup gets the best food to eat. When he gets his food, the pup sits up and says please! And the pup says thank you, too. At least, that's what Ed says.

rib   bed   tree   bag   bell   plum

ribs   beds   trees   bags   bells   plums

bibs   lids   legs   sails

       sounds   eggs   heels

100

guns   things   ears   paws

pans   kings   cheers   laws

spoons   oars   claws

sows   days   toys   upstairs

cows   ways   boys   downstairs

clowns

Paul thinks a lot. He thinks about lots of things when he is in bed. And he hears things, too.

He hears the wind in the trees and thinks it is a witch. He can hear odd sounds downstairs. He can hear odd squeaks on the stairs. Paul thinks, "Is it a bobcat in the house? Is it a bobcat that has big fangs and big claws? Will it eat boys?"

Paul creeps near the stairs. His hair stands on end from fear. He holds a toy gun that pops.

When he peeks down the stairs, he can see a thing. It must be the bobcat! On its big paws, it creeps up a step and then the next step. Paul can hear it breathe! It's near him. Bang-bang! Pop-pop! (That's Paul's toy gun.)

The beast on the stairs jumps up with a howl. Now its hair stands on end.

When Paul gets near the beast, he sees it's not a bobcat. It's Miss Spots, his cat.

Paul thinks to himself that it was fun to think it was a bobcat and not Miss Spots.

100

leaves	sleeves	elves	ourselves
loaves		shelves	themselves

About Elves

101

Last week, I saw six elves near this spot. An elf lives in this tree. Can you see him?

The elf slips down a twig, skims on the leaves, and lands near us. He cannot see us. We must stand still and wait. We cannot breathe! We must be still!

The elf has on red pants, a green vest, and a coat with red sleeves. He trots away from us. He meets an elf in a red outfit. This elf gives our elf three wee bran loaves. Then the elves jump and skip a bit. We can hear squeaks and small noises from them. We think that's how elves sing. We watch and stay still. The elf leaves our elf and hops and skips away. Our elf eats a bit of bran loaf and then he skips away, too.

We pinch ourselves. Did we dream about the elves, or was it real? We cannot tell.

102

Jill's hat

Jill has a hat.

It is Jill's hat.

Fran's coat

Fran has a coat.

It is Fran's coat.

Ben's hand

Ben's hand got cut.

It's Ben's hand that
got cut. Ouch!

Tom's toys

Tom's toys are cool.

We play with Tom's toys.

the boy's bag

The boy's bag is red.

Ted's bag is red, too.

the man's coat

The man's coat is black.

Dad's coat is black, too.

Ann has got a cold. Ann's got a cold.

Ann is sick. Ann's sick. Ann is sick in bed.

Pop's a big man. Pop is a big man.

Jean Hoyt lives in a big town in the east. Jean's mom has a shop downtown. It has bins and trays of nuts, mints, and sweet things. In the back of the shop they keep milk, eggs, cream, and soda.

103

A cat with big claws lives in the shop. Its job is to crawl on shelves and keep the rats down.

This week Jean's to help her mom at the shop. But when she went to the back of the shop with eggs in a box, the big gray cat sprang at her from a shelf. Jean let the box of eggs drop. Crash! Smash!

Jean's mom is glad to have Jean help her in the shop. But the cat is not a help. He's a big pest when he plays sick tricks.

The cat thinks Jean's his pal when she drops eggs. He can lick up as much as he can eat! It's a treat! Jean thinks the cat's a pest.

The Lunch Club

Meg and Joan and Bob have a lunch club. Each week they fix and eat lunch, and then they play.

103

This week the club will meet at Meg's house. This means that Meg must fix lunch and clean up, and then she can play with Joan and Bob.

When the club met at Bob's house, Bob did not fix lunch. He just did not think to do it. When Meg and Joan got to Bob's house, Bob did not have lunch. But Ann and Joan and Bob did have a grand lunch. Bob found chips and jam and toast and a bit of beef and a peach and cream. And in the end, not much mess to clean up.

Then the club went to see an owl's nest in a big oak tree. And they saw a muskrat slip in and out of his den on the bank of the stream. Bob says he will fix a big lunch next week.

miss	kiss	bus	box	tax
misses	kisses	buses	boxes	taxes

104

rinse	house	raise	praise	buzz
rinses	houses	raises	praises	buzzes

peach	reach	inch
peaches	reaches	inches

bunch	dish	wish
bunches	dishes	wishes

Cliff Cockroach lives in a house near our sink. As cockroaches live in wet spots, near a sink is the best spot a roach can choose to live in. I cannot see Cliff. He stays out of the way. If Bob spills when he rinses the dishes and pots, Cliff gets a free meal. When Bob and I are in bed, Cliff runs around and eats as he wishes.

104

In his house, Cliff has three chairs, a bed, a lamp, and a rug. Cliff's bed is cut from match boxes. He has a rug from a bit of a sock left on one of the benches outdoors.

Cliff has found out that the cat sleeps near the sink. This upsets him. If a cat will eat a mouse, will it feast on cockroaches as well?

Gus	Bess	Jess	Max	Rex
Gus's	Bess's	Jess's	Max's	Rex's

105

On our team, Fran Gray pitches and Bill Smith catches. Fran pitches well and Bill catches well. Fran cannot run and Bill cannot bat. But Bill can run well and Fran hits well. Let's see if Fran can bat and Bill can run for her. Then we can win!

Dad's Tugboat

Gus's dad runs a tugboat. Gus helps his dad clean up the tug. They paint it and grease it and oil it. Gus hands his dad the oilcan and the pail with grease in it. When Gus's dad needs a tool, Gus brings it.

Then Gus and his dad scrub down the tug. They scrub the deck and the boat well. When it's clean, they spray the boat to get rid of the soap. It is then a clean tug.

105

But Gus is not clean. When he helps out, he gets oil and grease and mud on his sleeves and on his pants legs. It gets on his socks and his cap, too. Gus's a mess.

When Gus got back in the house today, he got spots of mud and sand on the rugs and spots on the stairs. Then when Gus sat down on his bed, he got mud and oil and grease on the bed.

Gus's mom just groans and tells Gus that the tug may be clean, but Gus is not and spots are on the stairs. He can just jump into the tub and get as clean as the tug. Then he can mop up the rest of the spots in the house.

boil	cool	sail	clean	cheer	play
boiled	cooled	sailed	cleaned	cheered	played

smell	spell	film	buzz	dawn	haul
smelled	spelled	filmed	buzzed	dawned	hauled

106

Peg boils an egg. She thinks boiled eggs are swell.

Dan smelled a bad smell. It's a skunk. It stinks.

A bee will buzz. A bee buzzed in Jim's ear.

See the cat up at the top of that tree?

She clawed her way up the trunk.

Then she sat on that branch.

Next she cleaned her paws.

Then she yawned and stretched.

I think she will have a nap next.

A cheer went up from the crowd.

The crowd cheered when the team won.

live	please	tease	breathe
lived	pleased	teased	breathed

107

Say please and thank you. It will please me.

I was pleased when you did say please.

Jack's a tease. He teased Jill up and down the hill.

Jill socked Jack when he teased her.

The Smiths live in that house.

The Hoyts lived in this house, but they went to Spain.

You can hear the cow breathe.

She breathed in the cool fresh air.

Chet banged the lid down on the box.

Chet was mad. It was not the thing to do.

The lid cracked, and now Chet must mend it.

grab	nab	rub	stub
grabbed	nabbed	rubbed	stubbed

drag	beg	slam	drum	snag
dragged	begged	slammed	drummed	snagged

108

Kit snagged her coat on a twig.

The man dragged a big load on a handtruck.

The cops nabbed the bad man. The man had robbed
the bank.
The cops slammed him in jail.

Dick drummed a pen on the desk. Bill grabbed the pen
from Dick.
"Stop that noise, Dick. Get a real drum to bang."

I rubbed the rug until it got clean.

Nan begged to get a pet. She got a skunk.
It's a skunk without a smell.

108 Frank dragged his sled up the steep hill. Then he lay down on the sled and slid down the hill. Whiz! Swish! How the sled went! How it sped! Frank slid down the big hill. Zip! Then he hauled the sled back up the hill. Puff, puff! Next he whizzed back down the hill. Up and down, up and down.

land   mend   crowd   weed   nod   pad

landed mended crowded weeded nodded padded

lift   hunt   pet   pat   spot

lifted   hunted   petted   patted   spotted

109

On the Subway

When the subway train is crowded, Kit cannot get a seat. She must stand and grab a strap. If the train stops with a bump, Kit may get swung around.

At one such quick stop, Kit landed in a man's lap. The man had eggs in a bag on his lap. When Kit fell, she sat on the man's lap and on his eggs, too. The man got a bit mad at poor Kit. But when Kit got back up, the man did not have egg spots on his pants. The man just grinned at Kit, and Kit grinned back.

The man patted the bag of eggs. Kit and the man will tell you that a bag of eggs on your lap in the subway is a risk.

slip	rap	tramp	bump
slipped	rapped	tramped	bumped

110

jump	camp	pack	thank
jumped	camped	packed	thanked

milk	wink	sneak	soak
milked	winked	sneaked	soaked

pinch	scratch	brush	wish	fix
pinched	scratched	brushed	wished	fixed

rinse	fuss	miss	loaf	tip
rinsed	fussed	missed	loafed	tipped

Fran and the Peaches

Rick and Fran spotted ten big peaches up in a peach tree. Fran went up the tree to get them. But it had rained. The tree's leaves were wet. And now Fran was soaked, too.

110

When Fran got onto a branch and leaned way out and grabbed at a big peach, she slipped. She slipped and fell to the ground. She had missed the peach as well.

Fran landed on the ground with a thump and bumped her back. Rick ran to her. He helped her to her feet.

Fran brushed away bits of wet leaves from her pants and rubbed her back. She had just bumped and scratched herself in the fall.

"Thanks a lot, Rick. I needed help! Ouch! I think I will not sneak peaches from a tree."

"Yes! Me, too. Let's not get peaches from a tree when we can have them in a dish—with cream!"

Meg met a pal of Dan's at camp.

The pig got into a bag of peanuts.

The pig thinks peanuts are a treat.

A peahen sat on a mound of bricks.

Then she fixed a nest on top of them.

The crowd shouted with joy.

The train runs west of this town.

The bus runs to the east.

Miss Smith thinks well of Nan.

Nan reads well.

Tim's Clock

Tim had a clock with a bell. It clanged.

Its tick was too loud.

Tim's clock got fixed when it fell from the desk.

Now it cannot clang. It cannot tick.

It just sits on a shelf. Tim's glad about it.

The Toy Pup

Jean lived on Green Street. Chet, who lived in the next house, had a pup, Shep.

"Let's get a pup, too, Dad, " Jean begged.

Dad got Jean a pup—a black pup with a stub tail. But he had gotten Jean a toy pup, not a real pup. Jean did not feel bad that the pup was not real. She hugged that pup and petted it and played with it.

Jean hugged Dad, too, and thanked him. She thinks that next to a real pup, her pup is the best.

When Jean went to bed, she still hung onto that pup.

The next day when Jean and Chet went out to play, Jean left her toy pup on the back steps at Chet's. Shep went up on the steps; he saw the pup. He yipped at it, but the toy pup just sat.

Shep ran up to the toy pup and sniffed at it. The toy pup did not sniff back. Next he nipped at the toy and jumped back. It did not jump at Shep. Then he rushed at the toy and grabbed it in his mouth and ran with it.

When Chet saw his pup do that, Chet yelled, "Drop it, Shep!" But Shep did not drop it. He just ran. Chet ran, too. Round and round the house ran Chet and his pup.

When Jean saw Shep run away with her toy, she shouted and ran, too. Chet shouted, Jean screamed, and Shep just ran and ran.

Then Shep stopped, dropped the toy and lay down with his chin on his paws. He seemed to feel bad. And Chet felt bad, too.

Jean frowned as she picked up the toy pup. "Well, Shep, my pup is a bit wet and chewed, but he's not spoiled. I think Chet needs to get you a toy. Then you will not need to steal toys and run away with them. How about that, Shep?"

With a glad yip, Shep jumped up and licked Jean's hand. He seemed to say, "Yes, indeed! Let's get it now!"

Dan's Fish

The tenth of May was a cool spring day. On that day, Fred went to the pond to catch fish.

114

In the pond was a raft. Fred stepped onto it and floated way out into the pond. He dropped a string with bait on it to fish. Then a fish bit the bait. Fred slipped on the wet boards of the raft and fell into the pond.

"Help! Help!" Fred yelled.

Dan ran to help Fred. He swam out to the raft. He grabbed Fred's hands and hauled him to the raft. Then he got the raft to the bank. Next, Dan hauled Fred out of the pond.

Wet as a fish, Fred went back to the house. His mom met him on the steps. "Fred," she said, "it's too cool to swim!" Fred did not say a thing. He just sneezed.

Fred had such a chill that Mom sent him to bed and kept him in bed with just hot milk to drink. At noon the next day, Mom let him get dressed to eat lunch.

114

Mom had fixed Fred a poached egg on toast, but Mom and Dan had roast beef hash and green beans. Fred gulped down the toast and egg in a rush. Then he begged, "Hash and beans and lots of ketchup, please."

Fred had a lot of hash and beans and a lot of ketchup, too. He had such a lot, he had to have three cups of cool milk, too. Then Fred had a dish of peaches and cream.

When Fred's dad got back from town, he was glad to hear that Fred had had such a big meal. He slapped Fred on the back and winked at Mom. He said, "I'm glad you can eat now. You may be well, but you need to stay away from that pond!"

Mom grinned and said, "Fred may as well stay away from that pond. He cannot fish a thing out of it."

Dan grinned, too. He said, "But I can get a fish. I got Fred!"

one   The clock struck one.

        One fox got into the henhouse.

says   Sis says she can spell well.

        How can she? She's just three!

said   I said the goat did not eat my pants.

        Maybe I just ripped them.

are   May and I are pals.

        We are glad to see you.

were   We were glad to see you until you got mad at us.

been   I have been away on a trip.

        It has been a big job to fix the shed.

A ram is a he.

A hen is a she.

Sam and I are we.

I am just me.

Can we three be pals?

115

my	you	they	her
myself	yourself	them	herself
	yourselves	themselves	

| | your | their | hers |
| | yours | theirs | |

116

She skinned herself on the board that I scratched
myself on.

When you fell down, you bumped yourself on the steps.

Ten men got stuck in the mud. The men got themselves
out of it.

If you have a mouse, it is yours. It is your mouse.

If she has a mouse, it is hers. It is her mouse.

If they have a mouse, it is theirs. It is their mouse.

If I have a mouse, it is my mouse.

I	he	she	you	we	they
I'm	he's	she's	you're	we're	they're
I've			you've	we've	they've
I'd	he'd	she'd	you'd	we'd	they'd
I'll	he'll	she'll	you'll	we'll	they'll

116

If you're hot, you'll have to jump in the pool. You've
    got to get cool.

They're out in the truck they've rented, and they'll be
    back at seven.

I'll be in the shed, as I'm on the way to feed the chicks.

He is quick, and he is thin. He's an ant.
She is big, and she is plump. She's an owl.

He will run. He'll be hot.
She will sit. She'll be cool.

We will have a picnic. We'll eat a lot.

We have rats. We've got a cat. Soon we'll not have rats

We're in bed. We're about to sleep. We've had a big day.

had not	has not	have not	did not	need not
hadn't	hasn't	haven't	didn't	needn't

116

is not	are not	was not	were not	will not
isn't	aren't	wasn't	weren't	won't

It was hot. It wasn't cool.

It had not rained in six weeks.

It hadn't rained one bit.

Jeff and Jack haven't gotten up yet.

They'll get up at ten.

She hasn't had lunch.

She'll need to eat soon.

Bill and Al didn't see the hawk.

It wasn't out at the zoo.

You needn't fret. I'll fix it.

Jim and Kit aren't on the bus.

Didn't Frank tell them it left at ten?

sunset	blacksmith	mailbox	oatmeal
gumdrop	peanut	haircut	sailboat
grandstand	steamship	hairpin	billboard
	earmuffs		blackboard

116

| catfish | dishpan | content | hilltop | windmill |
| codfish | dishrag | contents | eggshell | |

Is This Catfish Cal?

It's hot, but Don's mom told him to cut the lawn. The sun's rays beat down on him. His cat rests on the back steps to the house.

As he cuts, Don daydreams. He isn't Don. He's Catfish Cal, the cowboy. He isn't on the lawn with his cat. He's in the ring with his trained fox. Around the ring is a grandstand. The grandstand is filled with kids. They clap and shout when Catfish and his fox do tricks. They shout, "Hooray, Catfish. Hooray! Do it Fox! You can do it Cat and Fox!" Catfish and Fox do their tricks well.

117

The shouts ring in Catfish's ears. He lifts his hat and bows to the grandstand. His fox bows, too.

In a wink, Catfish stops. Wait, that's not a grandstand. That's the lawn. That's not the sound of a crowd. That's his mom. She shouts to tell him to eat his lunch.

I wish I were Catfish, Don thinks to himself. And, cat, I wish you were Catfish's fox. But I'm just a boy, and you're just a cat. Let's get lunch.

teaspoon	plaything	haystack
toothbrush	railway	toadstool
toothpick	railroad	steamboat
toadstool	steamboat	playground

117

Wee Miss Teaspoon thinks she'll set up her tent next to a big toadstool. The toadstool will keep the rain from getting her things wet. She can sit under the toadstool and eat and read or play jacks. She will sleep in the tent. It will be the best house yet.

One day Miss Teaspoon went out from her camp. She found a wee railroad. She got onto the wee train, and it went chug-chug. She got down from the train in a wee town and saw shops. She went into a shop and got a wee sweet bun and a cup of tea.

117

She went around the town and found a playground. A lot of elves were at the playground. The playground had swings. Near the playground was a pond. On the pond was a steamboat. Miss Teaspoon got on it and went around the pond.

At dusk, Miss Teaspoon got back on the train and went back to her camp.

She had a grand day.

outfit	sandwich	insect	insult
outlaw		product	insults
seesaw	picnic	discount	

118

Frank's Paint Job

"Now that it's spring," Dad said to Frank, "we need to get out the red bench that you and Jess and Nick fixed last year. You can clean it and give it a fresh coat of green paint. But don't ask Jess and Nick to help!" They had spilled paint and then painted pink dots on it.

As Frank went out to the shed, he said to himself, "This will be a big job. How can I clean the bench by myself? With that dust, mud, grease, and red paint on the bench, it seems to me I've got too much to do. I think I'll see if I can get Chuck to help me. Dad did not say Chuck cannot help."

Frank went back to the house to get Chuck.

118

Frank said, "Can you help me with a job, please? I've got to clean the big bench out in the shed. If you help me, it will be a quick job." Chuck said he'd help Frank.

They got the bench and began to scrub it. Next they had to sand the paint off it.

Then Chuck said, " The bench tips. One leg needs to be sawed down a bit."

Frank got a saw and Chuck cut the leg. But he had cut too much from the leg. The bench still tipped. Chuck sawed the three legs to match it.

When the bench didn't tip, Frank and Chuck painted it. But it's just a green seat on the ground now. Chuck sawed the legs too much!

Anna   salad   flop   canvas   address

Linda   method   hammock   August

Wilma   instant

extra   different

119

Linda's Hammock

One hot August day Linda got a gift—a canvas hammock. Linda was pleased. She hung the hammock from a pair of trees. She laid down in it. It was a grand hammock.

Linda planned her days in the hammock. "I'll stretch out in my hammock," she said, "and sip cool tea, and maybe I'll read a bit. Let Nick and Sam and Anna gallop around and play tag and get hot. Not me!"

When Nick and Sam and Anna stopped at Linda's house to ask her to play with them, Linda sent them away. Sam said, "Linda thinks she's a queen with that hammock!"

Linda spent the day in her hammock. At noon she fixed a sandwich and had her lunch in the hammock.

119   The next day, from her hammock, Linda saw Anna and Sam and Nick as they played tag. She felt a bit left out and a bit sad, too. Maybe she missed her pals.

In an instant, Linda jumped out of her hammock and went to join them. "A hammock is just grand," she said, "if one needs extra rest. But not me! I don't need rest! I'm not weak! I need to play with pals."

attic	wicked	coolest	finish	active
comic	rugged	cleanest	foolish	olive
traffic	hundred	dearest	polish	
plastic	hundredth	thickest	punish	
rapid		thinnest	radish	
liquid	Kenneth	biggest	rubbish	
solid		fattest	selfish	
splendid	dentist			

120

Mouse Traffic

The mouse traffic in our attic is active. I think there is a big mouse town up there. The beasts live up in the attic with the cobwebs and dust and boxes and junk.

Each mouse has a truck. We can hear trucks speed round and round and up and down and back in the attic. The mouse trucks run up and down, up and down each day until sundown. And we hear crashes. The rapid traffic must end up in the biggest messes.

120

One day the fattest mouse had a wicked smash-up. He ran his truck too near the attic stairs and did not stop. Down the steps the foolish mouse crashed! He lay in a heap. His splendid truck was finished.

His dearest pals ran down the stairs in a panic. They dragged him from the smashed truck. The crash banged up his leg and bent his ear. Can his pals fix him up?

The noise from the crash sent Max, the housecat, upstairs. He needed to see it. Max thinks he's a traffic cop. He thinks he must punish the selfish mouse who crashed. But when Max got to the attic steps, he did not see one mouse. The crashed-up mouse and his truck and his pals had vanished. The cat found just a big mound of rubbish.

habit	blanket	pocket	blackness	tennis
limit	bonnet	rocket	sadness	promise
merit	bucket	tablet	sickness	Agnes
rabbit	closet	ticket	stillness	
spirit	cricket	toilet	sweetness	
visit	hatchet	trinket	weakness	
	helmet	trumpet	mattress	
	jacket	velvet		
	junket			

121

The chipmunks picnic. Each has milk and a peanut sandwich in a plastic bag. They sit on a blanket. But near the blanket, a hundred ants stand and wait to eat the chipmunks' lunch. The chipmunks must leave. They'll need to pack up their lunch and their blanket. They'll have to go to a spot away from insects.

121   Beet Tops and a Bus Ticket

Agnes got her red jacket out of the closet and went out to the bus stop. She planned to visit Beth, who had a rabbit. Agnes had promised to bring the rabbit beet tops as a treat. Agnes had stuffed her pockets with the beet greens. Now she waited till the bus got to the bus stop.

When she got on the bus, Agnes found she had left her ticket at the house. Panic crept upon her, but the bus man grinned and said, "I'll let you on if you give me one beet green." You see, he saw Agnes each day, and he let her get on without her ticket.

Agnes sat down in a seat and leaned back. In a wink, she fell asleep. She had a dream. At least, she thinks it was a dream.

She found herself at Beth's house, but Beth wasn't there. Instead of Beth, an odd rabbit greeted her. The blackness of its velvet coat was trimmed with patches of red fuzz.

The rabbit had a toy trumpet and played it. What a racket! Next, he said, "I greet you, Queen Agnes. You must stay to tea." They went into his house and sat on a mattress. The rabbit laid out milk and sweet buns on a blanket. Agnes waited as the rabbit grabbed his bun and gulped it down. Sweet buns were this rabbit's weakness.

As soon as they had finished their tea, the rabbit jumped up and went to his closet. He set a helmet on his head. He said that each day he played tennis with the toad who lived in the next house. Then he dashed out.

121

Agnes felt this rabbit was the limit! Such nonsense! "I must leave," Agnes said to herself. She did not wait till the rabbit got back. Instead, she got on the next bus. The next thing, Agnes found herself at the bus stop. How did she get there? It was an odd day, indeed! She slid her hand into her pocket. In it was a toy trumpet! Now, how did that get there?

mix	be	paint	bat	grab
mixing	being	painting	batting	grabbing
ending	sleeping	playing	getting	digging
singing	meeting	loafing	letting	swimming
catching	eating	soaking	sitting	running
pitching	reading	drawing		cunning
fishing	reaching	crawling		shopping
thinking	beating			stopping
drinking	hearing			
locking				
blessing				
spelling				
buzzing				

122

have	give	live	leave
having	giving	living	leaving

wedding	stocking	duckling
weddings	stockings	ducklings

The Fish and Swim Club had an outing on the weekend. The day was clear, and the kids in the club set out. At the dam, the stream runs clear, and it is swell to spend the day fishing and swimming there.

Ted left his lunch at Jim's house. Jeff did not think of bait. Well, Ted got a bit of lunch from each boy, but without bait, they will not be fishing.

When Frank was jumping into the pool in the stream, he slid on a rock and cut his hand. Ted had a Band-Aid in his pants pocket and let Frank have it.

Jess got a big lump on her cheek when an insect bit her. Ann fell in the pool with her pants on. But the kids kept jumping in, playing tag, and having fun.

Ted was floating on his back in the pool, peering up at the trees, when he felt a raindrop. Then three, six, hundreds of drops. The kids ran pell-mell from the dam, grabbing this and that, leaving in a rush, and getting soaked in the rain.

Now the Fish and Swim Club is the "Swimming in the Rain Club."

dress	upon	about	around	appear
undress	upset	adjust	surround	disappear
unless		admit	asleep	account
unpaid		afraid	allow	address
until		agree	attack	
		aloud	attend	raccoon
		amount		balloon
				canal

123

Chet's balloon got away from him when he failed to hang onto its string. It soared into the air and appeared to get stuck up in a treetop.

A chipmunk sitting up in the tree was afraid of the balloon as it floated in the air near him. When the balloon was about to land on him, the chipmunk attacked.

The balloon popped, and the chipmunk disappeared into his house. He stayed asleep in his house the rest of the day.

He did not appear until sunset.

clock	day	confess	content
o'clock	today	connect	contented
	protect	consent	contest
	collect	complain	increase
	correct		insult
			insulted

124

Pal thinks it is his job to protect the house. Pal yaps a lot when he's doing his job well.

When do they collect the mail? At ten o'clock?

At twelve o'clock I'll meet you at the bus stop.

Nell found a cocoon. It was attached to the trunk of a tree. Nell lifted the cocoon from the tree and set it on her desk in a nest of leaves.

We will attend the meeting if we can get train tickets. The meeting is at three o'clock today.

The cat seemed content as she lay stretched out on the rug.

fifteen	himself	indeed	instruct
fifteenth	itself	insist	intend
sixteen			invent
sixteenth			

125

Bee and Pig

Hank Pig was trotting by himself on a path to town. He was thinking about how the sun felt on his back and about eating lunch. (Indeed, pigs think about lunch a lot.) As Hank trotted on, he did not see an insect in the air near his ear. Instead, Hank just flicked, intending to stop an itching feeling. The insect caused the itch and caused him to twitch his ear. The insect was Chet Bee, and he intended to have a chat with Hank.

He said, "Hank, my boy. How about giving me a lift into town?"

Well, Hank just stopped still in his tracks. He said to himself, "Bees do not speak. I must have invented him."

125

When Hank did not say, "Yes, you can get a lift on my back," Chet got mad at Hank. He said in a loud way, "Hank, if you will not give me a lift, I'll have to sting your ear."

A pig cannot stand to be stung on his ear. Sixteen stings on a pig's back are better than one sting on an ear. And when a bee insists he will sting, a pig thinks it's better to do as the bee wishes. Which explains how Chet Bee got a lift on Hank Pig's back.

discuss	within	expect	enjoy
disgust	without	explain	employ
dismiss	withdraw	expense	misspell
display		exclaim	

126

Mr. Smith expects to finish the job within a week.

King Max will employ Rob Rabbit to mend his crown.

Mom was disgusted with the cat when he found a stick
of gum and got it stuck to his paws.

My pals and I must discuss our expenses. We need to
fix up our tree house.

I do not complain about rain. I just think about
how much I enjoy rain on a hot day. I think about
how cool it feels. I think about the sound of rain as it
splashes on the roof and on the ground. I think about
how rain cleans the air, and I think about how much
we need it!

because	defeat	repair	elect	request
began	defend	repeat	event	respect
begin	defense	reply	neglect	result
begun	destroy		meow	
beneath				
between				

127

We planned a grand event. We planned to give a feast and a play and to have lots of pals enjoy our event. But we neglected to send out requests for our pals to attend our event. The result was an event with not one extra pal to see it. That's a bad result.

The cat meows. When she meows, she is requesting a meal. If I reply, "Not now," she meows. If I neglect to stop and fix her food, she is not defeated. She begins to meow in a loud way. The result of her loudest meows is her dinner. When she has eaten, she does not meow. She just licks herself and has a snooze.

Kenneth and the Chipmunks

Each weekend in the spring the Hunts went camping in the hills. They set up a tent. Mom and Dad slept on cots in the tent. Agnes and Kenneth slept on the ground in sleeping bags. They had to keep their food in plastic bags and boxes. If they didn't, the groundhogs and chipmunks and ants and foxes got the food.

The Hunts had their lunch beneath the trees. They had sandwiches and canned beans and toasted franks and tea.

One weekend, Agnes exclaimed, "This is the best food! Let's give a bit of it to the chipmunks." And then Agnes flung the end of her sandwich to a chipmunk. Kenneth, too, began to feed the chipmunks.

The chipmunks sat on their haunches and picked up bits of food with their paws. They grasped the food between their paws and fed themselves. The chipmunks stuffed food into their mouths until their cheeks stuck out.

127

127

Agnes said, "Those chipmunks do eat a lot, and with such speed!"

The next weekend, the chipmunks stayed around the camp, and Agnes and Kenneth fed them now and then. The chipmunks got less and less afraid of them and began to get near them. They seemed to expect food from Kenneth and Agnes.

"They'll soon be eating out of our hands," said Kenneth. But the chipmunks did not get that near.

Then, on Sunday, when one of the chipmunks got near, Kenneth reached out and grabbed it. "We'll keep it as a pet," he said. "We'll bring him back to our house, and he'll be our pet chipmunk."

"Let him loose," said Agnes. "Let him live with the rest of the chipmunks."

But Kenneth did not let the chipmunk loose. He fixed up a box and put the chipmunk in it.

When the Hunts went back to their house in town, the chipmunk went with Kenneth. Kenneth did not neglect the chipmunk. He fixed a swing in its box. He got his pet a dish of milk. He went shopping to get greens and beets and peanuts, and he fed the chipmunk each day. But the chipmunk did not eat.

127

One day Agnes set out a feast of nuts and grain, but still the chipmunk could not eat. Food seemed to disgust him.

The plump chipmunk got thin. He seemed sad and weak.

Then Kenneth said, "This weekend when we camp out, I will set the chipmunk free. We'll let him loose at the camp, and when he can live in the brush, he will soon get his strength back."

When they got to the camp, Kenneth lifted the lid from the box. The chipmunk jumped out and ran away.

"I'm glad," said Kenneth. "Chipmunks are fun to see when camping. But it's not fair to keep them as pets."

Africa	holiday	Alaska	expensive	America
camera	opposite	Atlantic	detective	arithmetic
benefit	relative	astonish		umbrella
cabinet		banana		unfinished
definite		develop		unwilling
delicate		electric		
difficult		electronic		Thanksgiving
Santa Claus				

128

The opposite of down is up. The opposite of in is out. The opposite of me is you. There are lots and lots of opposites.

Is there an opposite of banana? I do not think there is one.

Is the opposite of a cat a rat? That's not a real opposite. But the opposite of "I can" is "I cannot," and the opposite of "I won't" is "I will."

Stan has his granddad's camera. It has film in it. You must develop the film to see your snapshots. You can go to a shop and pay to get the film developed. You can develop the film yourself.

Stan has an electronic camera, too. An electronic camera doesn't have film. And it will fit into your pocket. When Stan leaves his house, he slips the electronic camera into his pocket. It's a neat thing, and it's not too expensive. The best thing is that you can see your snapshots on the camera's screen.

128

129

winter	temper	sister
enter	jumper	blister
hunter	number	Buster
painter	lumber	Easter
pointer	limber	oyster
counter	member	rooster
under	slumber	shelter
thunder	banker	
yonder	sinker	

silver	reader	steamer
helper	leader	deeper
flower	cleaner	steeper
shower	eager	powder
power	heater	sooner
tower	speaker	cooler
	scooter	dealer
	shooter	

layer	lawyer	whisper	whisker
player	Sawyer	whispers	whiskers

Sinker Swims

129

Sinker Sailfish is a silver jumping fish. He leaps up into the air and then enters the sea with a splash. He sinks down but soon will jump into the air.

Roy Oyster is not as limber as Sinker. He lives deeper down in the sea, in a shell. He cannot swim with Sinker, and he cannot jump into the air. Roy just sits in his shell next to his sister, who has a thicker shell than his.

From their shelters, they see Sinker jump and splash. Sinker sees them, too. He is eager to be their helper. He swims to them, and tells them to latch on to his sail. Then when Sinker jumps into the air, Roy and his sister can enter into the fun, Sinker's fun of leaps and splashes.

130

Thatcher	thicker	bother	beaver
pitcher	flicker	gather	giver
catcher	sticker	lather	liver
teacher	snicker	whether	deliver
preacher	cracker	hither	river
singer	checkers	wither	shiver
chapter	locker		

ever	dresser
never	miller
clever	boxer
proper	
stiffer	
suffer	

Wilma's Dad's Umbrella

Wilma's dad was a lawyer. He had his umbrella with him. He never went without it.

When he got downtown to his job, his helpers snickered and whispered because he had his umbrella.

130

It had not rained in weeks and weeks. The sun had been out days on end without a drop of rain.

The river did not have much in it but dust and a bit of mud. A layer of dust lay on the town. The flowers drooped and suffered from the heat.

At the end of the day, the helpers left their jobs. "Clouds!" they said and pointed. Soon they heard thunder. At the bus stop, they were greeted by a big shower of rain.

Then Wilma's dad strutted up with his umbrella, and they crowded under it. The town got cooler and cleaner as it rained. Wilma's dad and a number of helpers crowded under the shelter of his umbrella, waiting for the bus and not getting wet.

131

batter	chatter	pepper	robber
butter	clatter	dipper	rubber
mutter	matter	copper	ladder
flutter	scatter		rudder
shutter	platter	stopper	shudder
stutter	better	shopper	
fatter	letter	slipper	
	bitter		
flatter	shatter	hitter	glitter

banner	hammer
manner	stammer
dinner	summer
thinner	simmer
winner	glimmer
runner	slimmer
	shimmer
supper	bigger

The Eager Beavers

Bill Thatcher is the pitcher on our team. Ed Singer is the catcher. Our teacher is the coach. I am a member of the team, too. We are the Eager Beavers.

It seems that our team can never be a winner. The players on the opposite team snicker and say, "Stick to checkers." At least we'd be cooler if we played checkers.

But we Eager Beavers keep on playing. We may never win, but we have lots of fun playing. Maybe one day we'll be better batters and faster runners.

doctor	collar	Richard	standard	conductor
mayor	dollar	custard	coward	visitor
sailor	beggar	mustard	Edward	September
tailor	poplar	backward	lizard	
author			wizard	
mirror		upward		
error				

132

"Richard," exclaimed Ann, "are you eating mustard on your custard?"

"Yes," said Richard. "I am fond of mustard. It's much better than cream."

"But, Richard," Ann protested, "mustard is not correct on custard. Cream is standard on custard."

"Not for me," said Richard.

"Richard, you'll get sick," said Ann.

"I'll not get sick. I saw the cat eating a lizard. The cat did not get sick."

"But you're not a cat," said Ann.

"Correct!" said Richard. "Cats are not fond of mustard. If I were a cat, I'd be eating cream."

Albert eastern record

Robert western

desert   lantern

133

The desert is a hot spot. It's in the hundreds in the western desert in summer. When it's that hot, you cannot stay in the desert sun. It's better to think about the desert than to be in the desert.

It doesn't rain much in the desert, but flowers do bloom there in the spring. Lizards, insects, mice, and owls live in the desert, too. They creep out at sunset to eat or hunt. When the sun is down, the desert is cool.

Albert and Viv had a grand outing in a sailboat. They didn't get back until the sun was down. They hung a lantern from the sailboat's mast. It helped them see. And it helped a passing boat to see them, too. They got back in a wink from their sail. The brisk western wind sped them on their way.

remember	sunflower	interest	whenever
semester	gunpowder	interested	understand
customer		interesting	together
			however

134

consider	Mr. Smith
entertain	Mrs. Smith
	Ms. Smith

How the Sawyers Spent the Day

One summer day, Mr. and Mrs. Sawyer, Richard Sawyer, and Sal Sawyer went out to the river to have a picnic.

When the Sawyers got near the river, they set their lunch down under a tree.

Richard and Sal helped get the lunch out. They helped unpack plastic dishes and cups and the bags of food. They laid down a big blanket. They set the lunch on it and sat on three rugs. Mr. and Mrs. Sawyer sat together on one rug.

134

They had a big lunch with ham sandwiches and cheese sandwiches and peanut butter and jam sandwiches. There were boiled eggs, cups of custard, and bananas. Richard and Sal drank lots of milk.

Soon they were finished and eager to go down to the river. However, Dad said, "Now let's clean up the cups and dishes. We can gather up the rugs and the blanket and pack them up, too."

When they had packed the things away, Mom said, "We must see the beavers on the river. Sal can lead the way." Sal did not think much of this plan. "The muskrat may be waiting. Maybe I'll step on a beaver," she said. But in the end, she led Dad and Richard and Mom down the hill to the river.

"See that!" said Mrs. Sawyer, pointing at the river. "Did you see it? A fish jumped. The fish are jumping! I think they are catching insects when they jump that way."

134

Richard complained that he didn't see one jump. His mom said, "Just wait. Soon you'll see one jump."

Then they did see one. A big silver fish jumped clear up into the air and fell back into the river with a slap and a splash.

Then they saw the beaver dam. It was on a stream that ran into the river. The beavers had to be near. Then Richard spotted a beaver. It was a big one swimming in the river. It had a stick in its mouth. You saw just its eyes and ears and a bit of its back—and the stick with leaves on it. It went under as the Sawyers got near. Maybe it had to repair its dam.

At three o'clock Dad said, "Now we'll have to think about getting back to town. It's too bad, but we must get back soon."

"I'm sad to leave the trees and the flowers," said Sal, "the river and the fish and the beavers. They're the best!" Richard and the Sawyers agreed.

ramble	candle	cackle	sample	ankle
scramble	handle	tackle	simple	uncle
thimble	bundle	pickle	crumple	
grumble		tickle		eagle
mumble	noodle	twinkle		measles
fumble	needle	sprinkle		
tumble				
stumble				
tremble				

135

nibble	apple	cattle	bottle
bubble	ripple	rattle	settle
gobble	topple	little	kettle
			brittle

wiggle	struggle	dazzle	drizzle
snuggle	juggle	sizzle	puzzle

Nibble, Gobble, and an Apple

135

Nibble Mouse and Gobble Rat had a battle about an apple. Nibble had settled on top of a kettle to eat the apple. "Impossible," grumbled Gobble. "That simple little mouse cannot sit on my kettle and eat my apple." Gobble jumped at the kettle. The kettle rattled, and Nibble wobbled.

Nibble hugged the apple and began to tremble. Then the battle was on! Nibble sat up on his haunches. He threw a bottle at Gobble—it sailed past his ear. Gobble struggled to pull the kettle down. Nibble toppled from the pot. He fumbled the apple. Gobble jumped at the apple, but Nibble landed on his ribs. He began to tickle the rat. Around and around they ran until, in the end, they fell in a giggling heap.

Was it possible? The apple lay neglected beneath a chair!

apple	cackle	settle	tickle	sizzle
apples	cackles	settles	tickles	sizzles
	cackled	settled	tickled	sizzled
	cackling	settling	tickling	sizzling
	cackler	settler	tickler	sizzler

136

A hen cackles when she lays an egg. We say she's a cackler. When ten hens lay eggs, we have ten cacklers and a lot of noise.

It was summer. It was too hot. A man set an egg down on the blacktop. The egg sizzled in the sun, just as if it were in a pan.

rattle	grumble	sprinkle	simple	possible
rattles	grumbles	sprinkles	simpler	impossible
rattled	grumbled	sprinkled	simplest	
rattling	grumbling	sprinkling		terrible
rattler	grumbler	sprinkler		probable

136

A grouch is a grumbler. This grouch mumbles his grumbles. That grouch mutters. And one grouch shouts. Too much grumbling!

Red apples fell from the tree. They rotted on the ground. Lots of bees settled on the apples to drink their sweet liquid. They buzzed and sipped and went from one apple to the next.

Robert is a grand runner. In fact, he is the best runner on our team. That means he has the best record of wins.

metal	camel	awful	devil
petal	panel	cheerful	
total	model	joyful	pistol
pedal	level	faithful	
royal	travel	fearful	Harold
several	gravel	helpful	
animal	barrel	painful	
mineral	tunnel	thankful	
capital	nickel	powerful	
hospital	towel		

137

A camel is an animal that lives in the desert. It has a hump. A camel can live without drinking for several days. It can travel in the sand with its flat feet and not slip. It is a powerful animal. You can strap a load on a camel and it will be your truck. Trucks do not travel well in the sand. But the camel is helpful for traveling in the desert.

138

kitten	madden	happen	given
mitten	sadden	Ellen	driven
bitten	gladden	Helen	linen
gotten	redden	chicken	children
rotten	hidden	weaken	
eaten	sudden	kitchen	

| seven | eleven |
| seventh | eleventh |

Ms. Cat kept her kittens hidden in a box in the shed.

We found them yesterday.

Ms. Cat went hunting and happened to be bringing her
kittens a fat mouse.

We saw her going into the shed with the mouse, and
we crept in.

We didn't think she'd enjoy unexpected visitors. We
stayed hidden, too, and kept still.

Helen has gotten bigger. She was eleven. Now she is

    twelve.

On the seventh, eleven of us met in the chicken coop.

The coop's not a clean spot, but it's better than

    meeting in our kitchen.

I have a list of things to do.

I must be cheerful.

I must not say awful things.

I must be helpful.

I must pick up the towels and hang them up.

I must feed the animals.

I think that's an awful lot to do.

button	cannon	lemon	prison	canyon
mutton	common	wagon	prisoner	crayon
cotton	summon	Stetson	poison	
ribbon	lesson	Dobson	reason	
Madison	gallon	Hobson	season	
Harrison				

139

The Ranch Hand

Bill Harrison went on a trip to the Grand Canyon this summer. He stayed at a ranch near the Grand Canyon. A man from the ranch picked him up at the train in a wagon. The wagon rattled down the road. It was a neat way to travel to the ranch.

The man, Sam Dobson, was a real cowboy. He had on a ten-gallon hat, boots, and jeans. Bill spent each day with Sam Dobson. He went with Sam when he rounded up cattle. He got Sam to teach him how to sit in the saddle.

Because Bill went west, he thinks he's a real cowboy, too. When I saw him in town, he had on a Stetson hat, jeans, and a pair of cowboy boots.

American   chairman   errand   second

husband

thousand

140

Maud thinks the best sandwich is an American cheese
sandwich.

Lil says she has a thousand errands to do.
But her list has just three things on it.

We have a pair of pigs. One is Mr. Henry. He is the
husband of Mrs. Sweet Pea.
Henry and Sweet Pea had a big litter of piglets. Henry
is proud of his children.

Uncle Sam went on a trip to Latin America.
He will be back in six weeks.

cabin	raisin	napkin
robin	Latin	Wisconsin
Robinson	satin	

141

The Robinsons have a cabin on a river in Wisconsin. Harold and Anna Robinson and Mrs. Robinson spend the summer at the cabin. Mr. Robinson travels to the cabin on weekends. That's because he has a job in town. But at the end of the summer, Mr. Robinson spends three weeks at the cabin.

It's cooler at the cabin than in town. And the Robinsons can swim in the river if it's a hot day. They can fish in it, too.

Living at the cabin is simple. They have simple lunches, without dishes or napkins. The Robinsons enjoy living next to a river in Wisconsin.

There is not a lot of noise at the cabin. It is possible to hear raccoons shuffle in the leaves. You can hear a skunk sniff around the trashcan. You can hear a jay mocking a robin. You can hear insects buzz. That's as much noise as you will hear at the cabin. Well, you may hear noise when Harold and Anna play catch or are swimming. But you will not hear cabs or buses or trucks.

Fred is chairman of our Trout Fish Club. He fishes with us club members as much as possible. And he fishes without us, too. He fishes if it's raining and if it's hot and if it's cool. He just needs to fish. He may not catch a fish, but that seldom happens. One day Frank said he got a big, big fish. He said it was too big to keep. We cannot tell if he did catch a fish. If he did, it's still swimming in the river. We cannot tell if it was as big as he said. Maybe it's there now, getting bigger and bigger!

141

captain   fountain   fashion

mountain

142

Seth Robinson was the captain of a big ship that sailed from America to Africa. Seth sailed the ship down the coast of Latin America. Then the ship sailed east to Africa. Seth saw mountains and beaches, big trees, and green hills on the coasts of Latin America and Africa.

Jenn had her pup, Zip, on a leash. She and Zip went to town to get some meat. Zip and Jenn got hot as they trotted into town. In town was a cool place to sit under trees. She and Zip sat down. Then Jenn saw the drinking fountain. It was just the thing they needed. Jenn got a cool drink from the fountain. Next she picked up Zip and held him up to get a drink. He lapped up a big drink from the fountain.

at	freedom	welcome
atom	seldom	
bottom	wisdom	problem
blossom	kingdom	

143

Mrs. Hoyt has a problem. She just got a letter from Jeff. The letter said he will visit next week. But Jeff has a pup, and the pup is the problem. The pup romps and jumps, crumples up the rugs, and bangs into the lamps and chairs. He's a terrible pup!

She thinks she must say yes to Jeff and let him visit. She cannot think how to tell him his pup is not welcome.

She thinks and thinks about the problem. She wishes she had the wisdom to solve it. She thinks maybe Jeff will not bring the pup with him.

In the end, Jeff does visit and the pup does, too. But the pup has solved Mrs. Hoyt's problem. He has gotten bigger and now has the best manners Mrs. Hoyt has ever seen!

Keeping Cool

"Isn't it a hot day?" said Chuck to Linda. "How can we get cool?"

144

"We can get out the sprinkler," Linda said. "If we sprinkle the lawn, maybe it will cool down the air a bit."

Linda and Chuck didn't wait to think about it. They got the sprinkler out of the shed. Linda held the sprinkler and Chuck went to get a lawn chair out of the way.

As soon as Chuck had set down the chair, Linda said, "This will cool you down, Chuck!" And she aimed the sprinkler at Chuck.

The spray was cool. Too cool! Chuck yelled and grabbed the sprinkler away from Linda. Then he sprayed Linda with it. She yelled, too.

But Linda and Chuck weren't hot now. They were wet and cool.

I saw a fashion model. She had on a splendid silk gown.

My dad fashioned a raft from three big planks.

My pal Fran runs in an odd fashion.
But she can run much better than I can.

This is a problem. A king runs his kingdom, and a queen runs her kingdom. How can a king have a kingdom and a queen have a kingdom? A king and a queen can run a kingdom together. Why don't we say a queen runs a queendom? How odd!

145

Jimmy	Sally	badly	correctly	pity
Jenny	Billy	gladly	cowardly	very
Bobby	dolly	quickly	suddenly	candy
Betty	Molly	simply	rapidly	jiffy
Patty	Polly	promptly	awfully	plenty
Peggy	holly	nearly		daily
Harry	jolly	really		
Jerry	jelly	clearly		fifty
Andy		possibly		sixty
Sandy	mommy	probably		twenty
Blacky				seventy
Henry				

In September, Henny Penny decked her house with
holly. She's awfully silly.

Sandy had a swim. Then he sat on the sand. If he's wet
and sits on the sand, Sandy will get really sandy.
He'll be sandy Sandy!

Jerry smears jelly on crackers. Jerry says jelly is jolly.
I say jelly is sweet and sticky!

body	laundry	daddy	puppy	blackberry
lily	pansy	buddy	berry	strawberry
fairy	daisy	piggy	cherry	cranberry
dairy	country	penny	kitty	gooseberry
		bunny		

146

| berry | penny | buddy | cherry | kitty |
| berries | pennies | buddies | cherries | kitties |

Henry is the delivery boy at Daisy Cleaners down the block from our house. On slippery days in the winter and rainy days in the summer, Henry tends to be very cranky. He cannot seem to keep the fresh laundry from getting wet. And he cannot keep his customers happy.

The plastic bags get splashed when trucks speed into puddles. The bags get stuck under his feet when Henry stumbles on the slippery streets. On a bad day, Henry thinks he may not have a job.

146

It was Mrs. Sawyer who had pity on Henry. She solved Henry's problem and helped him please his customers. She got Henry an umbrella and a pair of rubber boots. Now Henry and his customers are cheery and happy. And the bundles of laundry stay clean.

When you do your job promptly, you do it quickly.

Did you hear about the cowardly pig? He quickly hid in the shed when he saw a little mouse!

funny	chilly	rusty	rocky	weary
sunny	hilly	dusty	lucky	oily
fussy	silly	ugly	sticky	cloudy
fuzzy		cranky	noisy	rainy
dizzy		dandy	drowsy	breezy
muddy	sickly	sandy		sleepy
merry	empty	windy		

147

The Picnic

It was a sunny spring day. "Just the day to have a picnic," said Betty.

"It's too windy," said Peggy.

This annoyed Jimmy. "Bosh!" he said. "It's just breezy. It's a dandy day to have a picnic up on top of the hill."

Jimmy fixed sandwiches. Betty got a bag of cherries and a box of strawberries, and Peggy packed the lunch in a canvas bag. Then they began the trip up the hill. It was steep. Soon they ran out of breath. Betty said, "It's foolish to scramble way up to the top

147 now. We need strength to do that. Let's have our picnic now."

"Yuck!" said Peggy. "This spot is too muddy!"

"I'm not fussy. I need to eat!" said Jimmy.

"Well," said Peggy. "I'll think about it."

"I'm not thinking. I'm eating!" said Betty. "And when I've eaten, I'm going up the rest of the hill to the top."

And the three of them did just that.

carry	carries	carried	happy	easy
marry	marries	married	happier	easier
study	studies	studied	happiest	easiest
copy	copies	copied	happily	easily
			happiness	easiness
			unhappy	uneasy

148

Greedy Pup

Our puppy, Dolly, is the greediest puppy that ever lived. It seems that she never can get as much food as she needs to fill up.

When we feed our puppy, we feed our cat, Penny, too. Dolly gulps down her food greedily. Then she rushes to Penny's dish and grabs a bit of her food. She sneaks away with it in her mouth. Then she sits and growls as she eats it. Dolly thinks Penny will attack her to get the food back.

Dolly needs better manners. We wish she'd copy Penny's manners. Penny never gulps her food. When she has finished eating, she cleans her paws and her whiskers. Then she happily settles down to nap.

every	family	history	delivery	factory
everybody	salary	victory	slippery	satisfactory
everything				unsatisfactory
everyone				

149

Everyone in the family wished they were traveling to the west coast with Molly.

"Pack me in your bag," begged Lily. "I'm not too big to fit in your bag."

"Me, too!" begged Harry.

"Remember to pack your camera and plenty of batteries," Lily said. "Carry it with you and never be without it. You must not miss a thing!"

"Yes, we need to see lots of snapshots," Harry added.

Molly did just as Lily and Harry demanded. She clicked and clicked and clicked the camera at everything.

When Molly got back from her trip, Lily and Harry asked, "Tell us about the things you saw."

"I didn't see a thing," said Molly. "I was too busy clicking the camera. That's the main thing I did. I didn't see. I just snapped. But when I get new batteries, you can see everything. You can see everything the camera saw. And I can see everything, too."

149

Annie	brownie	Millie	Willie	alley	chimney
Frankie	Winnie	Milly	Willy	valley	
			willy-nilly		

150

Chimney Visitors

A bunch of chipmunks are living in our chimney. We need to get a chimney sweep to get them to leave. When the chimney sweep begins to clean the chimney, he is shocked. It isn't just a nest or a small family of chipmunks. It's a town of chipmunks living in the chimney.

The chimney sweep says that we need to tempt the chipmunks to leave. He tells us to drop peanuts and grain at the top of the chimney and also in a trail on the ground leading away from the house. When the chipmunks go to the top of the chimney to get food, they'll smell the food on the ground. The chipmunks will leave their town in the chimney to eat the food.

It's a grand plan. The chipmunks leave, and we have a clean chimney!

150

Willy says it's silly to think brownies are real. Brownies are not elves, he says. Brownies are sweets that have nuts in them. Molly says Willy's the silly one. She says brownies are teeny-weeny. She says she sees brownies under toadstools if it's raining. She has seen one brownie sneak into his house at the bottom of an oak tree. Is Molly correct? Or is Willy?

Billy did things willy-nilly. He did things every which way, which was really silly!

Sunday   Saturday   yesterday   maybe

Robert Rocket

151

Captain Robert Rocket waited on the launch pad next to his gleaming rocket ship. He was just ten and proud to be on his way to the moon.

Everything was packed on board. Now Robert and his men got aboard, sealed the hatches, and began the countdown. Robert flipped the switches that set the rockets throbbing. He felt the ship lift away from the launch pad. They were underway in a cloud of mist.

The rocketmen settled down. The ground fell away from them. Everything got black as they shot nearer to the moon. In about three days, they began to land.

Without the least bit of difficulty, Captain Robert Rocket landed the ship on the moon's crust. The men peered out of the ship and saw that everything was clear. They began to unload the gear. Soon they had set up camp and begun to scout around the hills and valleys nearby. Just Champ, the pup, was left in camp.

He fell asleep and did not hear the little red moonmen creep up. They peeped into the rocket and the tents; they inspected everything. Then they found the boxes of *Let's Read* that were packed in the ship.

151

Quickly gathering up the boxes of *Let's Read*, they jumped from the rocket ship. Just then Champ saw them. He bit at one of the little red moonmen but nipped himself on the lip in error. The moonmen were thinner than air!

When Captain Robert got back to his ship, he found red hoofprints on everything. Who had sneaked away with the boxes of *Let's Read*?

Suddenly Champ sent up an awful howl. As Robert got down from the rocket, he saw the problem. Clouds of red and green dust hung in the air, and from the next valley there was a very loud, rumbling sound.

151

As Robert's men ran to check out this noise, it got louder and louder. The moonmen were in the middle of a pitched battle! Red moonmen were hugging green moonmen and green moonmen were tickling red moonmen. Everyone was struggling to get a copy of *Let's Read*! What an odd battle! What a roaring rumpus!

Suddenly the moonmen saw the rocketmen and began to run at them. Robert and his men held their ground. The moonmen gathered around the Americans and began to jabber. Robert raised his hand. The leaders of the red and the green moonmen stepped up to him.

"We can speak as you do," the red one said. "But we cannot understand this!" And he held up his copy of *Let's Read*.

"Well," said Robert, "Americans can speak with scribbles. That thing can teach you to read the scribbling. But can you tell me the reason you had a pitched battle?"

"The reds have every one of them," said the greens' leader.

"Yes. They do seem to," said Robert, "but do you need them?"

"We hear," said the red moonmen's leader, "that you will soon be living on the moon. We must understand you and your scribbles! If not, we will end up in a big battle."

"We well may," admitted Captain Robert. "But I think I have a way to solve the problem and to help bring understanding between us. We rocketmen will teach you moonmen to read if you will teach us about your moon!"

"Yes! Yes!" shouted the reds and greens together.

And indeed Robert's men did teach the moonmen to read. And to this day, moonmen can read as well as rocketmen.

PART V

The Commonest Irregular Vowel Spelling Patterns

Guide to Part V, Lessons 152–199

art V is concerned with vowel patterns that occur far less frequently than those of the earlier parts and thus are highly irregular within the *Let's Read* sequence. Nonetheless, they are common enough and embody enough vocabulary that they could be considered "semi-irregular." Fortunately for the learner, this means that there are abundant reinforcing examples within the vocabulary of approximately 1,600 words, but the number of separate patterns to learn is fewer than twenty-five. Clearly, a lot of ground will be covered in part V. However, the learner, who is by now nearly an independent reader, will not be overwhelmed by the lessons.

In part V (and in part VI as well), the emphasis shifts from learning basics to learning not only the devilish 10 to 20 percent of English that is irregularly spelled (nonalphabetic), but also about the conventions of written English. The pupil will not necessarily be aware of this shift, but the reading, by example, stealthily leads to that result. The lessons adhere to the same general format and procedures established in Lesson 1. Therefore, even though the vocabulary is more sophisticated, it is presented in the familiar way, supported by practice reading.

SCOPE OF PART V

- *a* as in *game, bake*
- *ea* as in *steak*

- *are, ear, ere* as in *care, bear, there*
- *a* as in *father, car, ask, salt, wash*

- *o* as in *dog, go*
- *ow* as in *snow*
- *or, ore, oor, our* as in *for, core, door, pour*

- *i* as in *bite*
- *y* as in *by*

- *o, ou* as in *son, young*
- *u* as in *put*
- *oo* as in *book*

- *u* as in *cute, true*
- *ew* as in *few, chew*

- *ea* as in *head*
- *e* as in *even*

Suggestions for the Teacher

1. This part of the vocabulary explores territory that is more likely to be subject to variations in pronunciation, not only between one region and another but even within a pattern. *Dog, log,* and *frog* or the several ways to pronounce *donkey* are good examples; English speakers frequently pronounce each one slightly differently, but we consider them as one pattern. Just as the pupil accommodated to difference in pronunciation in earlier lessons (for example, in the case of *prom* and *from*), further accommodation will occur here. This may be especially noticeable in words like *father* that are liable to distinct regional variation. And, as the teacher has been encouraged from the beginning to respect the pupil's individual pronunciation system, so should the teacher likewise stick with the pronunciations that are familiar to and comfortable for him or her. At the risk of repeating the obvious, it is more productive (and probably more sensible) to let spelling pattern do the instructional work.

2. Some vocabulary has been encountered before, mostly as sight words inserted into the reading; in part V, the pupil will see many of these words as part of a larger spelling

pattern. When a long pattern is introduced, it might give the impression of being a case of overkill, but the lists are not exhaustive. They are merely large samplings of words within a pattern. And some patterns are very short because there are few words in English that follow them.

3. The pupil will also encounter homonyms such as *grate/great; steak/stake;* and *male/mail*. Some pupils do not even notice that they are learning an alternate spelling for a word that sounds the same as another but has a completely different meaning. The pupil will also become acquainted with homographs such as *read*, past tense of *read* (introduced earlier). As with unfamiliar words, the best course is usually the simplest: if the word is new to the pupil, define it simply, and if the pupil notices that there are now two spellings for words that sound alike, examples of use in simple sentences will make the point clear that context and meaning go together (as in *A boy is a male; a letter is sent in the mail. Something greater is bigger or better; a grater shreds cheese.*). For the curious pupil, these idiosyncrasies of English can lead to interesting supplementary activities.

4. The lessons of part V also include longer stories. They have been added for two reasons: students are ready for them; and we know from experience that they enjoy reading an extended narrative of more depth.

Interpretation will depend on the maturity of the reader, but even young readers should be encouraged to stretch their comprehension skills to grasp the content. After all, it is not unusual for a newly-minted reader to try to read a newspaper story.

5. In respect to comprehension and interpretation of the reading, the pupil's level of interest, life experiences, use of language, and similar considerations will determine how much attention to focus on content, either implied or expressed, in the reading.

6. Despite mention of complexity and irregularity and longer reading passages, the teacher should not anticipate difficulty. It is nearly a given that most pupils sail through part V, and troublesome words can be analyzed once trouble is evident. There is no need to analyze part V in anticipation of difficulty any more than it would have been useful to do the same for any other part of *Let's Read.*

NOTES

It is entirely possible to teach a pupil to read without ever doing a single supplementary activity. These activities are merely suggestions for either the older pupil, the pupil who likes these kinds of things, or for the pupil who actually needs more practice working with words.

1. *Word lists.* Encourage pupils to collect words that they find interesting on the computer or in a notebook. These words can be any the pupil has taken a fancy to, and can be of any character, such as adjectives in their different forms (comparative and superlative) or homonyms or definitions of homographs, etc.

2. *Dictation.* Writing sentences from dictation is often a useful reinforcement for those pupils who are able to write their letters with ease. Dictation can also be an effective way to encourage a pupil to write his or her own sentences and stories.

3. *Writing.* Pupils who like to write can be encouraged to write a sentence or two about a story. At first, the teacher will most likely need to initiate and complete this kind of activity, but with practice, the pupil should be able to do this independently.

   However, the teacher should not confuse the skills of reading and writing, because they are very different. Our concern is to teach reading rather than writing. If expressed as a formula, reading = decoding + understanding (a message). Writing is generative, and thus could be expressed as writing = encoding + creating (a message).

4. *Computer activities.* For those of us who learned computer skills later in life, it is sometimes daunting and often dazzling to see what a youngster can do with a computer keyboard. If a computer is available, and the pupil likes to use it, by all means incorporate it into the reading lessons. As with writing skills generally, computer use is not necessary to achieve reading mastery, but it can be a very effective reinforcement and perhaps even heighten enthusiasm. Use of the spell-check function, however, should not be encouraged. In fact, disable it.

ate	gate	rate	late	Kate
date	mate	crate	plate	skate
fate	hate	grate		state
bake	make	lake	take	quake
cake	sake	flake	stake	
fake	wake	Blake	snake	
Jake	rake	brake	shake	

152

	base	case	safe
	vase	chase	chafe

came	game	lame	gale	tale
dame	name	blame	dale	stale
fame	same	flame	male	scale
James	tame	frame	pale	whale
		shame	sale	

cave	fade	ape	cane	haste
Dave	made	cape	Dane	paste
gave	wade	tape	Jane	taste
pave	blade	gape	mane	waste
save	glade	grape	pane	
wave	grade	drape	sane	daze
rave	trade		lane	gaze
brave	spade	scrape	plane	graze
slave	shade	shape	crane	blaze
shave				

bathe	lathe	babe

Jim Blake, can you bake us a cake?

Yes, but my sister, Jane, says that you'll need a crane to lift it and an ax to cut it. My cakes are not the best!

152

Maybe you will think about asking her to bake a cake. Jane's cakes are fluffy. My cakes are simply bricks. You can make a house from them!

My dad ate a cake I made. He said it wasn't safe to eat! It's not too late to ask Jane to bake you a cake!

When the lake freezes, it is safe to skate. The flag is up today, and that means we can skate. Then we will sit around a blaze of brush. The flames will help take the chill from our feet and hands.

When we get back to our house, we'll sit around the grate and eat cake and drink hot tea.

James will slave at a job, and when he gets paid, he will waste his cash on junk. Dale will slave at a job, too. But she will save her cash till she can get a snake at the pet shop. James wishes Dale spent a little bit of that cash on stuff such as hair bands and sunglasses. Then maybe the snake will remain in Mr. Runyon's pet shop and not bother James.

skate	skates	skated	skating	gate	gates
gaze	gazes	gazed	gazing	crate	crates
rake	rakes	raked	raking	lake	lakes

153

name	names	named	naming	game	games
blame	blames	blamed	blaming	flame	flames

save	saves	saved	saving	cave	caves
shave	shaves	shaved	shaving	wave	waves
bathe	bathes	bathed	bathing	blaze	blazes
scale	scales	scaled	scaling	male	males

wade	wades	waded	wading	spade	spades
trade	trades	traded	trading		
chase	chases	chased	chasing		

Dave Baker had a snake named Wiggles. He kept it in a crate. Dave is fond of snakes, but Kate hates snakes.

Kate said to Dave, "I am afraid of that Wiggles. Can't you trade him? Get a goat, a pig, a pup? Just get rid of it!"

"Never!" said Dave. The next day when Dave and Kate went to take Wiggles out of his crate, Wiggles had vanished. Dave had really left Wiggles in a vase, but Dave said to Kate, "I let him go. He didn't wish to be in a crate."

"Is he safe?" asked Kate.

"He's as safe and as happy as Wiggles can be," said Dave.

grate	grater	wade	wader
skate	skater	trade	trader
bake	baker	make	maker

154

late	later	latest
brave	braver	bravest
pale	paler	palest
safe	safer	safest

Harry Bravest

Harry Bravest got up from his bed, stretched, and went thump-thump down the stairs. He went to the kitchen and got a snack of fish bits, liver, and milk.

Eating that much every day made Harry very powerful and made it simple for him to live up to his name, Harry Bravest. He was the one who tamed beasts hidden under rocks and in the trees. He snatched bugs from the air and chased snakes from under the leaves. Each beast yelled, "Help!" when it saw Harry Bravest.

But Harry was afraid, too. He felt silly about it, but if big brave Harry saw a mouse, it made him simply jump out of his skin.

Now Harry lived in a house that was filled with the little beasts, and not one of them was afraid of Harry. They felt safe around Harry. When he saw a mouse, that mouse squeaked with glee, because Harry got the shakes. Even if Harry was really brave about everything else, that still didn't make things better. Each mouse got braver around Harry Bravest. Oh! I forgot to say that Harry Bravest is a big tabby cat.

labor	paper	bacon	safety	salesman
favor	bakery			playmate
major		taken	David	pancake
razor		waken		airplane

became	awake	mistake	escape	operate
behave	awaken	mistaken	erase	separate
	ashamed		eraser	hesitate
lemonade				investigate

Who is Dave Gates?

Have you ever met David Gates? Well, he's just about the silliest boy in our grade, but he is my best pal, my playmate. You see, I am David's twin sister, and he's Dave to me. My name is Kate.

Twins are not just the same. I wake up and jump out of bed. But you have to shout at Dave and yank the blankets from his bed to get him up. I brush my teeth. Dave just fools around with the toothpaste. He makes toothpaste snakes on his toothbrush. He pretends his hairbrush is a razor or a rake, his socks are bags of coins, and he's just robbed a train.

At home, Dave fools around and pretends a lot. But when Dave leaves our house, he is a different boy. He can read as well as I do. He is quick at arithmetic. He seldom wastes his day. He is one of the best in our class.

salesman   cupcake   operate   hesitate

skateboard   seaplane   separate   imitate

Dave's Quick Thinking

156

Kids think a lot of Dave, too. Last week, he did a really brave thing. Nathan Baker can't run. He has a cast on his leg. Dave helps him. And last week, Nathan tripped and fell down in the street.

Nathan cannot get up easily, and he cannot run. Dave just ran to Nathan and got him out of the traffic and to safety. The kids in our class are proud of Dave Gates. And I am proud, too. I think my twin is quick and brave.

But when Dave gets back to our house, he gets back to his silly stuff. He will not sit still at dinner. He chatters. He spills. He is impossible!

One day, our dad met our teacher on the street. She asked our dad if he was proud of Dave for helping Nathan. Dad asked, "Who is Nathan?" So Miss Heath, our teacher, explained how Dave saved Nathan.

When dad got home, he said to Dave, "Well, Dave, you are one brave boy. Helping Nathan that way was a grand thing to do. I am proud."

Dave may be brave, but Dave is still silly. But maybe I'll be silly next. You cannot tell with twins. But I can say that Dave is the bravest boy in the class!

lady	lazy	navy	baby	Amy
shady	crazy	gravy		Katy

baby	lady	navy	crazy	shady
babies	ladies	navies	crazier	shadier
		craziest	shadiest	

157

able	cradle	label	acre	cable
unable		Mabel	apron	table
	maple	Hazel	April	tablespoon
			favorite	stable

Paul Pistol, Detective

Amy and David Chase and their pup, Hazel, were spending the summer with their family in a cabin near the Grand Canyon. The cabin had lots of shady trees around it.

One day Amy said to David, "Dave, have you seen my silver pin? I left it on the table."

"I haven't got your pin." David sounded disgusted. "It's probably in the pocket of your apron."

"But it isn't," said Amy. "Yesterday, it was on the table, and now it has disappeared."

"Impossible," said David.

"Please help me, Dave. It's my favorite pin."

Amy and David hunted and hunted. Hazel seemed to be helping, too. She sniffed around the rugs and under the table, but she did not sniff out the pin.

Then David said, "Well, it seems that it did disappear. Hazel, you and I must investigate. I'll be Paul Pistol, detective. You'll be my faithful hound, Gunpowder, and you can help me. How about it, Gunpowder?"

157

With a yip, Hazel made it plain that she'd be glad to help.

"Can I help?" asked Amy. "It's my pin."

"Well, lady," said David, "you employed me to handle this job. Now bring me up-to-date on this case of the missing pin."

"I had the pin yesterday," Amy explained. "And I left it on the table."

David scratched his chin, pretending to think about it, and said, "A robber must have sneaked in and escaped with the loot."

"You're crazy!" said Amy. "If a robber came in, he'd take lots of things—not just my silver pin."

"Maybe," said David, as he saw Hazel cock her ears at a scratching sound. It came from the sill near a rip in the screen. That got David really thinking; he said, "Maybe not men robbers, but how about animal robbers?"

"You *are* crazy, Dave," said Amy, but then she, too, saw the gap in the screen. "Maybe a little animal is the robber. Today I swept up nut hulls from the porch and in the cabin. Chipmunks can get in."

"Not chipmunks," said Dave. "I'm thinking of pack rats. They steal things and carry them away."

"Dave, you're a real detective."

"Mr. Pistol, if you please," said Dave smugly. "Now let's separate and investigate. You go that way, and Gunpowder and I will go this way."

The detective team disturbed a chipmunk, who scooted out of their way. A jay chattered at them. A robin flew off to the treetops.

157

Then David saw a little animal that was not a chipmunk, not a jay, not a robin. It scrambled out of a rotten tree stump and ran away. Gunpowder gave a yip and began to chase the little animal, but it scooted up a tree and disappeared.

Dave peered into the rotten stump. "Amy!" he yelled, "I've found it. I've found your pin."

Amy came running.

In the rotten stump they saw a little nest. It was made of twigs and leaves and bits of paper and cotton. In the middle of the nest lay Amy's silver pin.

Amy picked it up. "A pin's a funny thing to make a nest with. But that's a very odd nest. See, here are bits of string and even shreds from that scrub pad we threw out."

"It's a pack rat's nest," said Dave. "I saw the rat scramble out of this tree and run away." Dave pointed up to the top of the next tree. Hazel was still waiting and yelping under that tree.

"We're not taking a prisoner, Gunpowder," Dave said. "The handcuffs will not fit that little beast. Let's leave the robber and his shady nest."

"Mr. Pistol," said Amy, "you handled this case in a very satisfactory manner. How can I ever pay you?"

David grinned. "A plate of pancakes will be the best payment I can think of. I need a snack after such a difficult case. And Gunpowder agrees. Pancakes will be just the thing."

| break | breaks | daybreak |
| steak | steaks | beefsteak |

great	greatly
greater	greatness
greatest	

158

Mabel Gets Dinner

Mabel Oaks is just six, but she thinks she is a great help in the kitchen.

One Sunday, Mrs. Oaks was not feeling well when Mabel's Uncle Jim came to visit. As soon as Uncle Jim saw that Mrs. Oaks was ill, he said, "It's a shame to bother you when you're sick. I'll leave now and be back next Sunday."

But Mabel was fond of her uncle. "Please stay," she begged. "I'll get dinner."

"Yes, Jim," said Mr. Oaks with a wink. "Why not stay? Mabel will get the dinner."

"I'm really feeling better now," said Mrs. Oaks. "You must stay, Jim."

When Uncle Jim agreed to stay, Mabel got into her apron. Then she got out a box of brownie mix. "I can make brownies," she said. And she did. But her dad had to clean up brownie batter from the table to the sink. Mabel had blobs of batter on her apron and in her hair.

Mr. Oaks began to get the dinner. "Mabel, you can be the greatest help if you set the table."

"She is very helpful. Mabel is doing a great job," Mr. Oaks said to himself.

Suddenly a loud crash came from the next room. Mr. Oaks dashed in to see Mabel standing on a chair. At her feet lay several plates smashed to bits.

"I dropped them," sobbed poor Mabel. "And they were Mommy's best plates!"

Mr. Oaks lifted Mabel from the chair. "Well, you did not mean to drop them," he said. "Sweep them up and then finish setting the table."

When Mabel had swept up the smashed dishes, she began to feel a little better, but she felt ashamed of her mistake.

"Can I help fix the peas, Daddy?" she asked. "I can get them out of the freezer."

"Yes, and please bring me the steaks, too," added Mr. Oaks.

When the meal was on the table, Mr. Oaks sent Mabel to get her mom and Uncle Jim. "We can have dinner now," said Mabel proudly.

When they were eating, Mrs. Oaks said to Mr. Oaks, "I'm proud of Mabel. She helped a great deal."

"But I did break three of your best plates!" Mabel said sadly.

"Maybe you did, but you made the brownies and set the table and fetched the peas and meat. You have been a big help."

"The dinner is just great, Mabel. When you visit me, will you fix my dinner?" asked Uncle Jim.

"If I fix dinner at your house, Uncle Jim," Mabel said, "I think we need paper plates. I seem to break things!"

159

bare	care	barely	declare
dare	scare	scared	compare
fare	spare	daring	prepare
hare	stare		parent
mare		careful	
rare	share	careless	
ware	square	carelessness	

| Mary | canary | contrary | secretary |

bear	wear	there	prayer	elsewhere
pear	swear	where	Thayer	everywhere
tear		silverware		
unbearable				

A Bear Tale

Little Kerry Thayer thinks it is fun to play tricks. She plays tricks on her playmates and on her family. She simply plays tricks on everyone. It is unbearable!

Kerry has an uncle who happens to have a bad leg. Uncle Ned carries a cane. He was in a railroad crash and his leg was crushed. That made him lame. Kerry and her parents are very proud of Uncle Ned because he helped many get off the train to safety. Uncle Ned got a medal, but he never wears it. Now and then, Uncle Ned lets Kerry wear the medal as a treat. She struts around with the medal on her chest where everyone can see it. However, the medal and Uncle Ned's leg do not stop Kerry from playing tricks on her uncle.

One day Kerry got a thick brown rug and laid it on her back and said to herself, "I think I'll see if I can scare Uncle Ned. I'll pretend I'm a great big bear. Then I'll see how brave he is!"

Uncle Ned was sitting in a chair, reading. Kerry crawled up to him. Then she gave a loud growl and jumped at her uncle.

Uncle Ned was not bothered one bit. "A bear!" exclaimed Uncle Ned. "If I had my gun, I'd shoot it. Now I'll have to catch it with my bare hands and send it elsewhere!"

Uncle Ned grabbed the bear and held it. He lifted it up and began to shake it. Then he gave it a little spanking.

"Ouch! Help! Stop!" yelled the bear.

"I think I've scared that bear. I'm safe now," said Uncle Ned.

"Yes, yes! Stop! Stop, Uncle Ned. I swear it's me. It's Kerry!" wailed the poor bear.

"Well, I declare! It is Kerry! You gave me a terrible scare," Uncle Ned said with a chuckle.

As Kerry picked up her bear coat, she said to herself, "Uncle Ned must be a brave man, indeed. He isn't scared of a bear. And he isn't scared of me."

159

papa	father	what
mama	grandfather	whatever
mamma		what's

160

Mary Bacon's father was in the navy. He had just gotten back from a trip to Spain. As he stepped into the house, Wag and Mary jumped around him, waiting to be hugged and petted. He set his bag down, and, oddly, the bag said, "Mama." Mary stared. Wag growled. He began to claw at the bag. He was afraid of whatever scary things were hidden in it. To keep him from tearing the bag, Mary's father undid it then and there. What was saying "Mama"?

Captain Bacon felt around in the bag. He pulled out three socks, a pair of crumpled pants, and then a raincoat. He fumbled carelessly around and pretended that his bag was just full of laundry. Now the bag said, "Papa!" Mary jumped up and down. Wag backed away. Soon Captain Bacon found an interesting square green box. He handed it to Mary, who quickly lifted the top. It was stuffed with a lot of paper, but underneath lay a pair of little dolls in Spanish dress. One doll said "Mama," and one said "Papa." Mary was very happy.

However, Wag didn't care much about dolls. He simply sat there and stared in disgust, as if he were thinking, "Dolls. Crazy, stupid dolls."

LESSONS 152–199 | **345**

bar	tar	art	tart	barn
car	star	cart	start	darn
far	scar	dart	smart	yarn
jar	scarf	part	chart	
mar	are			

161

card	carp	bark	arm	arch
hard	harp	dark	arms	march
lard	sharp	lark	harm	parch
yard		mark	farm	starch
carve	park	charm		
starve	spark		marsh	
	shark			

Carl   Charles   Charlie   darling

Darling Charlie March plays darts. Darling Charlie thinks he can beat anyone at darts. But I am going to beat Darling Charlie. I am charming Art Mark. I will march up to Darling Charlie and ask to have a darts contest. We'll get Sparky Parks and Smart Bart Sharp to see who wins.

Mary had a little goat. She did not have a little sheep. Its coat was black as coal. And it did not go out with her. If she went out, it stayed on Mary's farm, and one day, it ate up her dad's pants. In fact, it ate all the laundry hanging up out in the fresh air. Now, whenever Mary leaves the farm, the goat has to stay in the barn.

garden	pardon	Martin	carpet	marble	darkness
sharpen	carbon	bargain	market	sparkle	harness
					harvest

162

barber	farmer	harbor	Arthur
partner	farther	parlor	Barbara
partnership	carpenter	armor	Martha

army	hardly	afar	apart	depart
tardy	party	alarm	apartment	department
hardy	partly			

boxcar	quality
hardware	quantity

A farmer plows the land. He makes a big garden.

We got a new sharpener to sharpen the ax. Its blade had gotten dull.

The game of marbles is fun. Do kids still play marbles?

A barber cuts hair. The barbershop is very clean.

I think it must have been difficult to run while wearing armor. Maybe it was impossible! I think the metal armor rusted and squeaked. Do you think it helped to oil its joints?

Jack has an army on the rug. You can hear the men shooting and shouting. They are very little men. In fact, teeny tiny.

We live in an apartment. It's not very big, but it's sunny.

fast	pass	ask	clasp	path
mast	class	mask		bath
past	glass	task	raft	bathtub
last	brass			
blast	grass			branch
	grasshopper			

163

aunt	can't	shan't	command	alas

after	master	basket
afternoon		
afterward	rather	nasty

Ant House

One lazy day I lay down on the grass in my garden. Little black ants kept passing by me, and I saw them make a house. I did not really see their house, because an ant's house is under the ground. Ants dig out a house by bringing the sand and soil up from under the ground grain by grain. They carry up each little bit and lay it down on the ground. These grains make an anthill. The ants' house is beneath the hill.

As I lay there, hundreds of ants passed in and out of the house. Their house must have been getting bigger because the hill was getting rounder.

163

Suddenly one ant ran away from the rest very fast. Maybe he had to run an errand. Then I saw that he had been sent to get a little twig by himself. As he began to drag it past me on the garden path, I saw what a difficult task it was. Each pebble in the path was a separate rock he had to scramble up.

Why did he need the twig? And which of the mean black ants commanded him to get it by himself? Maybe, I said to myself, they'll make a beam out of it to prop up a crumbling part of the house.

The poor ant had a terrible struggle dragging the twig near the ant house. I felt that the ant was very brave to tackle such a big job by himself.

As I lay there, sleepy as a cat in the sun, I began to think a lot about ants. Ants are careful, yet they are daring. Ants never play away the afternoon; they are able to spend an afternoon carrying things, doing a job. And I began to think how I am not daring and careful; I am not really brave; I am rather lazy. As I was thinking about this, I began to doze, and suddenly, I saw my ant stop still in its tracks. I raised myself up, and there was a grasshopper staring at the ant and at me.

The grasshopper began to speak. It said, "You have been staring at this anthill from ten o'clock, and it is now after noon. Why not have a real peek at the way ants live?"

A grasshopper speaking? Such a thing was indeed difficult to grasp, but I was not about to miss such a treat.

"Yes," I said, "that sounds interesting to me. Just how do I do it?"

"Get up, lazy one!" the grasshopper said. "Stand very still, and at my command, jump into the air.

163

I did just that, and as I landed on the ground, I began to shrink. Soon I became as teeny as an ant. Then the grasshopper jumped away, disappearing into the tall grass. Suddenly I felt afraid, but when the ant gave me a cheery greeting, my fears left me. The ant gave me a wave to say that I must go along with him.

On the way, I found out that this ant and the rest of the ants in the hill were under the command of the Master Ant. The Master ran everything.

When we slid down into the anthill, we went to see the Master. We bowed to him. The Master was sitting in his parlor with his sparkling armor on. His dark gaze scared me. I was glad when we left quickly.

Everywhere there was a swish of rushing ants. Every ant had a task. They hardly saw us as they ran up and down the tunnels.

At the beginning of each tunnel there was a mark. The mark told the ants what was in that tunnel. Ants don't read as we do, but ants understand what these marks mean, just as we understand what letters mean.

163

What did these tunnels have in them? There were tunnels to keep hundreds of ant eggs, tunnels to keep food, tunnels to sleep in on beds of leaves.

Too soon my ant declared I had to go. We went up a dark branching tunnel. Out we popped into cool air. He left me in the grass by myself and very afraid. Then I remembered how I made myself shrink, and with a deep breath, I jumped in the air.

Next, I found myself on my back in the grass. There was the anthill. Did I dream I went in it? I don't think I did!

all	wall	salt	bald
ball	small	malt	
call	stall	malted milk	false
hall	squall		

164

fall	tall	halt	Walt	walnut
fallen	tallest	halter	Walter	

always   baseball   basketball

war	warm	ward	wart	dwarf
warn	warmth	reward		quart
warpath				quarter

Walter's the tallest boy in our class. He says it's because he lives on malted milk. He always has one with each meal and after he plays baseball.

> Harry Hall was in a squall.
> His coat shrank till 'twas very small.
> Maybe an elf, if not very tall,
> Can wear the coat of Harry Hall.

swat	wasp	swan	water	washer
swamp		want	waterproof	washing
squat	wash	wand	watermelon	Washington
watch	wander	squander		watchman
squash		quarrel		

165

A teeny dwarf with a wart found a quarter but was not able to carry it. A quarter is much too big for a dwarf to pick up. However, the dwarf did get to spend part of the quarter, after he gave a nickel of it as a reward to Harold Hare, who was able to carry it. Better to share than not to have the quarter at all!

Casper's silly sister warned him not to run on the rickety wharf. She said it wasn't safe. After Casper fell into the lake, he felt that maybe his sister wasn't silly at all.

My dad said he read about kids who lived in a boxcar. He said it was nifty.

We went down to the harbor to see the tall sailing ships. They had sailed up the river and into the harbor.

dog	bog	song	long
hog	log	strong	along
fog	flog	throng	belong
foggy	frog	ding-dong	
	catalog		

lost	loft	off	onward	Jack Frost
frost	soft	offer	Boston	
cost	softly	coffee		
costly		coffeepot		

| boss | moss | cross | across |
| loss | toss | crossing | |

| mock | gone | moth | broth | tablecloth |
| honk | golf | cloth | froth | |

Arthur and Barbara Frost have dog now. They call him Toasty because he's a dark brown and warm as toast.

Jack Frost came when I was sleeping. He frosted all the roofs and shrubs and trees. They sparkled in the sun.

167

go	bone	shone	joke	hole
no	cone	throne	woke	mole
so	tone	lone	poke	pole
ho	stone	alone	spoke	sole
hoe	lonely	smoke	stole	
Joe			broke	
toe			stroke	
			choke	

nose	rove	hope	rode
rose	drove	lope	globe
pose	stove	slope	home
close	note	pope	
chose	vote	rope	
those		mope	

hoe	toe	go	poke	vote
hoes	toes	goes	pokes	votes
hoed	toed		poked	voted
hoeing	toeing	going	poking	voting

hope	close	rope
hopes	closes	ropes
hoped	closed	roped
hoping	closing	roping

Lost in the Marsh

David Cross and his sister Mary live on a farm in the state of Wisconsin. Near their farm there is a big swamp called the Great Sheboygan Marsh.

Their father always warned them about the marsh. "Never, ever wander too far into the marsh," he said. "It's easy to get lost in there."

One hot afternoon in August, David said to Mary, "Let's run down to the marsh and catch frogs."

Frogs are slippery and can jump away very quickly unless you sneak up on them. Mary was not too eager to hunt for frogs there. "I'm afraid of the marsh, Dave. Dad said the ground is soft, and if you step on it, you may sink down in the bog and not get out. We had better stay away from the marsh."

"Well," said David, "we'll not stray too far into the marsh." It's just a trip to get some little green frogs."

Mary agreed, and they started off with their dog, Scrapper, who was a big black dog. He always ran along after David and Mary.

When they got to the marsh, there was not a frog to be seen. "Where have all the frogs gone?" asked Mary.

"They must be a little farther this way," said David. "Let's just see. Maybe they are just beyond that clump of trees."

167

The trees were swamp oaks, and the children had to be very careful as they scrambled along the low branches. By now, David and Mary were really in the swamp. The ground between the trees had grass on it, but it was too soft to stand on.

"Be careful, Mary," David warned. "Crawl on the branches of the trees. Don't slip off. Scrapper can run fast and not get sucked in the bog. But we will sink in quickly if we land on the grass."

Scrapper was smart, too. He wanted to run back. But when David and Mary went on, Scrapper went along with them.

"Where are the little green frogs?" asked Mary.

"They aren't here," said David. "I'm afraid it will be dark soon. We'd better be getting back now."

They started back, hopping and crawling from branch to branch. After a few seconds the children saw that they were lost. "This is not the way we came," Mary said.

"I think the way we came is off to the left. Hang onto this branch, Mary, and I'll see if that's the way," David said.

The grass between the trees was long and very green. It seemed to David that in this one spot the ground must be solid. He slid down from the branch of the tree and let his feet hit the ground. They sank way down into the soft mud under the grass. It was up to David's ankles.

"I can't reach the branch. I can't get my feet out!" David yelled.

Mary scrambled across to the tree where David had let himself down. She stretched out her arms and grabbed onto his collar and held fast. Scrapper saw that they needed help. He barked and jumped at David.

167

"It's really getting dark," said Mary. She had to hang on to David. They needed help. Suddenly she shouted, "Scrapper, fetch Dad, quick!" Scrapper ran off to fetch their father, barking as he ran.

Mary held fast to David and waited for help. When darkness had fallen on the swamp, scary noises surrounded the children. Twigs snapped and odd things seemed to brush by them. Now owls and bats, weasels and bobcats were kings of the swamp, and David was stuck in the mud.

Scrapper ran as fast as his legs were able to carry him back to the farm. When he saw the children's father, he jumped at him, barking. Mrs. Cross ran from the house. "The children!" she screamed. "Scrapper never leaves David. Where are the children?"

"That's it!" said Mr. Cross. "He wants to take me to the children.

Scrapper gave a loud yelp and ran to the gate. Mr. Cross ran after him. When they got near the swamp, Mr. Cross saw that it was getting too dark to see. He ran back to the barn and got his lantern.

Mr. Cross made a second start into the swamp. Mrs. Cross ran after him but stopped to wait where the swamp begins. Mr. Cross made his way carefully along the branches of the swamp oaks.

167

Soon it was too dark in the woods to see Scrapper. Mr. Cross stopped; he fumbled around and got out his matches. When he had lit the lantern, he held it up to see better.

At last he saw Mary, and then he saw David sunk in the mud. With his legs hooked across a branch, Mr. Cross was able to reach down and grab David's belt. He tugged with all his strength and still he was not able to get David's legs free. Then he slid down nearer to the base of the tree. He had to stretch. Yanking and jerking each leg separately, he freed David's feet from the mud.

No one said much on the way back to the farm, but as they got near the house, Mr. Cross said to David and Mary, "If you had let Scrapper lead the way, you'd never have gotten lost. You have a great dog, but I have very foolish children. Maybe the swamp can teach its lesson better than I can."

broke	chose	open	swollen	over
broken	chosen	opening	swelling	Rover
token				Grover
				clover

168

go	no	home	toe	bone
ago	nobody	homesick	tiptoe	backbone
oho	nowhere	homesickness		wishbone

close   closer   closest   closely   closeness

explode   telescope

Joe broke his toe. He didn't think it was broken until it got swollen. It got so big, it seemed as if Joe had several toes and not just one broken toe!

Who did that? Who stole my telescope? Did Mr. Nobody do it? I need the telescope. A comet will explode in the heavens and I need to see it! Mr. Nobody, bring back my telescope.

Rover is a dog. Did you know a dog can get homesick? Rover's master went on a trip. Rover stayed with a family he liked, but he missed his master. His homesickness worried the family caring for him. However, Rover recovered when his master got home.

old	sold	bolt	roll	host	both
bold	told	colt	toll	most	don't
fold	cold	Holt	troll	post	won't
gold	scold	jolt	stroll		
hold		molt			
mold		volt			

169

Lizzie and Willie, who live in an apartment, have a game they play on rainy days. It is called Gold Rush Days. They are settlers going west to seek gold. They make a wagon from old boxes and blankets and get several dented pots and tin plates. If they are lucky, their mom lends them a milk carton to keep water in and a tin box to keep cookies in.

They have six oxen to haul their wagon over the dusty trail and across rivers. They are bold and brave, going west in terrible rain and cold.

When they stop to have lunch, they leave their wagon and crawl to the kitchen.

But they must look out for bears on the way to the table.

also	tomato	golden	poem	noble	sofa
banjo	potato	spoken	program	postal	soda
auto	buffalo	frozen		local	control
	hello	moment	November	locate	
older	piano				hotel
holder	Colorado		hopeful		
motor	tobacco		hopeless		
	cocoa				

170

| almost | cozy | only | rolling | October | suppose |
| mostly | pony | holy | clothing | | |

Cowboy Banjo Smith is a local seven-year-old who lives in an apartment on Sixty-fifth Street. One October day she rode her skateboard pony down the street and hitched him to a lamp post.

Banjo swaggered up the man selling sodas from a cart. "A slug of strawberry soda, please," said Banjo.

When Banjo finished, she plunked down her quarters and strolled back to her pony. Her mom, the boss, had told Banjo she was supposed to be back at the apartment (the Colorado Hotel) by six. The next moment Banjo was frozen in her tracks. The boss appeared! "I was hoping you had gotten the potatoes for me. Now I see you got a soda. Get rolling on that pony and bring my potatoes back with you!" the boss demanded.

low	mow	grow	blow	snow
row	bow	grown	blown	snowy
sow	crow	show	throw	
tow	glow	shown	thrown	
stow	flow			

171

slow	bow	grow	low	owe
slower	bowl	grown	lower	own
slowly	elbow	growth	below	owner

snowball snowflake rainbow rowboat

Nasty Abner Spinch lives on our street. He never mows his grass, so it grows as tall as your elbow. We stay away, mostly.

One afternoon Katie, Robin, Jamie, and I were playing ball. Robin hit a slow pitch way out. I missed the ball, so we all started to run after it. Katie got as far as Abner Spinch's hay and was just about to throw the ball back when out came mean old Spinch! We all ran. Abner Spinch ran after us, but we hid under an old rowboat. Spinch snarled about kids and slowly went back to his house.

Somebody said he's so low and mean that his own dog bit him, and we think it probably did.

bellow	follow	pillow	arrow	swallow
fellow	hollow	willow	narrow	Halloween
mellow			sparrow	
yellow		window		shadow

172

"Let's play follow the leader. I will be the leader, and you must follow me in every way," said Anna.

"Suppose you jump in the river?" asked Max. "Do you expect us to follow you there?"

"Yes, I do. You must do everything I do."

"What will happen if we all jump in the river?" asked Arthur.

"One thing is we'll all get wet," said Anna, "and the second thing is we'll all get a swimming lesson."

"And the next thing," said Max, "is you'll be playing follow the leader all by yourself. Arthur and I are going home."

or	cord	born	cork	horse
for	lord	horn	fork	horseback
nor		corn	stork	
north	form	scorn		sort
northern	storm	thorn		snort
	platform	popcorn		short

order	formal	stormy
border	normal	forty
corner	Norman	
former		important
formerly	organ	
forward	orchard	morning

173

The Storm

One April afternoon Sally and Jessie went strolling down the road. It was the sort of day for a stroll.

Much later Sally said, "Hear that thunder? We'd better get back." They started to run, but the storm broke. Home was still far away.

Suddenly a horn sounded, and a car stopped. "Mr. Short!" Sally yelled. "Are we ever glad to see you!" Soaked to the skin, Jessie and Sally scrambled into the car.

"I'll bet you didn't remember," said Mr. Short with a grin, "that it always takes just as long to get back."

Jessie grinned, too. "Not in a car!" she said.

Tommy said that a polecat is a cat that sits on a pole. But my teacher says that a polecat is a skunk.

Still, I think Tommy's joke is funny.

174

Dan did not get a ticket. He got on the train without one. He paid his fare on the train. He paid the conductor, but the conductor was grumpy about it.

Wilbert and the Cows

Wilbert, a great strong dog who lives on the next farm, is a devil. (The farmer calls him Bert.) About three days ago, Bert caused a real rumpus. He broke open the gate to the cow barn and let the cows get into the grass.

To begin with, nobody saw Rover romping around with the cows, so nobody can tell just what happened. But everyone saw the cows, mooing loudly and scrambling to get to the lush grass and clover close by. They ate and ate until they were stuffed, and as they gobbled clover, there was Bert yapping happily, as if he were proud to have let them out!

horrid	sorry	forest	forget	forgave
horrible	sorrow		forgot	forgive
	borrow	forbid	forgotten	forgiven
	tomorrow	forbidden		

175

Horrid little Norman wants a cat very badly, so he's always borrowing ours. Yesterday he went to the orchard, taking our cat on a cord for a leash. Soon he forgot that he had the cat and ran off to play. Kitty came home, dragging the cord. This morning he said he was sorry to borrow the cat without asking. We forgave him. Tomorrow I suppose Norman will put our cat in a box or leave it accidentally in the forest.

Isn't that Norman the limit?

Billy was sorry that he forgot to bring a cake for our class bake sale.

Martha remembered to bring her cake, but she found that she had added too much baking soda, and the cake tasted terrible. She wished that she had forgotten her cake, too.

Tomorrow we'll visit the zoo. We'll feed the animals, but not peanuts and popcorn. I was sorry to hear that they are forbidden because they are bad for the animals. Will they forgive us for not having their favorite treats?

In the fall, the chipmunk gathers nuts in the forest. He saves them for the winter. If the chipmunk forgets where he has hidden the nuts, can he borrow nuts from the chipmunk living in the next tree?

ore	sore	torn	fort	pork
bore	score	worn	port	porch
core	snore	shorn	sport	
fore	store	sworn	report	story
more	swore		airport	glory
tore	shore	ford	support	territory
wore	chore	forth		

176

before　　therefore　　moreover

At Fort Detroit, the settlers were afraid of the Crees who approached the fort. The Cree leader came forward, holding up a small branch from a tree. What did that mean?

The leader of the fort went out to see and held a powwow with the Cree scout. The settlers found out that the Crees had made their way to the fort to trade. They were starving after a hard winter. They needed to trade skins for corn and salt pork.

Later the brave men of the forest and the men of the fort held contests of shooting and running. And when the Crees left the fort, the settlers and Crees had sworn to help and support whoever was in difficulty. It was a great day for the Crees and settlers.

door	doorbell	pour	mourn	toward
floor	doorway	four	court	
indoors	doorstep	fourteen	course	
outdoors		fourth		

177

How Uncle Paul Came to America

Everyone was sitting on the porch enjoying the cool northern breeze. Uncle Paul was sitting in a rocking chair, and the children of the family gathered around him. The oldest one was Norman. He was fourteen. "Please, Uncle Paul, tell us a story," he asked.

"What story?" Uncle Paul joked. He pretended not to remember the story he told over and over.

"The best story!" shouted all the children. "The one about how you came to America!" The children always enjoyed the story. At each telling, Uncle Paul added details that he had forgotten to tell before.

"My story begins when I was fourteen years old," Uncle Paul began, "just as old as Norman is now. It was very long ago."

"I was born in Norway, in a seaport town. All sorts of ships docked there: ships from Spain, from Denmark, from Holland, from America, from South America, from the Far East—in fact, they sailed from every shore. We boys always went down to the harbor to watch the ships.

177

"One day I was watching the men load a ship. It was a small sailing ship that came from America. One of the men spoke to me. I asked about the masts and sails and ropes, and we got onto subjects such as visiting faraway lands. When I was just about to leave, he asked me if I wanted to sail on that ship. He said they needed a strong, smart boy to help. They needed a cabin boy. He explained that a cabin boy had to clean and polish the brass, help in the kitchen, or galley, and clear away the dishes from the table.

"I said yes, I had always wanted to sail on a ship, but I'd have to ask my father.

"The man I was speaking to was captain of the ship. He went with me to my house and asked my father to let me go on the ship as cabin boy.

"The captain said, 'It isn't an easy job. There will be lots of hard chores, but I promise to take care of your boy and feed him well.'

"My father agreed. We were poor, and in the olden days, boys left home for a job. And so I left my family very sadly."

177

"I slept in a hammock. All the sailors slept in hammocks, below decks. On a ship, 'below decks' means 'downstairs.' Only the captain and the mate slept in bunks. The mate is the captain's assistant.

"I got more to eat there than I did at home. We had hard crackers and salt pork and lots of peas and beans. We were able to eat all we wanted. I was glad to get so much to eat. The men all treated me very well; only the captain or the mate scolded me a bit now and then, when I did not finish my chores in the proper way.

"Toward the end of the fourth day, the wind began to blow very hard from the northeast. It poured down rain. The waves got bigger and bigger. The ship rolled and pitched the way a cork bobs up and down in the water. It was a bad storm. The captain said it was a gale.

"Of course, we got all the sails down before they were torn in the wind. We were very lucky at that, for the wind was blowing harder and harder.

"At last one of the masts cracked. It broke near the bottom, close to the deck. The sailors rushed to cut the ropes that still held the mast. When they got the broken mast loose, it fell into the sea.

"Then the captain said, 'Break out the boats!' There were three little boats on deck for the sailors to get into if the ship sank."

178

dine	dime	fire	hide	bike
fine	lime	dire	side	dike
line	time	hire	tide	hike
mine	rime	mire	wide	like
nine	crime	tire	ride	Mike
pine	grime	wire	bride	pike
vine	prime	sire	pride	spike
wine	slime	spire	stride	strike
twine	chime	squire	slide	
spine			glide	
whine			chide	
shine				

dive	bite	file	pipe	fife
five	kite	Nile	wipe	life
hive	mite	pile	ripe	wife
live	smite	tile	gripe	rife
lives	spite	mile	stripe	strife
wives	quite	smile	swipe	
drive	white	while	snipe	
		awhile		

like	side	wire	smile	time
likes	sides	wires	smiles	times
liked	sided	wired	smiled	timed
liking	siding	wiring	smilng	timing

white	ripe	wise
whiter	riper	wiser
whitest	ripest	wisest

kite	mile	life	wife
kites	miles	lives	wives

dine	mine	time	wipe
diner	miner	timer	wiper

The End of Uncle Paul's Story

"That was just what happened to us. The ship's hull began to crack and break open from the pounding waves. The water came pouring in. It filled the the hold, which is what a ship's bottom is called. I will never forget what a scary sound that was. But the captain did not act scared. He went about giving orders, and we did what we were told.

"We lowered the boats into the water. Then the captain gave the order to abandon the ship.

"We slid down the ropes and jumped into the boats as fast as we were able. The boats were tumbling about on the waves. It was hard to jump into them. One sailor broke his arm when he fell into the little boat.

"Soon after we got into the boats, the ship began to break up. Part of it sank and part of it broke up into boards that floated on the water. I was very cold and wet and scared.

179

"Soon the wind was blowing less and the waves became smaller. Late on our fifth day in the little boats, we saw a steamship. It was a long way off.

"We all hoped to be seen and so we yelled and waved a torn sail. The captain had a big bag that he opened. He got out a long, thick stick. It was a rocket. We lit it. It sizzled a bit, and then it shot off. It sent a big streak of red flame far up into the air and fell slowly to the water.

"The captain said, 'Maybe they will see that.'

"Then he got out a torch and lit it. A sailor held the torch.

"The men on the steamship must have seen us, for the ship began to head toward us. It was a big ship. We all yelled and sang because we were going to be saved.

"The sailors on the steamship flung ropes down and helped us get up onto their ship. When we were safe on the deck, there were tears of joy that we had to wipe away.

179

"We were glad to be on the big ship, and we were lucky because our captain was so wise. The kind sailors cleared out a corner of their own quarters and slung hammocks for us to sleep in. And of course, our captain thanked the steamship captain for saving us.

"Later, we were told that the ship was not able to take us back to Norway. It was on its way to North America, to the port of Boston. Our captain said that we planned to leave the ship after it docked in Boston harbor.

"When we did reach Boston, I left the ship and went into town. Later on, I made plans to stay in America and get a job.

"My parents were very happy for me. And that is how I came to be able to sit on this porch in America!"

alike	aside	admire	tiny	lively
dislike	beside	desire	shiny	
	besides	require	ninth	arrive
daytime	outside	inquire	ninety	arrival
bedtime	inside	entire	nineteen	revive
meantime	upside	entirely	revival	
	upside down		pilot	

180

campfire	invite	outline	divide
bonfire	polite	valentine	describe
	satellite	sunshine	recognize
firecracker			realize

Mary can add, but she cannot divide yet.
She can tell you that five times five is twenty-five.
And she can also tell you that nine times five is forty-five.
She will probably be able to divide numbers next month.

The forest animals are holding a Fall Feast. They will invite all the animals of the forest to the feast. They will invite the big animals and the small ones. It is the only thing to do. It is the polite thing to do. Besides, the forest animals are very careful to be polite to each other. They dislike bad manners.

181

bind	mind	kind	blind	mild
find	minded	kindly	blinds	wild
kind		kindness	blindfold	wildcat
wind	hind	unkind		child
rind	behind			grandchild
grind		pint		
grinder				

die	quiet	idle	final	China
lie		bridle	finally	Lima beans
pie	O'Brien	title		Ira
tie		Bible	silent	Iris
necktie				

tiger	lion	violet	ivy	Inez
tigress	lioness	violent	ivory	iron

Friday   library

A mole is blind. That's because he lives underground.
However, a mole has a keen sense of smell.

A wildcat is somewhat like a housecat but much bigger.
Wildcats live in rocky places and hunt small animals. A wildcat
will sometimes sleep in a tree or hide in the branches of
a tree.

Iris and her dad made a go-cart. It goes like the wind down
the hill.

fry	why	whys	spy	spies	shy

182

cry	dry	try	fly	type	dye
cries	dries	tries	flies	types	dyes
cried	dried	tried		typed	dyed
crying	drying	trying	flying	typing	dyeing
	drier		flier		
	driest			typist	

reply	die	lie	tie
replies	dies	lies	ties
replied	died	lied	tie
replying	dying	lying	tying

nearby	bye-bye	style	Ryan	Byron
butterfly	supply	styles	Bryan	

At dawn, Peggy Ryan and her black cat fly home on her stick. Halloween is over. Peggy stashes her stick in the closet. She must feed the bats who live with her. The bats cried when Peggy left. Then she will lie down and sleep for a week. After that she will check her hat and cape and dress. Are they faded and grayish? If they are, she will dye them black and hang them up to dry. After all, how can Peggy Ryan fly next Halloween if her clothes aren't really, really black?

son	month	one	does
ton	monthly	done	doesn't
won	Monday	none	
wonder	monkey	honey	front
wonderful	donkey		money

183

Some kids like to see the lions and tigers at the zoo. Some like to stand in front of the monkeys and watch them frolic about. And some prefer the seals. But none of the animals at the zoo seems as much fun to me as the little gray donkey called Monday in the petting zoo. She is named for the day on which she was born. Every now and then she gives rides to children when one of the ponies has a sore leg. And she is very smart.

My sister, Iris, says that an animal such as a donkey or a pig doesn't belong in the zoo at all. She says that wild animals belong in the zoo, and farm animals belong on a farm.

I think in a way Iris is correct. But I really think all kinds of animals belong in the zoo. If you don't live near a farm or on a farm, how else can you see cows and chickens and horses and goats and pigs and wonderful donkeys like Monday?

other	brother	comfort	come
otherwise	mother	comfortable	coming
another	godmother	uncomfortable	become
stepmother	company		
	grandmother		

184

some	somebody	sometime	quarrelsome
someone	somewhat	sometimes	lonesome
somehow	somewhere	something	meddlesome

I am in a temper. I cannot find my wand! Where is my wand? Who hid it? Somebody did it! How tiresome. I won't be able to do a thing without it. I need my wand!

I am a fairy godmother. I can do anything by just waving my wand. Sometimes I do really splendid things. I made a frog into a man. And I made a coach from a pumpkin. I made a horse from a mouse. And I made rags into a ball gown. I made a quarrelsome stepmother into a weasel. And if I want to, I can make the horse into a toad and a man into a mouse and a coach into a rock and a ball gown into a raincoat. But if I cannot find my wand, I will not be able to do a thing. Now where is it? It has to be here somewhere!

dove	shove	oven	color
love	shovel	cover	nothing
glove		discover	dozen
lovely	above	recover	among

185

When My Brother Shovels Snow

My brother just loves to shovel snow. He wears his down coat, and he covers up his ears with a big fuzzy hat. He wears about five pairs of socks, so his feet will fit into some big old boots. And snowpants. And a scarf. And big warm mittens over his gloves.

When my brother has shoveled all the paths at our house, he shovels the paths next door and a driveway down the block. He's a great shoveler! He must shovel a dozen paths.

When he's finished, my brother comes into our kitchen and gets warm by the oven. That's how he thaws out. We fix popcorn and hot drinks. My brother has plenty of both!

But sometimes I wonder if I'll discover that my brother doesn't really like to shovel snow. Maybe he just likes the popcorn and hot drinks afterward. Maybe he likes the money he is paid to shovel. But really, I think my brother just likes helping others, because when he is shoveling, he always seems so happy.

touch	double	young	cousin	blood
touches	trouble	youngster	country	flood
touched	troublesome			
touching		southern	couple	famous

186

Honey Parker and her chum, Sally Trask, watched a couple of fish swim back and forth in a tank in the pet shop window. After they had been standing there for some time, the owner came out and asked them if they'd like to come in.

Honey and Sally followed him into the shop. He showed them around, pointing out fish from warm southern waters, bloodhound puppies frolicking in a big box, a young and noisy monkey, and a parrot from South America, named Mr. Flood.

Then the owner said, "You can touch most of the animals, but do not get too close to the monkey. He's trouble!" But the youngsters were not able to keep away from the monkey. He chattered at them and hopped about. Finally they just had to go see him. He reached out and pulled one of Honey's braids. That made her giggle. But Sally was counting her money, and the monkey spotted the coins in her hand. In an instant he grabbed one. Then he swallowed it! And it was a quarter, too!

The next time Sally and Honey go into the pet shop, they'll keep their coins in their pockets!

push	puss	pull	bull	put	armful
bush	pussy	full	bully	butcher	handful
	helpful	fully			

bushel			bullet	pudding	
cushion			bulletin		

187

If you go backward to drag something, you pull it. If you go forward to shove something, you push it.

A bushel of corn is a lot of corn. It is as much corn as needed for a big feast.

Miss Pussy is a cross puss. She needs her fish dinner.

Do not let that bull scare you. He is not really a bully. He likes to run and butt the other bulls, but he is just frisking and is just being silly.

A butcher cuts meat and sells it in his shop. A butcher sells meat and fish and sometimes pickles.

Silly Willy dropped an armful of logs on the floor. Funny Frannie picked up a handful to be helpful.

book	took	rook	bookcase	lookout
hook	cook	brook	booklet	fishhook
look	cookie	crook	notebook	
nook	shook	crooked	cookbook	

188

hood	goody	wood	stood
good	goodness	woods	understood
goods	good-bye	wooden	

| foot | football | footprint | wool |
| footing | footman | footstep | woolen |

I got a book as a gift. I like to read books. With a book,
I can go anywhere and not even get up from my chair.

Frank took six oatmeal cookies and a bottle of milk and went
down to the brook. He sat by the side of the brook, ate
his cookies, drank his milk, and read his book.

Sandy cut his hand on his fishhook. Chet had a Band-Aid
in his pocket and put it on the cut.

Look at the rooks in those trees. Rooks are a lot like crows.

Ms. Goody Goodwitch had a hood on her cape. She did not
have a pointed hat. She said she did not like pointed hats at all.

room	roof	hoop	soot	bedroom
broom	hoof	coop	sooty	bathroom
groom	root	Cooper		classroom

189

We gave Cooper, our dog, a bath in the tub in our bathroom. First we ran the water, just warm, not hot. Then we put Cooper into the tub. Cooper began to howl. Cooper does not think much of baths. But Cooper had gotten into some coal left in a sack in the shed. He was all sooty from the coal.

He needed that bath. So we put lots of soap on him and rubbed him well. He looked like a snow-dog. Next we rinsed all the suds from him. Now he looked very skinny. Still, Cooper was howling. What a noise! Then we got our mother's hair dryer and blow-dried Cooper's hair. I think he liked the warm air blowing on him, because he stopped howling. Now Cooper is his clean, tan, and fluffy self again.

Of course, we got a lot of water and suds on the bathroom floor and on the tiles. We're glad no grown-ups came in before we cleaned up the mess. We forgot the pile of wet towels. Our mother made us put them in the washer and then the dryer. She was pleased about Cooper, however. She said he smelled like a rose and looked very pretty, too! Cooper didn't like that at all.

We gave him some treats for being such a good dog. Even if he did howl a lot.

fir	bird	birth	girl	firm	chirp
sir	third	birthday	twirl	squirm	
stir		birch	whirl	Irma	shirk

	dirt	skirt	first	thirteen
	dirty	shirt	thirst	
	thirty	squirt	thirsty	squirrel

Irma Squirt is a dirty little squirrel. Most squirrels are fairly clean, but not that little Irma. She shirks a bath if she thinks she can get away with it. When she's thirsty, she is very careful not to get her whiskers wet while drinking.

It was on Irma's third birthday that she developed her fear of water.

Scampering and twirling up in a fir tree, the big show-off jumped to a little birch but didn't get a firm grasp on the branch. Irma fell almost thirty feet into a birdbath. Now just thinking of water makes Irma squirm. At the first hint of rain, Irma is deep in her hole, sometimes for the rest of the day.

her	perch	jerk	fern	determine
hers	person	clerk	stern	
herd	perhaps		Ernest	

191

	term	serve	nerve
	Bert	servant	deserve

Earl	earn	heard
early	earnest	earth
pearl	learn	search

work	worse	worth	Myrtle
worm	worst	worthless	
word	worry		journey
world	worship		

My name is Bert. I am a cat. I live with Myrtle. She is a bird. I like her—and I don't mean to eat. When other cats find out that I've learned to love a bird, they make fun of me. Cats are supposed to hate birds. They are made for catching and eating. Most cats say birds are worthless bits of fluff.

Perhaps she is a bit small, but Myrtle is some bird. There isn't a better pal on all the earth. She is good company. She plays tag. But I worship Myrtle mostly because she sits on her perch and sings lovely songs to me!

fur	burn	turn	curve	burr
cur	burnt	return		purr
		overturn	curse	
hurt	burst	churn	nurse	
unhurt	burden	church	purse	

curl	hurry	murder	curdle	purple
curtain	furry	turkey	hurdle	turtle
	flurry	Thursday		

furnish   purpose   further   surprise

192

Thanksgiving

It was the fourth Thursday in November. The curtains in Sally Perkins' window were flapping wildly as the rain beat down outside. For most families, this was Thanksgiving Day. For others, like the Perkins family, it was just another day.

Sally's father was out of work. The coal mine in Lancaster had closed more than a year ago, and her dad wasn't able to find a new job. The family's savings were running out. This Thanksgiving there was to be no turkey dinner.

Sally shut the window and burst into tears. Life had been better when her father had had a job. Sometimes it hurt to be poor. But at least she had a home. Some families didn't even have houses or apartments to live in.

192

Still, Sally missed the sounds of hurry and flurry in the quiet apartment. On Thanksgiving, her mother had always gotten up very early to start cleaning and stuffing the bird and fixing the pumpkin for the pie, getting out dishes, banging pots. There had been a flurry and purpose on Thanksgiving Day. The apartment was too quiet.

The sound of church bells from down the street interrupted Sally's tears. She got back in bed and pulled the covers up over her like a turtle to drown out the sound. She soon fell asleep.

Later in the morning, Sally poked her chin out of the covers. The rain had stopped and the sun was trying to break out between the clouds. The smell of turkey drifted into her room. Perhaps one of the families in a nearby apartment was already cooking their turkey. Just then, fur tickled Sally's ear. It was the cat. Somehow Simkin had shoved the door open. Time to get up!

Sally slowly realized there was a great deal of noise outside her room. It was the sound of her mother working in a flurry. And that smell came from their kitchen! What was going on?

"Goodness, Sally," said her mother, opening the door. "Are you going to sleep till dinner? I really need some help with the pumpkin pie. And you'll have to set the table."

What had happened? The world seemed overturned. First no Thanksgiving. Now a turkey dinner! The fact was that Father had just gotten part-timework in a small steel mill.

use unite continue fuel
used United States perfume mule
useful music
useless

193

excuse cute compute
refuse computer

pupil pure figure fury January
human cure regular

Davy sat in bed. He had his regular January cold, and he was in bed to cure it. Davy was feeling pretty grumpy. His mother told him it was useless to be in a fury over a cold.

Davy was a pupil in second grade and had to keep up with his class work in spite of his sneezing and blowing. So he continued to figure his arithmetic, do his spelling, and then make up a story about a mule.

After Davy had finished his lessons, he was lying back on his pillows. Suddenly his mother came in, saying, "Davy, don't feel so sorry for yourself. Getting a cold is just a human thing. Look, it says in the paper that the President of the United States has a cold today, too. You see, everyone, big and small, gets a cold now and then!"

rule	rude	June	July	blue
ruler		tune		blueberry
		prune	Ruth	bluebird
true	cruel	ruin	truth	blue jay
	gruel		truly	

194

A Pet Like Tune

June had a pet canary. Its name was Tune. June's cousin, Stuart, also had a pet, a dog named Duke. Duke was a brave and clever dog. He had saved a little boy from drowning. Stuart was very proud of the medal Duke got for being so brave.

Of course, June had heard all about her cousin's dog. When she heard about the medal, she wished she had a dog like Duke. She wanted the mayor to give her pet an award for bravery, just like Duke. But Tune was just a canary.

Still, Tune was a pretty good pet. Tune was not stupid at all. She liked to hop on June's ruler. She was never rude. She learned to eat a blueberry from a spoon so politely. So what if it was true that Tune liked the taste of glue? Glue will ruin a canary's beak, so June hid it.

duke	due	tulip	stupid	numeral
duty	duel	Tuesday	student	numerous
	during		Stuart	avenue

Tune's Trick

June figured out how to teach Tune tricks. Tune was a good student. When June used the computer, Tune liked to hop on the keys and watch the screen. So June began to teach Tune to tap numerals onto the computer screen.

Soon Tune learned to tap the numerals 911 when June asked her to. It seemed like such a cute trick, as useful as any trick Duke had learned to do.

Last Tuesday, June fell and hurt herself badly. In her fall, she broke her arm and bumped her head hard on the floor. No one was in the apartment but June and Tune. And June lay so still on the floor that Tune was really puzzled. Was this a game?

195

Tune hopped on June's chest to get her up. She pecked at June's cheek numerous times to awaken her. June didn't even blink her eyes during all this time. She didn't do a thing. Tune became frantic. The poor bird went from June to the computer and back again. She began to play with the keys. As if June had asked her to, Tune typed in 911 again and again.

When Mrs. Tulip came home, she called and called June. She didn't see her. June wasn't in the kitchen or upstairs. Where was she? Mrs. Tulip didn't hear one sound! She was very worried. Then she saw Tune hopping on the computer keys and 911 all over on the screen. She said, "No tricks now, Tune. What does 911 mean?" All of a sudden, she figured it out. 911 said "HELP!"

Of course, Mrs. Tulip found June. She was on the floor behind the couch. And after June got her broken arm fixed up, everyone heard how Tune begged for help by working a computer. Tune was even on TV!

In July, June will visit Stuart. And Tune will meet Stuart's brave dog, Duke. What will Duke think of a canary who can work a computer keyboard?

new	pew	Jew	drew	crewman
news	few		grew	screwdriver
newsstand	fewer	blew	crew	chewing gum
	dew	flew	screw	Jewish
	stew		strew	
		chew	threw	

196

A birch tree grew on the slope of a hill. In the winter its branches were bare, and its bark was as white as the snow. When spring drew near, and the snow began to melt, the buds on the birch tree swelled. Finally they grew into new leaves as the grass came up at the foot of the tree.

In the fall the birch tree strewed its golden leaves all over the grass. They made a carpet to keep the roots warm during the long cold winter.

There was a boy who watched the birch through all the seasons. Sometimes, when its leaves rustled in the wind, it seemed to be talking to him. "Take care of me. Watch over me," it seemed to say. And the boy did just that. And so the tree and the boy were like a family.

As the boy got older and the birch grew, new young birches grew around it. When the boy grew to be a man, he still went to see his trees and listen to their leaves whisper to him. But maybe because he was older, it became harder and harder to understand what the birches said.

197

dead	bread	ready	deaf	weapon
lead	tread	already	death	pleasant
read	spread	steady	breath	breast
head	thread	instead		breakfast
ahead	dread		heavy	
overhead	dreadful	meadow	heaven	

dreamt	sweat	threat	feather	dealt
	sweater	threaten	leather	
meant			weather	

	health	wealth	jealous	
	healthy	wealthy	jealousy	

Dead leaves are dry, like paper. They rustle when a breeze
  swirls them around.

You can rake fallen leaves into a big pile.

Then you can jump into it over and over.

You'll get leaves in your hair and caught in your sweater.

The leaves make a crinkly noise when you jump into the pile.

A feather is soft and strong. A feather is not heavy.
Feathers are like fur coats or raincoats for birds.
Really soft feathers are called down.
Chicks have down. So do ducks and geese.
Down is very warm.
Some feathers are long and stiff and help birds fly.

197

Ben Franklin, who was the first postmaster of our country, said,

"Early to bed and early to rise
Makes a man healthy, wealthy, and wise."

That means if you get plenty of sleep and get to work early in
the morning and don't dawdle, you will do well.

When I sweat, I take off my sweater, because I'm hot.
If I'm cold, I put it on. The same is true of a sweatshirt. I can
wear one or the other and warm up or cool down. Long ago,
sweaters and sweatshirts were worn only by athletes, who
sweat a lot. Now everyone wears them.

be	we	Eve	Steve	Pete	Jesus
he	she	even	Steven	Peter	
me	these	evening			

198

	athlete	evil	idea	secret
	fever	equal	theater	frequent

The Deeds of a Witch

Years and years ago in a kingdom far across the sea, there lived an ugly old witch who was stone deaf. Hazel Goodwitch was dreadful to look at, and when she flew across the sky, most wise persons put their heads under their pillows.

But instead of doing wicked things, this witch tried hard to undo or repair the spells of her six evil sisters. This work didn't give her time to catch her breath, but it was a pleasant burden. She had her helpers—the meadow mouse families, the crickets, and some creepy old trolls for heavy work. Her ugliness and her goodness were her only weapons, but she used them well.

here　　mere　　　severe　　hero　　material

here's　merely

More Deeds of a Witch

Now it happened that Hazel Goodwitch was getting old. Her strength was not what it used to be; she was not as healthy as she had been in years gone by.

Here in West Sussex, life had been quiet for years. But now her evil younger stepsisters, the Badwitches, were grown up and more troublesome than ever. They were flying all over the county on their own, causing great trouble. A few humans had threatened to go on a witch hunt. Even the animals were worried.

Hazel's sisters did more harm in one evening than she was able to undo in four or five evenings. If she fell behind in undoing the evil antics of her sisters, life for a witch was going to become unpleasant, indeed. This meant that she had to rely on help, and it was the meadow mouse families that were able to help most because of their great number.

199

On Halloween, the mayor of Meadow Mousetown held a meeting to discuss this problem with Hazel Goodwitch. His ideas were new. He wanted to put an end to the evil deeds of her wild sisters. His method interested Hazel. They determined then and there to put the mouse plan to work as soon as possible.

The first task was to collect the materials needed. This was completed within a month by all those taking part in the plan. The mouse families were able to round up several of the items; the rest were supplied by an assortment of local helpers, including the trolls, who also worried about the possibility of witch hunters. (Sometimes trolls were mistaken for witches.)

Finally, all was ready.

The next afternoon, Miss Nasty Badwitch and her five sisters heard noises in the brush outside their den. At first they were alarmed, but nothing happened. They soon got used to the noises, and so they went about their regular affairs.

That evening, as the sun was setting, each of the six Badwitches prepared to fly off on her wicked rounds. One took her bag of goat whiskers, another picked up her mouse tails, and a third counted the rats' feet she carried with her.

Soon they had left the cave. At that moment, from behind each bush came the followers of Hazel Goodwitch, led by the mayor of Mousetown. In no time at all, they finished stuffing the mouth of the cave with bits of paper, broken glass, rocks, old boards, and other junk. Then they settled back to wait.

199

Dawn was near as the Badwitch sisters flew home. Each swooped down toward the mouth of their cave. Each crashed into the wall of trash that sealed the doorway and fell flat on the ground.

Each had a look of terror—the sun was only a few seconds from rising. It is a common rule that if a bad witch is hit by rays of the sun, she will go up in a puff of smoke. No wonder the Badwitches were in a panic!

Now, years and years after that fateful day in West Sussex, the residents of the countryside don't even think about evil or witches or secret plans. Nobody suffers from evil deeds.

Hazel sometimes chuckles quietly about those six balls of smoke that floated over the valley one morning about three hundred years ago. The great-great-great grandchildren of the meadow mouse families beg Hazel to tell them the story over and over.

The Commonest Irregular Consonant Spelling Patterns

Guide to Part VI, Lessons 200–245

The *Let's Read* pupil about to begin part VI is like a climber close to the top of a mountain. Although at times subject to fatigue and discouragement, the steady pace has brought the pupil to the last stage of the quest. And like adventurous climbers, the pupil and teacher should begin to feel some exhilaration from their impressive achievement. But they're not quite there—yet.

Part VI teaches the most irregular consonant and some irregular vowel spelling patterns (*would, friend, heart,* for example). Their singularity within the *Let's Read* sequence is their irregularity, but they are integral to the common vocabulary and almost irreplaceable in English: Can one manage without the conditional *could, would,* or *should*? Is it possible to get by without *language, machine, nation, Russia,* or *question*? Though their written forms may be different, nonalphabetic, some of them comprise very large patterns and are prolific contributors to the basic English vocabulary.

SCOPE OF PART VI

- Group I: Irregular Consonant Spellings
  - *c* as in *cent, face*
  - *g* as in *gem, page*
  - *dg* as in *edge, bridge*
  - *k* (silent) as in *knee, knock*
  - *g* (silent) as in *gnaw, gnome*

- *w* (silent) as in *write, whole*
- *b* (silent) as in *lamb, doubt*
- *l* (silent) as in *talk, calm*
- *h* (silent) as in *hour, school, John*
- *t* (silent) as in *often, whistle*
- *n, c, th* (silent) as in *autumn, scene, clothes*
- *gh* (silent) as in *caught, high, bough, though, through*
- *gh* as in *rough*
- *ph* as in *phone, orphan*
- Group II: Irregular Vowel Spellings
  - value of *u* as in *put: woman, could*
  - value of *u* as in *cute: shoe, soup, fruit, beautiful, view*
  - value of *i* as in *pin: build, busy, pretty, hymn, sieve, spinach*
  - value of *ee* as in *beet: field, ceiling, people, key, gasoline*
  - value of *e* as in *bet: any, again, guess, bury, friend, leopard*
  - values of *a* as in *date* and *German: vein, obey, foreign*
  - values of *o* as in *note* and *aw* in *saw: soul, sew, broad*
  - value of *i* as in *bite: eye, buy, guide, island*
  - value of *ar* as in *car: heart, guard*
- Group III: Irregular Consonant and Vowel Combinations
  - as in *finger, angle, onion, Julia, champion, language; sure, Russia, ocean, special, anxious, machine, nation; rouge, measure, occasion, picture, question, soldier, education, exact*

These irregularities are best presented as patterns and learned as patterns without phonics-based apology for how they are spelled. The sheer volume of vocabulary in these lessons is a great help to pupils; it deemphasizes the deviation of the patterns in part VI from earlier patterns, making these irregularities appear quite logical.

Suggestions for the Teacher

In general, pupils have little difficulty with the new vocabulary of part VI. If difficulties do occur, by this time the teacher will have at the ready many tested ways to get around them.

The challenges of part VI for the pupil and, occasionally, the teacher are mainly: to accept sound-letter correlations that are both different and logical; to accept a range of pronunciation variations common to the vocabulary; and, sometimes, to learn new words and their meanings.

Suggested procedure:

1. The pupil is ready for more extended reading passages. While their purpose is to demonstrate the use of the vocabulary in narrative text, the stories certainly demand more attention to meaning than earlier connected reading. A pupil's interpretation of the stories will, of course, be at a level appropriate to his or her age and experience; therefore, when discussing a story, the teacher should keep the pupil's maturity in mind.

2. A pupil's enthusiasm for and desire to talk about a particular story is a good indicator of comprehension. Not all stories will be equally enthralling to a pupil, and this judgment will be reflected in the pupil's interpretation of them. In the interests of maintaining a high regard for the art of reading, therefore, it is probably the wiser course to discuss more fully the meaning of reading that captures a pupil's interest, which is not to say that a pupil should skip or gloss over what fails to measure up to his or her personal standard.

NOTES

1. *Additional activities.* Continue with whatever reinforcements and other activities seem appropriate or that the pupil likes to do. Surely for the computer-literate pupil, the computer can be a vehicle for practicing and using what has just been learned. However, as has been pointed out many times, ancillary activities are entirely optional and not an essential part of learning to read.

2. *Free reading.* Before finishing *Let's Read*, pupils usually try to read almost anything available. With completion of formal reading instruction in sight, it is a good time to take a trip to the library with the pupil to choose some books to read without supervision and just for fun. Youngsters often gobble up books and should be encouraged to do so. And they will enjoy getting to know the library as a personal resource for really independent reading.

cent	cedar	cell	recent	license
center	cease	cellar	recess	necessary
central		celery		
		celebrate	December	proceed

200

certain	grocer	cereal	city	cinder
certainly	grocery	sincere	cities	cinnamon
	groceries	sincerely	citizen	

cigar	decide	recite	circus	civilized
medicine		recital	circle	uncivilized
				narcissus

Grover Martin is my hero. He works for the Circle Grocery on Cedar Street. He works at the checkout counter. If you need something, Grover can tell you where it is. If somebody is sick and cannot get out to get groceries, Grover takes their groceries to them. He can drive because he got a license recently. Grover delivers newspapers on Sundays, too. He works very hard. He told me he's saving his money to study medicine.

But Grover is my hero because he helped me out when I needed help. He let me help with the newspaper deliveries and paid me to do it. I needed to earn money to buy a gift for my dad. Now that's what Grover is like. A really great pal.

A narcissus is a pretty white flower. The Greeks told a tale about it: There was a handsome man called Narcissus. He was vain. He liked to stare at himself in a pool of water. He was unable to cease looking at himself in the water and did not eat or drink. He vanished, and in his place grew a flower, called the narcissus.

ace	lace	race	brace	
face	place	trace	bracelet	
pace	space	Grace		

201

dice	rice	slice	ice	ice cream
mice	price	spice	vice	vice president
nice	twice	spicy	advice	
nicely				

peace	voice	sauce	scarce	truce	reduce
peaceful	choice	saucer	force	spruce	produce
fleece	rejoice		source		introduce

necklace	terrace	notice	practice	office
surface		justice	service	officer
palace			Alice	lettuce

Alice Dice

There was a cat who lived down the street from us. Her name was Alice—Alice Dice. Her owners, the Dices, had a very nice little house. Mostly Alice lay about on the terrace, sunning herself. She wore a red leather collar but pretended it was a necklace made of rubies. She pretended her house was a palace, too, and that she was the queen.

Most cats chase mice, but Alice took no notice of them, even when they ran under her nose. She claimed never to have eaten mice, even on lettuce.

dance	lance	France	chance	ounce
dancer	glance	prance	advance	bounce
				pounce
distance	pence	difference	since	pronounce
entrance	fence	Florence	wince	
attendance	sentence		prince	
allowance	absence	excellence	princess	once
importance	silence	excellent	principal	
ignorance				

202

Alice Dice Leaves Home

Alice was happy to leave the practice of catching mice to those uncivilized tomcats living in alleys. Then one day Mr. Harry Dice found a mouse staring at him from behind a loaf of bread. "This is too much," he bellowed. "Cats are supposed to catch mice." He tossed Alice out of the house and into the rain. Alice was shocked. She was being treated like a common alley cat. "The injustice!" she meowed.

What a difference to be tossed outside after living like a princess! Alice sat in silence for a long while, getting soaked. She decided she'd better find shelter. Alice jumped down from the steps and glanced back at the house in anger. "I'll show them," she said. "I'll be a princess somewhere else!" She pranced off down the path and slipped under the fence. She headed toward town, all the while thinking nasty things about Mr. Dice.

When Alice reached the Circle Market, she saw an open cellar window. She slipped inside to get out of the rain.

As she licked herself dry, Alice looked around the cellar. She saw cartons of products. She advanced along one row of boxes and read labels that said "Choice Quality" and "Produced in France."

(To be continued . . .)

gem	germ	gentle	gist	ginger
generous	German	gentleman	giant	gingerbread
George	Germany			

203

age	change	ranger	lounge	bulge
cage	exchange	manger	large	huge
page	range	danger	charge	urge
rage	arrange	dangerous		
wage	arrangement			magic
sage	angel	engine	imagine	vegetable
sagebrush	strange	engineer	pigeon	suggest
stagecoach	stranger			

More than a hundred years ago, a German gentleman came to America to visit the Wild West. He traveled by stagecoach and wagon and train. He saw the huge grasslands and giant mountains. He saw buffalo, eagles, and wild horses, farmers and cowhands. But he wanted most of all to see an outlaw.

One day, while riding in a bouncing wagon to the next railroad line, the gentleman got his wish. The wagon was suddenly halted. A bunch of lawless men on horseback surrounded it. The passengers had to get out. The outlaws waved guns in the air. One man took the German gentleman's watch. Before riding off, the outlaws tied up the passengers from the wagon.

The German gentleman said to himself, "Now I have really been in danger! This is the Wild West, indeed! Just what I was looking for!"

damage	garbage	sausage	cottage	college
savage	bandage		cabbage	
courage	postage	orange	village	energy
voyage	package			energetic

204

manage	passage	message	carriage
manager	passenger	messenger	marriage

Alice Dice Begins a New Life

"Don't touch that spice," said a voice above Alice. A big cat bounced to the floor. She seemed to be very energetic. "I'm Florence, and just who let you in?"

Alice explained how Mr. Dice had put her out in the rain. She tried to be polite, but it was hard. She had never had to explain herself before. And this cat had such a nasty tone of voice.

"Well, of all the nerve! Some humans!" said Florence. "You just sit down here, my dear. I'll be back after I've had a chat with Prince, our manager." When Florence came back, she showed Alice a saucer of milk hidden behind some boxes. "Now drink this, and then you can meet Prince."

When Alice had finished, Florence led her down a passage to Prince's office. It turned out that Prince was a dog. Alice lost all her courage. She trembled in the doorway. "Please come in, Alice," Prince said kindly. "Don't be shy."

Alice advanced slowly through the doorway. Prince seemed a different kind of dog. He was old and he wore spectacles. Alice wasn't afraid of him at all. Prince looked at her carefully. "You are pretty fancy. Maybe too much like a princess for our hard work here."

edge	budge	nudge	dodge	ridge
hedge	fudge	drudge	lodge	bridge
ledge	judge	trudge		
wedge	judgment	grudge	badge	fidget
		smudge	Madge	midget
			gadget	Bridget

205

Alice Dice Gets a Job

"Oh, I can succeed if you'll give me the chance," Alice replied. "I can see well in the dark," she added hopefully.

"How far can you pounce?" Prince asked. "How heavy is the heaviest mouse you can catch? Three ounces? Five ounces?" Alice had no answer because she had never chased mice.

"I can't hire you," Prince said. "Here, you have to catch mice and other intruders. You have to hunt them without mercy." Alice looked down after hearing Prince's judgment. But after thinking a moment, Prince asked, "Can you count? Can you use a pencil?"

"I can count, and I can work a pencil," Alice said. She had learned numbers when she lived with the Dices.

Another cat spoke from a ledge in the shadows. It was Madge, a small but powerful cat and an excellent mouser. "I think the principal thing is to want to do well," Madge said. "I say let her work the numbers, and I can give her some lessons in mousing. Then the council can vote on whether she stays or goes. We need another cat in attendance here after dark. The rats are increasing in number and boldness." She nudged Prince. "What's the harm in giving her a chance?"

And so it was settled. Alice was to learn to be a store cat. She helped Prince keep track of the supplies in the storeroom. Also, Madge and Cecil, a champion pouncer, tried to teach Alice how to pounce and catch.

But Alice was a flop. She was certain she was going to be asked to leave Circle Market Security, as the group called itself. But Cecil and Madge liked Alice. They said they were going to tell the others on the council to let her stay.

The evening of the meeting, Alice waited on top of some boxes outside Prince's office with her pencil and ledger. She was very sad, thinking about leaving.

Alice heard Prince's chair squeak. She knew he was getting up to leave for the meeting. Then she heard a scratchy voice shouting from the doorway. "You flea-bitten old bag of bones, we've come to take this joint over. You're too old to keep this job." As Alice watched, a troop of rats burst into the office, overturned the desk, and broke Prince's glasses. Now Prince was unable to see a thing!

An icy chill ran down Alice's back. She sprang to her feet. Her paws began to sweat. Suddenly she slipped off the boxes and fell smack into the middle of the rats crowded in the doorway of the office. She landed on top of three big rats and they crashed to the floor.

205

knot	knit	knelt	knife	knew
knob	knitted	knee	knives	know
doorknob	knock	kneel	jackknife	known
				unknown

206

Alice Saves the Day

As other rats began to circle around her, Alice grabbed her pencil. Without thinking, she used it as a lance, dancing about, poking the pencil this way and that, jabbing at the beasts. Soon, she had backed all of the rats into a corner!

The next thing Alice saw was Cecil, Florence, Frances, and Nancy—a cat from the drugstore—dashing into the office. Fur flew everywhere. Loud squeaks filled the air, and suddenly a bunch of rats lay huddled in the center of the office. The cats were all kneeling on the squealing, squeaking rats. Then they netted up the crooks. Alice looked at the rats with disgust and helped knot the strings to the net.

After the cats tied the prisoners' net to the doorknob, Prince asked Alice to come into his office. "Alice," he said," "I know you're a terrible pouncer and a really bad mouser. But you are good with numbers, and you're very good with a lance. You are also brave. Alice, you saved the day. I'd like you to join Circle Market Security. What do you say?"

Alice said yes. She knew that at last she had found her place in the world.

gnat   gnaw   gnome   sign   campaign

gnash   gnarled   gnu

207

A new gnu has come to the zoo. His name is Moo Gnu and he came all the way from southeastern Africa. He's got big curved horns and a long beard. He looks a bit like an antelope. He also has a waggy tail with a big tuft of fur at its tip.

One lazy summer day, Becca said to Nancy, "I'd like sitting out here on the lawn if it weren't for these nasty gnats." Nancy agreed. She was lounging in the hammock. "They just keep gnawing on me. I think they wait in the trees gnashing their teeth. When they see me, they say, 'Here comes Nancy. Time for dinner.'"

"How can we get rid of them?" Becca wondered. "They just love insect spray. They gulp it down like lemonade!"

"And they're too small to swat," added Nancy.

Just then, Katy came by. She had heard the girls' complaints. "Why don't you just put up a sign?" she asked, "that says 'NO GNATS ALLOWED!' That will keep them away!"

"No," said Becca. "Those stupid gnats can't read."

wrap	wren	wrist	wrung	sword
wrapped	wrench	wring	wrong	
	wreck	wringer		answer

208

write	writing	wrote	typewriter	whole
writer	written		handwriting	

Steve broke his wrist. Now it's wrapped in a cast, and Steve cannot write. His handwriting was never very clear, but now it's impossible to read. So here's Steve with no way to write, which he likes to do. He wishes he had his computer, but it's back home. And besides, he's living in a cabin this summer and has no electricity to run a computer. He can't go hiking or swimming, either, because of his cast. Now he's getting very grumpy sitting around with nothing to do but read.

He goes out to the shed behind the cabin. He just wants to poke around. He finds old paint cans and stiff brushes, bits of chain and rope, boxes of screws and nails. There's an old engine. Then he spies a typewriter. "A typewriter! The perfect answer to my problem!" he says to himself.

The machine is so old, it doesn't work at all. It's clogged with dust and grease. So Steve lugs the typewriter outside and cleans it. Then he oils it. He takes it indoors and sets it on a table. He puts a ribbon in it. Now Steve has the perfect machine. He can type with his good hand, and he doesn't need any electricity!

| dumb | crumb | lamb | comb | debt |
| numb | thumb | limb | climb | doubt |

209

Once upon a time there was a little girl who was very lonely. She lived with grown-ups who were always busy. They had no time to stop and play with her. So she used to go to the woods to find company. She watched the animals, the birds flying from tree to tree or the little field mice that scurried among the leaves. She really liked the squirrels, always climbing trees and jumping from limb to limb. The animals were busy, too, but the little girl felt less lonely when she was with them.

After a few days, she began to bring some old, dry bread with her and broke it into crumbs. She scattered the crumbs on the ground. At first the animals were too shy to come near the girl. But gradually they became bolder. The little girl scattered crumbs each day until the winter snow came. All the animals retreated to their nests and dens. The little girl had to stay in her house, just like the animals.

In the spring, she went back to the woods. The little girl was certain the animals did not remember her. But just as if by magic, when she stooped down to scatter her crumbs, the animals began to creep toward her. They seemed to be glad to see her again. And she was happy to be among her small pals.

walk	sidewalk	calf	calm	alms	yolk
talk	beanstalk	calves	calmly	almond	folks
stalk	cornstalk	half	palm		polka
chalk		halves			polka dot

210

I am Jack Crow. I live in southern California. I love palm trees, and where I live, there are lots of them. Palm trees are very tall. They sway in the wind. Some palm trees look like giant skinny sticks with fuzzy tops. If I sit in one of them, I can see for miles and miles around me. I can see cockroaches and other bugs crawling on the ground. Then I can swoop down and catch them. I can see humans on the sidewalk. They drop food and paper. I snatch the food. I like to eat the nuts and berries that hang from the tops of the palms. When I'm perching in a palm, I can also keep an eye out for other birds. I shout at them to keep them away because I don't want to share my food.

Jenny is a cow. She had two calves this spring. One calf is a girl named Dolly. She has big brown eyes. The boy calf is called Rufus. Rufus is very handsome. He will grow into a very big bull.

Sometimes I wonder about words. They are so strange! One queer thing is the word polka. That's a kind of jumpy dance. But I cannot understand why we say "polka dots." Polka dots don't dance. They are colorful spots on something, like an umbrella or a scarf. Probably long ago the dancers doing the polka had dots on their costumes.

honest	John	oh	school	schoolboy
honesty	Johnny	ah	scheme	schoolteacher
honestly	Johnson	hurrah		schoolhouse
honor			ache	schoolbook
hour	Thomas		headache	schoolroom
	Thomson		toothache	schooltime
ghost	Thompson			schoolwork
				schoolgirl

211

A Ghost Story

There are not a lot of big old houses still standing these days, but there is one big old house not far down the road from us. Nobody lives in it now, so kids often play in it after school. One day Johnny Johnson and his chum, Thomas Thomson, hopped on their bikes to explore the old house. Just as they got inside, it began to rain. Johnny and Thomas looked for some wood to make a fire in one of the fireplaces.

"That's some rain," said Johnny. "I'm glad we got here before it started!"

"Me, too," said Thomas. "But we can't stay here too long, or somebody will worry." Tommy said this because he was feeling a little scared. The house was getting darker as the clouds got blacker, and the wind was blowing, too. The boys began to sing, just to keep their courage up.

listen	often	fasten	castle	bustle	gristle
Christmas	soften		nestle	hustle	whistle
		hasten	jostle	rustle	bristles
				mustn't	

212

The Small Ghost

As the boys sat before the fire, Tommy stopped singing and began to listen. Outside he could hear the wind whistle through the tree branches. He wasn't certain, but had he heard a noise inside, too? The sound of a door closing upstairs? He felt the hair on his head stand up like the bristles on a brush. Thomas was scared. The stairs began to creak. He and Johnny hastened to the door. The latch was stuck! The door was fastened shut!

Johnny turned to look. There on the stairs was a ghost. It wasn't an awfully big ghost, but even a ghost just one foot tall was still a ghost. When the boys realized how small the ghost was, they forgot to shout with terror.

In fact, the boys were so curious that they walked toward the ghost. The ghost also edged a little closer to them. As the three of them stood there looking at each other, a tear rolled down the ghost's face. Next he began to sob. "I've got a awful toothache, nothing stops it from aching," he said. "I used to be a whistling ghost; everybody called me 'The Whistler,' but now it hurts my tooth too much to blow air between my teeth. Listen!"

He made a windy sound, not whistle.

autumn   clothes   scent   scissors   muscle
column   scene   science

Ghost Troubles Improve

So the ghost told the boys all his troubles. He told them about his toothache and about the people who were coming in autumn to fix up the house and live in it.

He said life for him was looking bad. He sometimes didn't even have a clean sheet to put on in the morning. He was running out of clothes. Sometimes he felt like taking scissors and cutting his sheets into little bits just so he'd not be seen.

"You mustn't talk that way," said Tommy. "You're just feeling bad because your tooth aches. Let us pull it."

Johnny and Thomas got the ghost to sit down. They began to work on the aching tooth. You can imagine that it was a very funny scene with Thomas trying to pull the bad tooth. Johnny tried to hold the ghost down, but the ghost kept slipping between his hands, for, as you know, nobody can hold a ghost down. But finally, after much pushing and wiggling, the tooth began to budge. Then, pulling with all of his muscle power, Tommy got the tooth out.

"Hurrah!" yelled Johnny. "What a tooth. It was like a stone column. I hope you don't ever have another toothache."

213

Then Johnny pulled Thomas over to a corner of the room and whispered in his ear for a moment. Thomas nodded, and they walked back to the little ghost.

213

It was Johnny who did the talking. "If things are looking so bad for you, and you're going to be driven out by the new owners of the house, maybe you can come and spend the winter with us, in my house and in Tommy's."

"I don't know. What if it isn't safe for me in your houses?"

"Oh, you'll be perfectly safe. My dog won't find you, because you have no scent. And Tommy doesn't have a dog. Please, come and give it a try, just until Christmas. If you don't like it, you can leave."

So it was arranged. The ghost moved in with Johnny and then Tommy. He stayed until Christmas was over. Johnny's dog was not the problem. It was Thomas's cat, who sniffed out the ghost and chased him every day. It was simply too tiring.

Did the boys miss their ghostly chum? Of course they did. Did they ever forget him? Of course they did not.

caught	slaughter	ought	bought	straight
taught		fought	brought	straighten
daughter	naughty	sought	thought	

Mrs. Whiskers had a naughty little daughter. Even if she was a cat, her daughter's behavior made her anxious. Mrs. Whiskers was an excellent mother. She had taught Violet everything she ought to know to go out into the world. And Violet was a good student, but she liked to daydream. She liked to imagine herself working a computer, keeping a pet mouse, going on a trip, taking an airplane, or going to the moon. Mrs. Whiskers thought Violet ought to think about other things.

Frank is not naughty very often. But when he's naughty, he's really bad.

If you straighten your room, you put away all your stuff.
If your teeth are crooked, a dentist can straighten them.

I bought a big bunch of tulips with my own money. I brought them to my mother.

The cat and dog fought so much that we thought they hated each other. But when the cat got lost, the dog was sad and lonely. He was happy when the cat came back.

214

high	sigh	fight	right	tighten
higher	thigh	light	fright	frighten
highest		might	bright	
highly	sight	night	flight	lightness
highness	tight		slight	brightness
			knight	

215

highway	height	flashlight	tonight
lightning	heights	sunlight	midnight
		moonlight	delight
mighty		overnight	

Hocus Pocus Thomas

One very dark night, Tommy had a visitor from a different planet. The visitor brought him secret powers. That is how Tommy began to play tricks on his family and his pals. All he had to do was to think of a trick, say, "Abracadabra, hocus pocus, zip," and the trick happened.

His brother, Francis, was always picking on him. So Tommy played a trick on him. His magic powers let him keep filling up Francis's plate with pancakes. Their mother said, "Francis, eat up your pancakes! What's the matter, don't you like them?" Francis said, "I like them, all right. I've eaten ten, and you keep putting more on my plate!"

Tommy laughed to himself.

bough

More Hocus Pocus

Next Tommy made some calves appear in Francis's closet.
Francis opened the door and yelled. Tommy secretly laughed. Then
Francis came rushing downstairs to tell his mother that the house
had gone crazy. He had calves in his closet and one of them was
eating his schoolwork! Tommy thought that trick went very well.

216

Tommy's father was not so pleased. "I don't know what you're
up to, Thomas," he said. "But I must tell you that your tricks are not
funny at all. In fact, they're giving me a headache. When I get home
tonight, I expect no more tricks. Do you understand?"

Tommy felt a little ashamed, but not very ashamed. "I'm sorry,
Father," he said. "I won't play more tricks. Really."

"Good," said his father. "Now, off to school with you. And
tuck in your shirt and tighten your belt. You look like a fright!"

On the way to school, Tommy thought about the trick he had
played on his brother and chuckled. He thought about that so much
that he forgot to walk fast. He walked slowly instead, smiling and
whistling. He even stopped to swing on the bough of a tree.

Of course, he was late to school. I'm in trouble, he thought.
If I can't think of a trick to play on Miss Bridget, she'll send me to
the principal's office. He thought of a great trick. "I'll be a knight in
shining armor. That will keep me out of the principal's office!" So
he said, "Abracadabra, hocus pocus, zip!" and opened the door to
his classroom.

dough	doughnut
though	although
thorough	thoroughly

217

The End of Hocus Pocus Thomas

Everybody gaped at Tommy. He strode into the room saying, "I'm sorry, Miss Bridget, to be late. But this armor is heavy, and it slowed me down."

Miss Bridget was not amused. "What kind of trick is this? I'm thoroughly disgusted with you!" Her voice got louder and louder. It sounded oddly like his mother's. "Tommy, Tommy! Come now! What sort of trick are you playing?"

Tommy opened his eyes, confused. "It's after seven o'clock," his mother said, "and you are still in bed. Get up and get dressed. We have fresh doughnuts for breakfast this morning." She went back downstairs.

"Aha," Tommy said to himself. "That abracadabra stuff was all a dream."

Tommy realized that he had no magic at all. Nobody had the magic to make things happen just by thinking about them.

through   throughout

Nancy Wonders about School

Nancy was six years old. She was going to start school in the autumn. All through the summer she talked about it and wondered how it would be. Toward the end of the summer, she became more excited than ever and began asking her big sister all sorts of things.

218

"Will school be fun?" she asked Franny.

"Well, yes," said Franny. "You will have fun at school. You will have to work, though."

Nancy thought about that for a while. Then she asked, "What kind of work? Will I have to take out garbage and sweep the floors? Maybe I had better take along my own broom."

"No," said Franny, smiling. "You won't have to sweep out the schoolroom or empty the rubbish. Each night Mr. Beasley sweeps the school throughout."

"Cooking?" asked Nancy. "I can cook sausage."

"No cooking," said Franny. "Mrs. Cooper and her daughter fix lunches for everyone. And we seldom have sausage."

"Then how will I work? What kind of work?" Now Nancy was very puzzled.

"Schoolwork," Franny told her. "And that is something no one else can ever do for you!"

rough	cough	laugh
tough	trough	laughing
enough		laughter

219

Westward, Ho!

Years and years ago Americans did not live from coast to coast as they do now. West of the Mississippi River was the land of the great buffalo herds. The grass there was tall, the mountains were high; there were no farms and no cities on the Great Plains.

In those days, people wanted to move there to start farming. Even though very few people knew much about the geography of the west, they wanted to make the tough and dangerous trip there. The Jacobs family was one of those groups of settlers.

Mr. Jacobs had read about settling the west in a newspaper. The family decided to leave New York. First Mr. and Mrs. Jacobs sold almost everything they had. Then they and their children took a train to the small settlement where they would begin their journey in a wagon train.

The railway trip was hot and dusty. All of the passengers were covered with soot from the engine's smoke and cinders. The train stopped often to take on water and to allow the passengers to eat. But the Jacobs were excited to be starting a new life.

The settlement, really a small town, was not as civilized as New York. People's manners were rough, but folks were cheerful. There was much shouting and laughter. The citizens dressed differently. But the Jacobs did not mind. They were busy getting the wagon and enough supplies to last on their journey west. They needed warm clothes, boots, hats, blankets, pans and pots, tin cups, and most of all a strong wagon and strong oxen to pull it.

Phil	phone	photo	telegraph	autograph
Philip	telephone	photograph	paragraph	phonograph
		photographer	geography	

	Ralph	orphan	elephant
	Joseph	hyphen	nephew

220

Wagon Train

The Jacobs were going to travel with a group of settlers from Kentucky. The wagon train was to be led by Mr. Thompson, a tall man who had already made other trips with settlers going west. He told Mr. Jacobs and his family about the dangers of the trip. He also showed them how to pack the wagon and how to manage the oxen. The members of the Jacobs family might not have known a lot about the geography of the west, but they understood the dangers of the trip and were certainly excited about going west. Before leaving, the Jacobs had their photographs taken. They also camped outside town, to practice living in a wagon.

Finally the Kentucky settlers arrived and the wagons got arranged into a long line. Slowly they began to move. The wagons creaked and groaned; whips cracked in the air to spur the oxen; people chattered with excitement. At last, they were going west!

The first week of the journey was like going to school. The settlers learned how to manage the oxen. They learned to cook meals over a fire and not to waste water. It was a hard life. But each day, the settlers saw something wonderful. Sometimes a settler went hunting and got meat for the others. Sometimes people had fights. Sometimes people got sick and the wagon train had to move ahead without them.

woman	wolf	could	couldn't	he would	he'd
	wolves	would	wouldn't	they would	they'd
		should	shouldn't	I would	I'd
				you would	you'd

221

Sick on the Trail

One of the Jacobs boys, Phil, got measles, which makes a person very sick. He had a high fever and was covered with spots. He hurt all over. Mr. Thompson told Mr. Jacobs that he had to leave the Jacobs behind. You see, Mr. Thompson couldn't risk the rest of the settlers' health and safety for just one wagon. So the Jacobs were on their own. Mr. Jacobs hoped to catch up with the other wagons when Phil got better, but now he and his family were alone. It was lonely and dangerous, and at night when the wolves began to howl, it was scary, too.

After a few days, the Jacobs could not travel at all. Phil was too sick. Mr. Jacobs and Max, the older boy, guarded the wagon and hunted for food. Mrs. Jacobs and Clara, Phil's sister, took care of Phil.

One day, a band of riders and ponies surrounded the Jacobs' wagon, shouting and yelling. They were braves. One man jumped from his pony into the wagon where Phil was lying. Mrs. Jacobs grabbed Clara, and Phil suddenly stood up. The man saw that Phil was covered with spots. He and the others feared the settlers' sicknesses. The man jumped back onto his pony and the braves rode off like a shot. But one of them stopped a short way from the wagon. He told Mr. Jacobs to give him what was in the wagon, but to keep Phil away from them. Mr. Jacobs gave him some chairs, which the brave accepted. Best of all, no one got hurt.

two	lose	prove	shoe	remove	movement
who	loser	move	canoe	improve	improvement
who's		movie		approve	
whose					

222

Back to the Trail

As Phil got better, the Jacobs could go further each day. Each morning Mr. Jacobs or Ralph, the older son, hunted for quail or rabbit. If they didn't catch something, the family just had corn mush and dried beef to eat. And each day, of course, they had to fill their water bags.

One day, Mr. Jacobs went out to hunt for quail. He was thinking about how tasty the birds would be. He was lucky and got two birds to take back to the wagon. Then he saw a third bird lying dead behind a rock. "Whose bird is that?" he wondered. He didn't remember shooting three of them. As he got nearer to it, he saw that it had an arrow in it. "That means a hunter is near," he thought. Just then he spotted a tall man with a bow and arrow looking around, probably for the bird. Mr. Jacobs snatched the bird, grabbed his own quail, and ran as fast as he could back toward the wagon.

"Who's hungry?" he called out as he approached their camp. After eating the tasty birds, Mr. Jacobs told his family how foolish it was to go off hunting when they were all alone, without any help on those huge, vast plains.

soup	Lou	juice	beauty
soupy	Louis	juicy	beautiful
group	St. Louis	fruit	
wound		suit	view
youth		nuisance	review

223

Through a River

The Jacobs were trying to catch up to the rest of the wagon train. They had to travel farther and longer each day to reach their goal. It was hard work for the oxen and for the family. And there was always danger someplace. Each person had to be extra careful. But so far, they had been lucky. The wagon rumbled along, and it was quite a peaceful journey for the Jacobs.

Sometimes they found fruits to eat along the trail. One day, Clara found a bush filled with juicy, beautiful blueberries. The family feasted on them for two whole days!

A few days later, though, the Jacobs came to a halt. There, in front of their wagon, was a wide river. They knew it was also a long river because they had seen it on the map. They would have to cross it with their oxen and their wagon. This would be their biggest challenge.

Mr. Jacobs looked for the best place to ford the river. He and the boys led the oxen across first. One of them slipped and nearly went under the water. But in the end, they got safely across. With ropes hitched to the oxen on one side and to the wagon on the other side of the river, the Jacobs got the wagon through the river. Everything was wet. One chest was lost. But everyone was safe. The family felt quite proud. And they named the oxen in honor of their loyalty and bravery. One was called "Hero" and the other "Beauty."

build	busy	pretty	system	cycle
building	busily	sieve	mystery	cyclist
built	business	women	sympathy	unicycle
guilt			hymn	bicycle
guilty			physical	tricycle
			lynx	recycle
				recyclable

224

A Westerly Cloud

The Jacobs family rested for one day after fording the river. Hero and Beauty munched grass. The wet clothes and blankets began to dry. The cover on the wagon was pulled back to allow the things inside to dry.

The next day, the family started out at dawn. Mr. Jacobs was pretty certain the wagon train was near, and he wanted to reach it. And he was right. They passed by the remains of a campsite left by the other settlers. For a week, Hero and Beauty and the Jacobs family pushed ahead. The whole family walked alongside the wagon to make it lighter.

Each day they thought they would see the other settlers ahead. Each day was a disappointment. But then, when they weren't thinking about it, ahead they saw a puff of smoke. Or was it? No, it was a cloud of dust stirred up by the wagons ahead. The Jacobs family had made it! They were back with the wagon train! The women and men and children of the wagon train all shouted and waved and welcomed them back.

spinach	mischief	minute	biscuit
	mischievous		minutes

225

When I want to give everyone a treat, I bake a batch of biscuits. It only takes a few minutes.

Spinach was a mischievous rabbit. She got her name because of her mischief. It was always a mystery to Bonnie and Jack how that little rabbit could get out of her pen. It was supposed to be rabbit-proof. But she did get out. All the time. She would get out of her pen, raid the spinach patch in the garden, and then return in minutes to her pen. And that's how she came to be called Spinach.

I am going to be the greatest cyclist in the whole wide world. I have a system for building up my muscles. I ride my bicycle up hills each day. And each day my legs get stronger and stronger. I just wish the hills weren't so steep and long. It's hard work to become the greatest cyclist in the whole wide world.

The circus clowns rode unicycles and went so fast we thought they'd end up in a huge pile-up.

Some garbage is good for compost. Some trash can be recycled.

field	chief	brief	belief	niece
yield	thief	grief	believe	piece
shield	thieves	grieve	relief	apiece
airfield			relieve	fierce

neither	receive	key	Louise
either	deceive	ski	police
ceiling		people	

magazine   gasoline   automobile

226

Going to Montana!

Madge and Lou Field were waiting for a letter. They had written to their Aunt Louise to see if they could work on her ranch. Their mother had explained to Aunt Louise that the children believed they could help out. They were city children. Living on the ranch would be exciting and different for them.

Finally, a letter came. The children were to go to Montana to spend the summer with Aunt Louise and Uncle John. Uncle John was a retired police chief. Aunt Louise was a good cook. Madge and Lou believed they were the luckiest people on earth!

again	any	anyhow	anywhere	anybody
against	many	anyway	anything	anyone

friend	friendly	guess	leopard	bury
friendship	unfriendly	guest	Leonard	

227

Ranch Lessons

Uncle John met Madge and Lou at the airfield. They had to drive over a mountain pass to get to the ranch. Madge noticed how the pine trees scented the air with their perfume. "You'll smell something even better when we get to the ranch," Uncle John said. "Aunt Louise's hot cakes and sausage!"

After breakfast, Uncle John took Madge and Lou to meet Leonard, who worked on the ranch. Leonard explained that the kids could be a big help. But first, to get around the ranch, they would have to learn to ride a horse. And to milk a cow. And to keep the calves from drinking all the milk from the buckets. One calf knocked Madge down he was so eager to get at the milk. At first the kids were very clumsy. But Leonard was a good teacher. Soon Lou could milk a cow almost as well as Leonard. Madge wasn't quite so good, but with practice, she and Lou each milked a cow as fast as Leonard milked the other two cows. The children learned quickly which animals were friendly and which to stay away from.

grey	vein	sleigh	eight	neighbor
prey	reins	weigh	eighty	neighborhood
hey	reindeer	weight	eighth	foreign
obey	reign	freight	eighteen	foreigner

228

Ready to Ride

Soon after Madge and Lou got to the ranch, Uncle John went to town to pick up some packages from the railroad freight office. After dinner, the kids and Uncle John undid the packages. In them were reins and saddles and saddle blankets and strong boots for both Madge and Lou. "Oh, thank you, thank you, Uncle John," both Madge and Lou shouted. "Just what we need to ride those ponies."

Uncle John and Aunt Louise looked pleased. Aunt Louise said that now Madge and Lou could really join the ranch workforce. Now they would be able to ride from one end of the ranch to the other.

When Lou went to sleep that night, he dreamed of chasing cattle and thieves. When Madge went to sleep, she dreamed about how she and her pony would become best friends.

The next morning, Lou and Madge came into the kitchen to find Aunt Louise waiting for them. "There's been a problem, and you two will have to help us out," she said. Lou said, bravely, "But Aunt Louise, that's why we're here."

Aunt Louise smiled and told the children that Uncle John and their neighbor had gone out to see if Leonard was all right. He was camping out, watching the cattle and there'd been a high wind in the night. "You two might have to do some of Leonard's chores for him," she warned the children.

soul   sew   broad   broadcast
shoulder   abroad

Real Ranching

229

"Here they come," yelled Madge, who had been watching for her uncle out the window. They all ran to the porch and saw Leonard lean on Uncle John's shoulder and limp to the house.

Uncle John told Aunt Louise to call Doc Stitch. He needs to sew up Len's leg. "Can't you just call 911?" Lou asked. Aunt Louise just laughed. "No 911 out here!"

Madge, Lou, and the neighbor, Mr. Broadbeam, helped Uncle John settle Leonard onto the couch. Leonard was hurt pretty badly. Uncle John said, "Well, it could have been much worse. Len's lucky. The cattle got spooked in the wind and one of them tramped on Len's leg." Then, looking at Lou and Madge, he said, "Now, you two will have to pitch in right away. You'll have to learn everything on the job, now, right now!"

And that's how Madge and Lou got into their saddles and out on the range right away. They found the cattle grazing peacefully in a nice valley full of grass. A river ran through the middle of it. They camped near the river and built a fire. Uncle John showed them how to do it and how to make it right for heating branding ions. Tomorrow they would be branding the calves. They ate next to the campfire. It was cold at night in the mountains. Both Madge and Lou were tired. Lou went to crawl into his sleeping bag and heard a buzzing noise. Uncle John jumped up and ordered Lou and Madge to the other side of the fire.

"What's wrong?" Len asked. Uncle John showed him. It was a big rattlesnake that had curled up at the bottom of the sleeping bag. "See what can happen on the range?" Uncle John asked. "You have to watch and be careful all the time." Lou dreamed of snakes all night long.

They saddled up the next morning and began to drive the cattle into the narrow part of the valley. Lou rode along one side of the steers and Madge on the other. Uncle John rode at the back of the herd. Now the cattle were hemmed in by the mountains on either side.

They separated the calves from the herd and began to brand them. Madge didn't like it at all. But Uncle John explained it was the only way to show which cattle belonged each ranch. It was like dog tags, but a bit more scary because the brand is burned into the calf's fur.

The city cowboys stayed on the range for three days. In the middle of the third night, Uncle John woke up to see a cow moving uneasily with her calf beside her. Then he saw a sleek shadow moving around the herd. By this time, all the cattle were standing up and moving about. All of them seemed worried. By now the cattle had begun to move in a circle. All of them were anxious.

Uncle John woke up Madge and Lou and instructed them to get up and onto their ponies as quietly as possible. He was planning to circle around the cattle to calm them down. But suddenly the cattle began to move wildly. Their hooves raised a choking cloud of dust. The cattle were bellowing with fear and running this way and that.

229

buy	eye	guide	island	isle
guy	eyebrow			aisle

Danger on the Range

230

By galloping to the wider part of the valley, Uncle John hoped to turn the herd around. He galloped to the front of the herd to head them off. But the cattle were afraid. They simply wanted to run away. The only way to stop them was for Uncle John to fire his rifle into the air. The shots made a huge, cracking noise. The cattle headed the opposite way. Lou and Madge and Uncle John were able to control them now. They rode around the herd to keep them from turning and running again. The cattle began to move in a circle and quiet down.

Lou was the first to get back to the campsite, just as the first streaks of daylight brightened the sky. He could see that most of the herd was standing or lying down. Lou slipped off his pony. It had been quite a night! Soon Uncle John and Madge rode up. The children helped their uncle build a fire and fix breakfast. While they ate, each of them kept an eye on the herd.

Although the cattle were calm, Uncle John told the city cowboys that they had to leave this beautiful campsite and move the herd to other fields. "But Uncle John," Lou protested. "You promised to let us explore the island in the river today."

heart   hearth   guard

sweetheart   lifeguard

Real Cowboys, at Last!

"Sorry, kids," said Uncle John. "An old mountain lion lives on that island. I thought maybe he had died, but I saw him last night. That's what spooked the cattle. You're not going to explore there, believe me! That guy may be too old to kill a cow, but he's not too old to spook a whole herd. And we can't be lifeguards for a bunch of edgy cows."

So the city cowboys and their uncle headed back toward the ranch with the herd. When they got to the edge of the ranch, Aunt Louise was waiting for them. Mr. Broadbeam and Len were there, too, and took over driving the herd.

Aunt Louise insisted first the cowboys have a bath. Then she gave them a grand dinner. "Well, you'll have a lot to tell your parents, won't you? You'll probably be glad to get back to the city."

"Oh, no, Aunt Louise," both children exclaimed. "We'd like to stay here forever. The city is no place for real cowboys like us!"

231

longer	younger	anger	tangle	finger	England
longest	hunger	angry	dangle	jingle	English
stronger	hungry		jangle	tingle	
strongest			angle	single	
			jungle	shingle	

232

Needles

Any kind of food is the main thing, if you are hungry. My younger brother used to catch birds or mice or even rats, but hunger never drove me to do that.

My name is Needles. In England, a place across the sea where I lived when I was new, there was a boy who used to pinch my tail in his fingers when he was bored. It made my tail tingle, and I'd get so angry I scratched him. That English boy must have been crazy!

I know dogs are crazy. They run and jump around making loud noises. That just jangles my nerves. They obey people, too. Being a cat, I do not obey anyone. If I am called, I only come when I think I might get something to eat. I move so slowly I don't jingle the bell on my collar.

When I was young, I liked to play with a ball of yarn. I would get in an awful tangle. The English woman I lived with would scold me. And I liked to play with the little English girl. I would pounce on her shoulder. The girl complained, "The kitten is digging its claws into my shoulder! Ouch!" Then her mother would say, "I hope we don't have to give this kitten away. But we can't keep it if it scratches."

onion	junior	familiar	Julia	California
million	senior	peculiar	Celia	Pennsylvania
companion	behavior		America	Virginia
			William	Italian

233

Daniel   convenient   convenience

To America?

One day a man from America visited the English woman I called "Mrs. Meanie." Mrs. Meanie was complaining about me to him. So he said, "Julia, ask my daughter, Amelia, if she wants this kitten. Since she's one of your companions at school, you could ask her at recess or lunch."

Now Julia was the English woman's little girl, and I did not like her at all. But I did want to meet this Amelia person.

The next day, Julia brought Amelia home to meet me. I liked Amelia right away. She did not dangle things in front of me to tease. Her behavior was good, for a human, and so I jumped up on her shoulder and perched there at an angle.

"Hey," Amelia said, "your little claws are sticking into my shoulder. They feel like a million tiny little needles. I am going to call you 'Needles.'"

So, when Amelia went home, I went home with her. In Amelia's family I discovered two boys called William and Daniel. William was the senior—that means he was older than Daniel. Both William and Daniel, the junior brother, were kind to me. The whole family was kind!

One day the father said, "We must go back to California. And Needles, I'm afraid, will have to go to another family."

Amelia wanted to take me with her and made a speech. She said, "If Needles stays, I stay! Leave dear Needles because of convenience? Pooh! Convenient or not, I love her."

233

We traveled for a long time. We went to Pennsylvania. I didn't like it there. It was too cold. But once we got to California, I liked it right away, because it's warm. I am on my best behavior, and if I leave a claw out, Amelia is never angry. "Needles," she says, "keep your needles to yourself!"

Sometimes Amelia holds me up and says, "I can tell the time by Needles' eyes. Early in the morning and in the evening the black part in the center of Needles' eyes is round. But at noontime the black part of her eyes is just a narrow slit."

I wonder if Amelia can really tell the time by looking at my eyes?

Now, Amelia's brothers have a dog. They call her Virginia.

I was afraid Virginia and I might tangle, but she came up to me and sniffed. Then she said, very plainly, "Why, you're a cat! Put your claws away, and we'll be friends." I didn't have to fight with her. But, like all dogs, Virginia is a little crazy.

So I have learned to obey—at least sometimes. And I like a few humans. I even like crazy Virginia, except when she eats some of my food. And I really, really love Amelia. For a cat, I think I've made a lot of changes to please others.

India   Indian   radio   period   Muriel
Columbia   guardian
Philadelphia   champion   obedient   language
Sylvia

234

curious   furious   serious   glorious

Daniel Montour

Daniel Montour was a boy who lived in the state of Wisconsin more than two hundred years ago, long before the time of computers or TV or trucks and cars. Back then there wasn't even a state of Wisconsin. There were no railroads or roads of any kind. There were just a few settlements of farmers and traders in the middle of Indian country.

Daniel and his sister, Sylvia, and their parents, had come from the city of Philadelphia. The family had built their house on the bank of the Fox River. Here there was a settlement of just five houses. And just like the Indians who lived in this mostly empty land, the settlers traveled on foot through the woods or by canoe on the rivers. It took a whole day to get to the nearest town of Portage.

When Daniel was seven years old, his father took him to visit his uncle and aunt and cousins. They lived near Portage. Daniel had such a good time he didn't want to leave. He pleaded with his father to let him stay just for another week. And so it was that Daniel's father agreed to let him stay for another week. He would travel home in a big canoe with a man who would act as his guardian on the trip.

sure	insure	issue	Russia	discussion
surely	insurance		Russian	
sugar				

235

Daniel Goes Home

At the end of the week, these men came and Daniel's guardian put Daniel in their canoe for the trip home. It was a glorious, clear and bright day, and Daniel was glad to be going home. The group had paddled only a few hours when they were attacked by robbers.

Some of the robbers took the canoe and all the things in it. The others led Daniel and the men into the woods. They walked all day long. Daniel felt as if he had walked all the way to Russia. He didn't know where they were going. He just knew they were going farther and farther into the woods. And he wondered how he could escape and find the river.

When night came, the robbers camped around a fire. They tied up the men, but they did not tie Daniel up. They thought he was too little to run away. And Daniel tricked them into thinking he was obedient, so they would not watch him.

As the men sat around the fire, Daniel heard them talk of selling him and the other men as slaves in Indiana.

special   social   commercial

specially   financial   official

ancient   precious   appreciate   suspicious   physician

sufficient   gracious   suspicion   ocean

236

A Brave Escape

When Daniel was sure the men had fallen asleep, he ran off into the woods. He ran at a furious pace as far as he could, and then he rested. He began to run again, afraid that the robbers might catch him. He did not know where he was going. It was just important to keep moving. But when he was too tired to go another step, he lay down under a tree and fell asleep.

Daniel was awakened by someone pulling at his coat. He was sure it was one of the robbers, but a man was leaning over him. He was an Indian. Daniel knew many Native Americans because they came to his house. Most of the people who lived in that part of the country were Indians. Still, the man was a stranger, so Daniel had reason to be suspicious.

"Hello," said Daniel bravely. "I am Daniel Montour. Some robbers took us off into the woods. I ran away and now I am lost. Please help me get back home."

machine   mustache   Michigan   anxious

machinery   Chicago   anxiously

Daniel Meets a New Family

237

The stranger only smiled and shook his head. Daniel saw that the man didn't understand him. This made Daniel afraid. He said to himself, "Now the issue is to get away from this man as soon as I get a chance." The man did look scary. He was tall; he carried a gun. The man spoke. Daniel did not understand the man's language, either. He made signs for Daniel to get up. Daniel got up anxiously. Then the man made signs of eating and drinking and of a house, and Daniel felt a little better.

So it was that Daniel went with the Indian through the woods. Finally they came to a path and then to an open place in the woods. There was a house made of sticks and bark from trees. A woman was cooking over a fire in front of the house, and three boys and a girl were playing there.

When the children spied Daniel, they came running toward him and talking all at once in their own language. It seemed they wanted to be friends with him, but Daniel wasn't sure. After all, he knew that sometimes there was trouble between the Indians and the settlers. But then the woman got a wooden bowl and put some meat and a big piece of cornbread in it and gave it to Daniel with a cup of water.

nation	information	explanation	motion	mention
station	decoration	vaccination	notion	attention
vacation		civilization	caution	

238

	section	collection	action
	infection	correction	contraction

	position	constitution	patient
	addition	expedition	impatient

Daniel Begins to Learn

Daniel was very hungry and thirsty in addition to being afraid. The whole family watched him eat and drink. Daniel appreciated the food and thanked the Indians, although he knew they couldn't understand what he said.

Soon the boys tried to ask Daniel his name. They asked by pointing. Daniel finally understood and said, "Daniel Montour." The boys tried to say his name, but it sounded like "Danien Mondoon." The older boy pointed to himself and told him his name. When Daniel tried to repeat it, the children laughed because Daniel didn't say it right. But Daniel kept trying and the children pointed to their parents until Daniel learned their names. When they pointed to their house and said "wigwam," Daniel knew that word. Then he knew they were trying to teach him their language, which was Chippewa.

occasion	decision	measure	usual	garage
occasionally	division	pleasure	usually	
		treasure	unusual	rouge

239

Almost a Chippewa

The next morning, when the children's mother gave Daniel some food, she smiled at him and pointed to him and then to her own children. She held up first one, then two, then three and four fingers and then her thumb. Five. Daniel knew what she was telling him, that he was an addition to her family and one of her children now. She was kind and gracious to Daniel.

The boys took Daniel out in the woods to shoot with a bow and arrow. Shooting well brought Daniel pleasure. And all the while, his Indian brothers were teaching him Chippewa words. They pointed to trees and rocks and plants and birds and got Daniel to repeat the words for them. Being able to speak Chippewa was unusual for a settler's boy. Daniel thought he was lucky.

Later, the father came home with some beaver pelts and a small deer. Daniel helped skin the deer and cut it up. He helped stretch the beaver pelts, too. Daniel learned to help out just like the Indian children did. They smoked fish to dry them and grew some corn and beans and squashes and onions.

The father's name was Bear Claw, the older boy was Little Bear, the younger boy was Two Bears, and the littlest boy was Four Bears. The mother's name was Red Sky and the little girl's name was Sunrise. The Indians thought it was very odd that Daniel's name did not mean anything special as their names did.

Red Sky made Daniel a pair of deerskin moccasins. He wore them proudly.

Daniel saw how respectful and obedient to their parents the Indian children were, and he acted the way they did. He thought about his parents and how much he missed them. Daniel knew he had to be patient. He really wanted to return home.

Bear Claw tried to find someone who knew of Daniel's family. Sometimes Daniel would hear him talking to strangers. Some of them came from far away along the shores of Lake Michigan. But none of them knew of any family called Montour.

At last, someone Daniel knew came to see Bear Claw and Red Sky. It was Tom Feather. Tom Feather had been at Daniel's house many times. Daniel ran to greet him. Tom Feather and Bear Claw made the decision that Tom should take Daniel home.

Daniel was excited to think about going home but very sad to think about leaving his Indian family.

239

After Daniel was back with his real family, he asked his father if he could see his Indian family again. He was so happy to be back home, but occasionally he missed Bear Claw and all the family very much. His father didn't really answer Daniel. Daniel wondered why there was no discussion about his wish.

Then, when the winter had passed, Daniel's father went away for a few days. Daniel worried about his father. Maybe he would be taken by robbers, too. But Daniel needn't have worried. His father had gone to bring Bear Claw and Sunrise and Red Sky and the boys to visit.

The Indian family stayed for a month. They made a house in the woods like the one Daniel had lived in and the families shared meals. The children played and went hunting and fishing with their fathers. The Indians learned some English and Daniel's parents learned more Chippewa words. The children spoke a mix of Chippewa and English to each other.

When Bear Claw and his family had to leave, he told Mr. Montour that they would be back next spring. Bear Claw said that Daniel was like his own son, and he wanted to see how this unusual son grew. He also said he was proud to have Daniel as a member of the Chippewa nation.

picture	feature	signature	adventure	natural
lecture	creature	furniture	century	naturally
capture				

mixture	future	literature
pasture	nature	temperature
		manufacture

240

The Winter Queen

When Olga was a little girl she liked to ride in the sleigh with her father. He would hitch up a team of horses, and they would go part way around Stor Lake. It was like going on an expedition or adventure, and she nestled in the blankets till she had a snug, warm nest.

But when her father mentioned skating, Olga always had some explanation of why she couldn't go. Olga did not want to skate. The thought frightened her.

At first, her father and mother were very patient about it, but as Olga grew older, Olga's family became impatient. In Sweden, where Olga lived, everyone they knew skated. Skating came naturally to them and their friends.

statue	actual	mutual	fortune	question
	actually	situation	fortunate	suggestion

Olga Worries

241

The place where everyone went skating was a section of Stor Lake near the village. Olga's house was right on the shore of this lake. If you stood on the porch, you could see the deep woods on the hills around the lake, which seemed wide as an ocean. Nobody lived in those woods except animals. To Olga, civilization seemed to stop at the edge of those woods.

When Olga turned seven years old, she began school. She felt fortunate to be going to school, even if some of the schoolwork was very hard. And she liked her classmates. So it happened that when it started to get cold, she found she wanted to go skating with her class. Then she began to worry. She did not know how to skate. So she had to force herself to pick up her skates and go to school.

Olga's teacher, Miss Anderson, said to the class, "Soon it will snow so much it will cover up the ice. Then there won't be any more skating. That's why we need to go skating now! And it's so beautiful on the lake."

soldier   individual   gradual   graduate   education

cordial   gradually   schedule

cordially

Olga Skates

242

Miss Anderson was a good skating teacher, too. She helped Olga and held her hand while she skated. Olga skated quite well for a beginner. Soon she graduated to skating on her own.

Olga gradually became more and more comfortable on the ice and soon began to love skating. Gliding over the smooth ice made her happy. She could go so fast. She didn't even mind when it got very cold and the ice would make a singing noise as she was skating along. Sometimes it made a big, thundering noise, even if nobody was skating. People would say the ice was settling. They meant that the ice was shifting, shrinking, and changing shape because it was so cold.

The year Olga learned to skate, there was not as much snow as usual. Everyone was happy to be able to skate even after New Year's Day. The children of the village went down to the lake every day. But one January day, Olga did not go with them, because she had to help her mother lay out and measure some cloth for a new quilt she was making. As soon as Olga finished helping out, she put on her warm skating clothes and went down to the lake.

The sky was a rosy red. It looked as if someone had smeared rouge on it. The other children were already leaving. So Olga skated alone along the shore, looking at the hills and woods and the far side of the lake. Mostly people skated near Olga's house and farther down the shore to the railway station. That day she went farther than she'd ever gone before.

exact   exactly   example   examine   examination

Olga Meets the Winter Queen

She felt so happy with the cold air on her cheeks and the ice singing under her skates. She decided to go a little further. She thought, "If I skate fast, I'll get home before dark." The ice was singing so much, it was like music. As Olga went around a small bend in the shore, she saw a figure skating toward her. Soon she could see it was a woman dressed all in white.

Olga examined her carefully as she came nearer. How beautiful she was! All her clothes had decorations of white fur: her cap and her cloak and her mittens, and even her boots. She had golden hair and blue eyes and pink cheeks. She looked like someone from one of Olga's fairytale books.

"Come, skate with me, girl child," she said to Olga. "I will show you the shore and the hills where no people live." She came to Olga's side and turned and put her hand on the little girl's shoulder, skating with her. Naturally it was a very beautiful hand, but Olga could not feel it on her shoulder.

How fast they went! The woman did not seem to be exactly pushing Olga, yet they skated faster than Olga had ever seen anyone go. "Look at the woods, girl child," the woman said in her odd way. They skated on and on, Olga completely forgetting about time and darkness coming.

Finally Olga gathered up all of her courage. She asked, "You are so beautiful, but who are you?"

"I am the Winter Queen."

grandpa   pumpkin   handkerchief   Wednesday   February
grandma

forehead   chocolate   tongue   guarantee

244

Skating with the Winter Queen

Olga didn't really understand her answer. This was such a wonderful adventure, Olga didn't want to ask any more questions. They skated on and on, faster and faster.

Suddenly the ice thundered. The thundering came from the middle of the lake. It sounded as if the lake were angry with them.

Olga and the Queen stopped skating. The Winter Queen stood as still as a statue. It was getting dark. In the west, a huge cloud almost covered the setting sun. Now the wind was blowing in Olga's face. Again Olga found the courage to ask another question. "Isn't it time for me to go home?"

"Yes, girl child," the Queen answered. "It is time for you to go home, because soon the snow will fall and cover the lake. And then I'll have work to do."

The Winter Queen kept her hand on Olga's shoulder, and they swung around, skating back the way they had come. The wind was pushing them now, and Olga felt as if she were skating faster than ever. But the ice was no longer singing under her skates. From time to time, it thundered angrily.

Olga was afraid now. Even the Winter Queen seemed a bit afraid.

244

The snow began to fall in big flakes, covering the ice. Olga was afraid that soon it would get so deep that she wouldn't be able to skate all the way home. And it was dark. But the Winter Queen kept her hand on Olga's shoulder and they skated together to a place close enough to Olga's house that she could see it. Everything was quiet. Even the ice had stopped thundering.

The Winter Queen told Olga, "You must get home quickly, and I must go away. When I leave you, you will not be able to skate. The snow will be too deep. Walk home as fast as you can, straight toward the lights of your house. Farewell, girl child!" Olga's beautiful Queen of winter glided away on her skates until all Olga could see was big flakes of snow.

Olga hurried toward home. Soon she heard someone calling her. It was her father and her brother, who both ran to meet her.

Her father scolded her. "Where did you go? Don't you know that you mustn't go off alone like that? We have been very worried. How could you stay out so late?"

Her brother, Rolf, asked if she had skated by herself. "Yes," she said, "part of the time. Then I met the Winter Queen." She tried to tell her father and brother about the beautiful woman dressed all in white. They could not understand at all how an imaginary queen dressed in white could explain Olga's thoughtlessness.

"Well," said Olga's father, giving her a big bear hug. "I'm glad we're all home together again. Perhaps I'm too old or have too much education to appreciate your beautiful Winter Queen. I prefer to think you forgot darkness comes so quickly."

perfect   direct   syrup   Asia   route
perfectly   directly
              direction   diamond   envelope

The Picture Country

245

Florence was an only child. She had no brothers or sisters to play with. She lived with her father and mother in a big apartment building, and there didn't seem to be any other families in the building who had children. The street in the big city where they lived was noisy, because trucks and cars drove that route day and night. Sometimes men would set up machinery outside the apartment building to dig up the street. Her mother told Florence that the men used the machines to get ready for new electric or gas lines or water pipes.

When Florence went downstairs she was not allowed to cross the street. There was a garage just across the street and her mother was afraid Florence might get hit by a car. Florence had to play indoors or in the hall or on the sidewalk, but the sidewalk was crowded most of the time with people going in all directions. So there was not much for Florence to do. She stayed upstairs at home most of the time, and she was very lonely.

Sometimes she tagged after her mother, and then her mother would say, "Oh, Florence! I'm busy! Go and find something to do." Later her mother would pat her and say, "Well, I suppose you do get bored. I wish you could live in the country."

And she would tell Florence about her life in the country when she was little, the way children live in the open country, and how there is lots of space to play and many things to do.

245

One summer Wednesday, when Florence was casting about wishing she were in the country with many things to do, the doorbell rang. Florence opened the door. There stood an old man with a long gray beard. He carried a big bundle slung over his back. Hanging round his neck he had a tray with all kinds of things in it: pins and needles and ribbons and combs, little mirrors, and pieces of lace from Asia. He was a peddler, and although peddlers were not allowed in the building, somehow he had gotten past the superintendent. The peddler was going from door to door selling his wares.

When Florence's mother went to the door, the old man asked her if she wanted to buy some of his things. He began lifting bracelets up from the tray to show them, and telling about the other things he had in his bundle.

"I'm very sorry," said Florence's mother. "I am sure your things are very nice, but I haven't any extra money to spend on things like these. Thank you for letting me see some of them, but I really can't afford to buy any."

The old man smiled and thanked her. He started down the hall toward the stairs that went up to the next floor of the building. He walked very slowly.

"Oh, Mother," said Florence, "that man is very tired. Look at the way he walks. Maybe he would like to come in and sit down for a rest."

Florence's mother patted her on the head and said, "You don't ask strangers in, my dear."

"I would," said Florence. "He seems like such a gentle old man."

Her mother thought for a moment, watching the old man walk slowly down the hall.

"Perhaps you are right. It is indeed a very hot day, and he does have a heavy load. Run and ask him to come back. I'll go fix him a glass of iced coffee."

Florence ran down the hall after the old man. When she had caught up to him, she said, "Please, sir, won't you come in and rest? My mother wants you to have some iced coffee."

245

The old man turned slowly toward Florence. "Thank you, dear," and back he went with her. Florence's mother invited him to sit in the big chair by the window. While the old man rested, he talked with Florence's mother. They talked about the city and the country and how hard it is for children to grow up in the city, where there is little room to play. Florence listened because she liked the old man. From time to time he looked at Florence and smiled. His beard and mustache covered his mouth but the twinkle in his bright blue eyes showed he was smiling.

When the old man got up to go, he opened the bundle he carried over his back and said to Florence's mother, "This young lady has been very kind to me. I wish I could give her a present. I can't do that, but I have a picture here that will please her. I will lend it to her, if she will hang it up on the wall. It will give her a great deal of pleasure. I will come back and get it someday."

The old man got out a picture in a wooden frame. The picture showed a great stretch of land with a lake at one side. On the lake there was a big ship. There were also several little sailboats with men and women and boys and girls in them. At the edge of the water people were fishing, and there was a landing place with some people just getting into a little launch to go for a ride. On the land you could see many things, too.

245

There was a track with a railroad train on it and people sitting at the windows. The train was just coming to a station. People were waiting there at the station—men and women and boys and girls. Beyond the tracks there was a big farm with men plowing, a funny-looking old woman tending a herd of cows, and children playing under the trees in an orchard. You could see a road in the picture with horses and wagons on it.

Florence and her mother thanked the old man for letting them borrow the picture. As he turned to go, the old man leaned down and said, "Child, when you are lonely you can walk into the picture and let all kinds of things happen, and when you want to leave, you can walk right out of the picture again."

That evening, Florence and her mother told Father about the old man. Florence's father hung the picture up on the wall above Florence's bed.

"It's not a very beautiful picture," he said. "There are too many things in it. But the colors are bright, and it will entertain Florence."

The next day Florence's mother and father had to go to work, so Florence was left alone for a while. She stood in her room looking at the picture, remembering what the old man had said.

"It doesn't seem natural that I could walk into it," she thought. "I wonder how I can step through the frame."

She lay down on the rug and looked up at the picture. Then she got the answer to her question. The picture seemed to get bigger and bigger. It reached right down to the floor, as if her bed had disappeared. Children were playing in the orchard! The first one to notice Florence was a girl about her own age.

245

"Hello!" said the girl to Florence. "What's your name?"

"Florence Smith," said Florence. "What's your name?"

Florence had a feeling she wanted this girl's name to be Mary Ryan. Mary Ryan was one of the girls she sometimes played with at school.

"My name's Mary Ryan," said the girl.

Florence played with Mary and the other children. She had great fun. Whenever Florence had a feeling she wanted something to be a certain way, then it happened exactly that way. One mischievous boy climbed way up to the top of a tree. He began to tease the others. "I bet you can't climb up and catch me." Florence thought, "He might fall down now. He's showing off, but I don't want him to get hurt."

Suddenly the boy lost his grip and came crashing through the branches right in front of Florence. When he got up, he looked very surprised and a little ashamed but said, "It didn't hurt me at all. I just had a good tumble."

After a while Florence said to Mary, "Let's go for a ride on the train. It will take us to the shore."

245

Even though the railroad station seemed to be miles down the valley, Florence and Mary walked just a little while. They went around some big bushes, and there right before them was the station. Inside the station Florence asked the man at the window for two tickets to go all the way to the shore.

Out on the platform the conductor cried, "All aboard!" Florence and Mary climbed on the train and found two seats by a window. The girls enjoyed watching the countryside pass by.

At last the train came to the station at the shore. Florence and Mary got out to find two sailors ready to take a party of children out sailing.

Florence thought, "I am sure they will invite us to go along."

One of the sailors turned around and said, "Come on, little girls. There's room for two more in the boat."

Florence and Mary got into the boat. The sailors hoisted sail, and as the boat sped through the water, the spray flew in the children's faces. They sailed far out to sea where the boat began to pitch and toss on huge waves. Florence thought this was very exciting. Perhaps just a bit too exciting. Then the boat turned around and sailed back to the landing place just in time for lunch.

"I must go home now, Mary."

She turned and ran along the beach. "Now I am coming to the end of the picture," she said. "I'll just step out of it and into my room."

She took a step or two, and there she was, back in the room lying on the rug. The picture was up on the wall over her bed. Her mother was getting lunch ready.

"Well, Florence," asked Mother, "where have you been all this time? Have you had a nap?"

Florence did not quite know how to answer her mother's question. "Why no, Mother. I've been in that picture the old man lent us."

Her mother smiled and said, "That's natural enough," and said no more.

After that, whenever Florence was lonely she walked into the picture. Sometimes strange or frightening things happened. Once Mary Ryan and Florence walked on the road and passed the old woman who was tending the herd of cows. A cow turned to look at the girls and said, "Run for your lives! I used to be a little girl like you. The old woman can turn you into cows."

The girls started to run, but the old woman caught up with Mary. When Florence looked back, there was Mary Ryan standing the road. She had the body of a cow. The old woman was poking her with a stick to drive Mary in with the rest of the herd.

That time Florence ran to the end of the picture and jumped out of it, back into her room.

No matter how long Florence stayed away in the picture, her mother never seemed to be worried or anxious. Florence's trips were becoming quite natural.

That autumn Florence began going to school again. She did not have so much time now to walk into the picture. Still, on Saturdays, Sundays, and holidays, she could visit if she wished. She and Mary, who was no longer a cow, had some grand adventures together.

In the spring, Florence began to bring home books from school, because by this time she could read quite well. One day her father bought her a storybook. Florence liked the stories in this book. She spent most of her time reading them. After the end of the school year, when she was at home much more, she spent more time reading than she did in the picture.

One day the doorbell rang, and there was the old peddler with his tray and his bundle.

"Oh, hello, do come in," said Florence. "I want to tell you what wonderful times I've had walking in the picture."

The old man smiled at Florence with his blue eyes. He greeted her mother cordially—just like an old friend.

"I am glad you liked my picture," he said to Florence. "But I know you haven't been going into it so much lately. Now you can read about many more wonderful things than just the few things in the picture country. In the future, books will keep you company. You do not need my picture any more. So now I am going to lend it to some other child who has not yet learned how to read books."

Florence's mother helped the old man take the picture down from the wall.

When the old man got up to go, Florence went with him to the door. Looking down at her with his bright and kindly blue eyes, he said, "If you should ever need me, I'll come to see you again. But I don't think it will be necessary, because you will never again feel bored and unhappy when you are alone.

"Now you know how to read."

Index to the *Let's Read* Vocabulary

This alphabetical index lists the words included in the vocabulary of *Let's Read* (inflected forms—plurals, past tenses, etc.—are generally omitted). Numbers refer to lessons.

About the Authors

Leonard Bloomfield (1887–1949) was a professor at the universities of Wisconsin, Illinois, Ohio State, and Chicago. He was Sterling Professor of Linguistics at Yale at the time of his death in 1949. Among his many significant writings, three stand out as basic to modern linguistic science: "A Set of Postulates for the Science of Language" (*Language* II.3, 1926); *Language* (New York, 1933); and "Linguistic Aspects of Science" (*International Encyclopedia of Unified Science*, I.4, Chicago, 1939).

Clarence Barnhart (1900–1993) is best known as the editor of the Thorndike-Barnhart school dictionaries (Chicago, 1952–1971) and of the *World Book Dictionary* (New York, 1963). During his career, he introduced many important innovations now common to most dictionaries, including the simplified pronunciation key, a single alphabetic entry list, and placement of common meaning first. Consistent monitoring of English usage and reliance on an active editorial advisory committee assured the authority of Barnhart dictionaries.

Robert K. Barnhart (1933–2007) was a dictionary maker who combined his knowledge of language and vocabulary with considerable gifts for storytelling, which he put to good use in creating reading passages for *Let's Read*. In addition to the 1976 edition of the *World Book Dictionary*, his most important dictionaries were the *Barnhart Dictionary of Etymology* (1988, now titled *The Chambers Dictionary of Etymology*) and the *First, Second,* and *Third Barnhart Dictionary of New English* (1973, 1980, 1990).

Cynthia A. Barnhart is also a dictionary maker with a special interest in new words and usages. She has been involved with *Let's Read* since its initial publication and was the first Barnhart family member to teach a child to read, working from the manuscript of *Let's Read.*